The Phoenix Economy

The
Phoenix Economy

Work, Life, and Money

in the

New Not Normal

FELIX SALMON

HARPER
BUSINESS

An Imprint of HarperCollinsPublishers

HarperCollins books may be purchased for educational, business, or sales promotional use. For information, please email the Special Markets Department at SPsales@harpercollins.com.

FIRST EDITION

Designed by Chloe Foster

Library of Congress Cataloging-in-Publication Data has been applied for.

ISBN 978-0-06-307628-0

23 24 25 26 27 LBC 5 4 3 2 1

For Erika

Another plague year would reconcile all these differences; a close conversing with death, or with diseases that threaten death, would scum off the gall from our tempers, remove the animosities among us, and bring us to see with differing eyes than those which we looked on things with before.

—Daniel Defoe, *A Journal of the Plague Year*

Contents

Prologue

THE HOHOKAM WERE one of four prehistoric cultures in the US southwest, alongside the Anasazi, the Mogollon, and the Patayan.[1] Starting around the year 1 CE, they settled the valleys of the Gila River and its tributaries—the Santa Cruz River, San Pedro River, Verde River, and, most importantly, the Salt River. Into the harsh and arid Sonoran desert they brought agricultural technology imported from Mexico, growing maize, beans, squash, and even cotton.

Life was not easy, with just about eight inches of rain per year and often none for months on end. Temperatures fell below freezing in winter; in the summer, they would rise above 120 degrees Fahrenheit. But this was home, and around the year 50, the Hohokam started building their first small irrigation canals.

The canals became much larger starting around four hundred years later, when the first houses were built at a small hamlet now known as Pueblo Grande, or Large Town, using the woody ribs of saguaro cacti as building materials. By the year 750, Pueblo Grande was a fully-fledged village with ball courts and trading relationships. By 875, it was producing magnificent ceramics and was at the center of a network of ten irrigation canals. By 1150, the village had become a walled town, which became increasingly elaborate. In the early 1300s, the Hohokam started building "big houses," including one at Pueblo Grande—elaborate multistory structures made of adobe, at least one of which was used for astronomical purposes. The town, more than a mile wide, became legendary; 135 miles of canals fed thousands of acres of fields, and agriculture extended even to fish farming, based in the Salt River.

Then, within just a few short generations, it was gone. By around 1450, after growing crops in the region for more than a thousand years, the last Hohokam left Pueblo Grande. Its structures remained but its inhabitants had all moved on.

Archaeologists have not reached a consensus about exactly what happened. It certainly had nothing to do with European settlers; Christopher Columbus wouldn't arrive in the New World for decades yet. War with the Apache and Navajo is perhaps more chronologically feasible, but even they hadn't appeared on the scene by the time the Hohokam civilization collapsed. One possibility is that some kind of localized plague or waterborne disease spread rapidly throughout the population.

The most likely explanation is just that Pueblo Grande got too big. The desert can support some folks, but not a lot, and a drought could have forced neighboring populations into Pueblo Grande, whose land and canals weren't fecund enough to be able to feed all who needed sustenance. Hohokam buried in the fifteenth century were malnourished, and floods in 1358 and the 1380s might have taken out enough of the irrigation system that the productive capacity of the town was already strained. Oral legends from the Pima, who are probably descended from the Hohokam, hint at political unrest, with the leaders being overthrown.

Ho-Ho-Kam was not the name these people gave themselves; it came later and translates to "people who are gone." Gone, but not forgotten. In 1867, just over four hundred years after the Hohokam civilization ended, a man with the magnificent name of Jack Swilling moved into the Salt River valley and started building his own canals, feeding crops that closely resembled the ones grown a thousand years previously. The area became known as Swilling's Mill, and Swilling himself wanted to rename it Stonewall, after Confederate general Stonewall Jackson.

Swilling's friend Phillip Duppa was underwhelmed by that idea. An Englishman and pioneer who had sailed all the way to South America and then made his way north from there, he felt the original pioneers of the land, who had worked it on a grand scale for well over a millennium, deserved the honor, not some general.

What Duppa envisaged was a rebirth: a city, bigger and bolder than Pueblo Grande, growing out of its historic ruins. Duppa had studied classics at Cambridge University and spoke five languages; he was deeply familiar with the most lasting legend in the history of civilization, one millennia older even than the Hohokam. It was known as Bennu in ancient Egypt, Huma in Persia, Garuda in Sanskrit, Feng-huang in China, Chol among the Jews. It's an everlasting symbol of rebirth, of resurrection, of the idea that the end is never really the end, it's just the beginning of something new. The Hohokam might be gone, but their spirit would live on in the name of the city that sprung up where Pueblo Grande had once stood, and that's now home to some 1.6 million people.

Phoenix.

Introduction

THIS BOOK ORIGINATED with an email from my agent at the beginning of April 2020, raising the prospect of a book about "pandemic economics." I came up with the concept of "The Phoenix Economy" immediately, long before I had a clue what the book itself might be. The name was an attempt to reflect some of the optimism that my agent hoped I might be able to bring to the table—stories of businesses thriving during and after the pandemic, that kind of thing—even as my own outlook, and that of most economists I was talking to, was pretty relentlessly bleak.

At the time, I looked at the economy and saw a plunging stock market, a pandemic of insolvency ("A Tidal Wave of Bankruptcies Is Coming," said one *New York Times* headline[1] as late as mid-June, long after the recession was over), an increasingly likely financial crisis, and of course a deadly virus rampaging across the world in a manner that was largely unchecked by a manifestly incompetent US president. No one believed that the Covid crisis would turn out to be economically much less damaging than the financial crisis and Great Recession of 2008–9; one of my former employers was even warning darkly[2] of what he called an "I-shaped recovery" that would end up being even worse than the Great Depression of the 1930s.

In that context, it seemed to me that concentrating on a handful of bright spots—the rise of telecommuting, say, or a newfound appreciation for homemade bread—would be tasteless at best. "Never mind the death and immiseration of millions, have you thought about how great this pandemic has been for dogs?"

The pandemic did turn out to be terrible. Hundreds of thousands of Americans died, and millions globally. Millions of American jobs were vaporized in a matter of weeks, many of them never to return. A national and possibly global mental-health crisis started to emerge as a result of stay-at-home restrictions and the educational and parenting nightmare that is virtual school.

It was easy to look around and see ashes—not only of individual loved ones but also of entire ways of life. People who used to spend their lives on airplanes, or who at least would leave their home country on a regular basis, found themselves grounded for years. The human integration of China into the rest of the world was thrown sharply into reverse, with travel both into and out of the country effectively going to zero overnight. The omnipresence of fatal infectious diseases, a constant for substantially all human history, became a background fact again, a morbid drone much louder for some than for others, after a few blissful decades of being all but forgotten in day-to-day life.

And yet, as the ashes piled up, it became increasingly easy to see the outlines of the phoenix emerging from them, certainly in the United States. Wealth soared, not just among the rich but also among the poor. An ultra-tight labor market precipitated a "great resignation" where people were able to quit their unloved jobs and find something much more to their liking. Where you lived, physically, similarly became much more of a choice and much less of a necessity than it had ever been in the past—at least within countries, if not across them. And for all the fractiousness and shouting, there was hope even in the way the world really did come together.

in 2020, with billions of people just *not moving* for weeks on end in a successful attempt to flatten the Covid curve and buy time for genius mRNA scientists to invent a magical vaccine that came more quickly, and proved more effective, than anybody dared hope during the early days of the pandemic.

It didn't take long, once the vaccines started getting rolled out in early 2021, for a wry refrain to start being heard, especially in the more cautious and Covid-averse populations: "Haven't you heard? The pandemic is over." The elderly, the immunocompromised, the people who retained a level of shock and dismay at the deaths of thousands of people every week—they would look around in disbelief at what they considered to be reckless and dangerous behavior by the unvaxxed or unmasked and wonder what those people were even thinking.

I was one of those people—until, at some point in 2022, I started using the same words with much less irony. In September 2021, I helped to organize a big birthday party where we took a lot of Covid precautions and ended up with no infections; by June 2022, I was attending a wedding where five people got Covid and the general reaction was "yeah, that's pretty good, it's less than I would have expected." Epidemiologically, the pandemic was still raging; anthropologically, it had become a fact of life, an inevitability, even something people started to hope they would get at a convenient time.

When people behave as though the pandemic is over, then the pandemic *is* over, on a behavioral level. Still, two things are certain. Firstly, the pandemic is extremely unlikely to be eradicated on an epidemiological level any time soon. Covid is with us for the long haul. To live in the world is to live with Covid, now and for the foreseeable future. Secondly, there will always be people for whom Covid is a stark and terrifying reality, one that changes how they live their lives in profound ways. Those people can't or won't live in denial of Covid, as though the pandemic is behind us.

This book is not about the epidemiological effects of Covid. Instead, it's a look at the lasting ways in which the microscopic SARS-CoV-2 virus changed the world, some of which are extremely large. Covid isn't the all-purpose causal agent behind any effect you might be looking at, but if you're reading this in the 2020s, there's a very good chance that its influence is being felt in a lot of the ways that today's world has changed from pre-pandemic days. That might be obvious when it comes to things like the degree to which you're able to work from home; less obvious when it comes to the contents of your Coinbase wallet. But it exists, to a greater or lesser extent, almost everywhere.

As this book went to press, for instance, the biggest economic issue in the rich world was that inflation was too high, for the first time in decades. Some of that was caused by supply chain problems traceable back to the pandemic. Some of it was a function of fiscal decisions that similarly were made only because of the pandemic. Some of it was the result of sudden pandemic-related changes to the labor force. And a large chunk of it happened because Vladimir Putin invaded Ukraine—something he may well have done even if there wasn't a pandemic, but that's ultimately impossible to know. Go down a couple of layers from almost anything, and there's a good chance you'll see the pandemic there somewhere: It's not something we can just move on from and put behind us, declaring that we're back to how things were before.

From the earliest days of the pandemic, the media was full of "this changes everything" arguments, some of them honest predictions, others based more in hope than in rational expectation. Against that stood what I thought of as the "mean-reverters"—people saying that most things would go back to their pre-pandemic *status quo ante*, and that anybody foolish enough[3] to proclaim that New York City was dead forever, to take one example, would soon enough be proved wrong. (New York, for the record, is still very much alive, and I say that not only as of the date I'm writing this, but also as of the date you're reading this, possibly many years hence. This isn't a predictions book, but that's one prediction I'm very comfortable making.)

By nature, I'm a mean-reverter. Journalists tend to have highly sensitive bullshit meters; we're also quite cynical, and broadly believe that extraordinary claims require extraordinary evidence. We're more likely to pooh-pooh world-changing forces and technologies than we are to overhype them. That said, no global event of the magnitude of the Covid pandemic is going to touch the planet lightly. It *will* have effects, and long-lasting ones at that. They will be profound, and many of them will be unexpected.

My hope is that this book will give you a deeper understanding of some of the huge changes that have already happened, and will prepare you to understand others, as and when they arrive. The legend of the phoenix is one of renewal and rebirth: a cycle, but not a slow-and-steady one. The phoenix exists in largely unchanged form for hundreds of years before a spectacular inferno brings its life to a brief end and creates the ashes from which the immortal creature is reborn. My thesis is that the Covid pandemic is one of those rare conflagrations that precipitates a whole new era. Most of us aren't old enough to remember the last time that happened, in 1945, but those who are never forgot it. Covid is likely to be similarly indelible in the memories of everybody who lived through it—and similarly far-reaching in its global repercussions.

If you want a simple gauge of just how momentous a big event is, one thing you can do is check to see how long it sits in the P1 position. P1, which may or may not stand for "position 1," is a concept that President Barack Obama reportedly used, and that cable TV news channels—especially Jeff Zucker–era CNN—understand intuitively.

At any given point in time, there's exactly one issue that everybody is fixated on above all others. From a news and public-sentiment perspective, that is the most important thing happening in the world, and if you devote airtime to it, people will watch. If you devote airtime to anything else, they'll get bored and click away.

In America, Donald Trump was in the P1 position for roughly four years before the pandemic hit. His presidential campaign and his presidency were extremely effective at sucking the air out of everything that wasn't Trump; while under most other presidents it was easy to go weeks without really thinking about who was in the White House, under Trump that was impossible.

Covid proved to be the one force capable of trumping Trump, of pushing him down into the P2 position. All but one of the biggest Trump stories of the Covid era were Covid related, and even during the one exception to the rule—the attempted coup of January 6, 2021—the lack of masking among the rioters, precious few of whom were vaccinated at that point, drove home the way in which Trumpism had become a cry against Covid restrictions.

The segment of the population that railed at what it perceived as a global overreaction to the disease still had Covid as their P1—and it stayed in that position not for weeks, not for months, but for two whole years (and then some). Only when Russia invaded Ukraine at the end of February 2022, at a point when vaccines had brought down fatalities impressively and when the big Omicron spike was starting to die down, was there an event big enough to displace Covid as the world's P1.

This was the single biggest difference between Covid and the Spanish Flu of 1918. The pandemic of 1918 came at the end of a devastating world war, and also at the end of an era when infectious diseases were a tragic fact of life; the result was that the terrible pandemic never became P1. Events that capture the world's imagination aren't always measured in lives lost. The attacks of September 11, 2001, for instance, were P1 for months and drove history for two decades, on the back of less than three thousand casualties. Celebrity trials, like that of O. J. Simpson, can be P1 for weeks.

Covid was P1 for two years. During that time, it killed about six million people worldwide, roughly one million of whom were in the United States. In other words, it was far more lethal than most wars, *and* it dominated the conversation for much longer than most wars do. There is no way that any phenomenon can share those two attributes without having major long-term repercussions. And the repercussions of 2020 are going to reverberate for decades, mostly in negative ways, for all the best efforts of governments to alleviate the medical and economic damage.

As the social-media cliché has it, Covid "lived rent-free in our heads" for two years solid, putting down roots and sprouting tendrils. It upended lives, reconfigured economies, and changed the way we perceived space and time.

More worryingly still, it could so easily have been much, much worse. The Covid vaccines, for all that they were distributed in a deeply unfair manner, arrived in record time. The virus itself, while deadly, was not nearly as lethal as many other infectious diseases have been over the course of history—and, as of this writing, it seems reasonable to hope that our ability to create and deliver vaccines, at least in the developed world, is going to be able to stay one step ahead of the various Covid mutants that will continue to emerge.

Possibly most importantly, the rise of internet bandwidth over the previous twenty-five years had *just* become broad and ubiquitous enough to allow companies and economies around the world to continue operating with surprising efficiency, even as their employees were physically unable to go to the office. And the United States, in particular, had what economists call "fiscal space" to spend trillions of dollars on keeping its domestic economy afloat—something that had significant positive spillover effects on other countries, too.

None of this went unnoticed. A global pandemic was not only predictable, it was also predicted. We knew this was coming—but almost nothing else went according to expectations. An elaborate 2019 wargaming exercise[4] conducted by Johns Hopkins University, the Nuclear Threat Initiative, and the Economist Intelligence Unit listed the countries most prepared for a pandemic—and put the US at the top of the list. Yet America soon skyrocketed to the top of the global mortality tables, for reasons only partially due to its incompetent president.

Financial markets displayed astonishing volatility over the course of the crisis—a key indication that they were extremely bad at anticipating what was going to happen next. Analysts were almost universally too pessimistic in their projections, both for how badly companies were going to be hit by the pandemic, and also for how quickly they might recover.

In the more outré corners of the market, speculative frenzies erupted over and over again—GameStop, AMC, cryptocurrencies like Dogecoin, NFTs like CryptoPunks. *Ex post*, it's easy enough to gin up a narrative as to why that might have happened: the Fed, excess liquidity, lockdown boredom, social media, something something something. *Ex ante*, however, these events were entirely unexpected—as was the sudden takeover by China of Hong Kong, or the successful storming of the Capitol in January 2021, or the way Black Lives were all of a sudden generally agreed to Matter in May 2020. (Pollsters were astonished at how swiftly public opinion on that question changed, relative to the first wave of Black Lives Matter marches in 2014—and, just months later, were equally astonished at how swiftly public opinion on the same subject reverted back to where it had been before the pandemic.) Even smaller changes, like the emergence of outdoor dining as a permanent part of the New York cityscape, were entirely unforeseen.

To live through so many unexpected events was to experience on a visceral level the idea that life is not normally distributed, that the things we expect to happen often don't, and that things we never dreamed could happen might upend our lives tomorrow. The pandemic itself is Exhibit A: For all that many of us knew in theory that it was a serious possibility, very few of us had given much if any thought to how we might react were such an event to actually arrive.

The idea behind this book is that the unexpected isn't over. The shock and trauma of the pandemic, its long-term downsides as well as its unexpected upsides, are not entirely in the past: They will continue to emerge for decades to come, just like the shock and trauma of World War II shaped personal and geopolitical behavior for half a century after the war was over.

I, for one, am not capable of anticipating the surprises—if I could, they wouldn't be surprises. Instead, what I want to do is to try to understand a bit about how Covid has already changed the world, and provide a framework for thinking about those future surprises—to make it easier to understand what might be underlying the unusual and unexpected things that are certain to surprise us, and how much of that might be usefully traced back to the feverish days of the pandemic.

I learned a lot during the pandemic, in a process that was quite exhausting. I'm in the back half of my life now, and so it's natural for me to want to understand the world by applying everything I learned in the forty-eight years I had on this earth before the pandemic hit. That's how growing older works: You learn fewer new things, you change your mind less frequently, and you increasingly rely on heuristics and shortcuts that have served you well in the past. But anybody who approached the pandemic with such a mindset will have missed a huge amount—and might well have ended up in a dark and dangerous place.

Take GMOs (genetically modified organisms), for instance—crops genetically engineered to feed the world more efficiently. They have saved lives and fed the hungry; they have also made a lot of money for private corporations and have proved extraordinarily controversial among people who think that anything unnatural is probably bad, or somehow harmful.

Before the pandemic, anti-GMO sentiment was in large part a tribal thing—an easy way of belonging to a certain group of people who care about the environment, eat organic food, and generally assume that things that are natural are good and things that are un-natural are bad. Such people find value in the "no GMOs" label on food packaging and are willing to pay extra for it, or at least feel reas-sured by it. Meanwhile, many of the rest of us, who have no problem with GMOs, saw little harm in such labeling—it was just a way of making the product appeal to as many people as possible.

That changed during the pandemic, when many of the people who were hesitant to eat genetically modified food became hesitant to take genetically engineered vaccines that proudly flaunted their heritage in mRNA technology. Such folks were not generally a huge part of the anti-vaxx problem—libertarian or MAGA types on the right were, as a rule, much more vocal and much more societally harmful than crunchy-granola types on the left. But the root prob-lem was the same on both sides: The less likely you were to change your pre-pandemic beliefs, or priors, the more constrained you were in the way you reacted to the novel coronavirus and the demands it made upon society. It turns out that many of those constraints proved unhelpful at best, and downright harmful at worst.

Call it the epistemic Covid crisis. Millions of people felt their easy reliance on solid facts was being ripped out from underneath them.

The epistemic crisis is hard to measure and was never as visible as the public-health pandemic, although the two were closely entwined. But it's plunged a large part of the population into the uncomfortable realm of what economist John Kay and former Bank of England governor Mervyn King call radical uncertainty.[5] It's a realm that technocrats are slowly coming to terms with, but it's far from accepted among the population as a whole.

After all, by 2020 we had long reached a stage of scientific and technological sophistication at which most of the things we need to know about the world could be found out very easily. Google, a company founded in 1998, became worth almost $2 trillion during the pandemic as a result of its unrivaled ability to fulfill the promise of its corporate mission: "To organize the world's information and make it universally accessible and useful."

As we all disappeared into our various screens over the course of the pandemic, we had become accustomed to finding all the facts we might ever want or need within seconds. And yet the new reality was one in which almost *none* of the facts we most urgently wanted to know about the world were known by anyone at all.

The result was, at least for me, a crash course in epistemic humility. I've long prided myself on having the classic trader's disposition of "strong opinions, weakly held"—it's a very handy professional skill, if you're a blogger. Posts where I change my mind, or admit that I was wrong, are the most important things I write. But the sheer frequency with which I found myself having to change my mind, during the pandemic, was like nothing else I'd ever experienced.

At the beginning of the pandemic, for instance, Covid was basically understood to be a germ. It lived on surfaces, for scarily long amounts of time, and then people would touch those surfaces, and then they would touch their face, and that was how they would get Covid. The whole country, more or less overnight, adopted a new purity ritual—

washing hands with soap for a solid twenty seconds. Once you'd done that, you could then touch your face, but touch almost anything else, especially if it was *out there* in the world, and that would immediately put you back into the impure state that only another twenty seconds of handwashing could address.

Handwashing brought the country together, at least until it slowly dawned on some of us that the twenty seconds thing turned out to be based on basically no science at all, and that fomites—inanimate objects that can become vectors for disease—were not the way that Covid was actually being spread.

That was one of the first areas of epistemic forking. I embraced the idea that I didn't need to worry about fomites, and consigned to the back of a utility closet the boxes of thin white art-handling gloves my wife had bought us to wear when we left the apartment. I would use the word "fomites" in conversation, and people would understand what I was talking about, or at least pretend to. (I did draw the line at "nosocomial," however.)

Millions of others, however, either didn't change their mind or changed it much more slowly. There's something reassuring about purity rituals, and there's something difficult about changing your mind, and at no point did anybody in authority come out and say explicitly that we *didn't* need to worry about catching Covid from, say, an elevator button.

Hygiene theater, then, would never really go away, certainly not in the hospitality industry. Once a fact gets accepted, it's going to stay accepted for many people—and the good thing about hygiene is that it's something that individuals have quite a lot of control over. They can practice good hygiene themselves, and they can expect good hygiene from their vendors, and that in turn creates a reassuring degree of agency in the face of a heartless, amoral virus.

Thus was the stage set for the next two years, at least. Covid was an epistemic double whammy: It overshadowed the global economy and became the foremost source of conversation and concern at exactly the point at which we knew the least about it. Everybody learns at a different pace—and everybody has a different propensity to unlearn what they thought they knew as new information emerges. Which is one reason why there were few reasons to scale back on performative-cleanliness responses to Covid, and is also a reason why many populations took a long time to start wearing masks.

As a financial journalist, after the economy bounced back with astonishing and unexpected speed, I rapidly lost count of the number of people who would talk to me about the unemployment crisis, or the way the rich got richer while the poor got poorer—even as all the data showed quite clearly that the poor got richer, during the rebound, even faster than the rich did. The crisis moved so fast that it allowed almost everybody's pre-existing opinions to get reinforced at some point—and, as is only human, most people were much more likely to embrace that kind of information than they were anything pointing in the opposite direction.

At the beginning of 2021, a new purity ritual, in the form of getting vaccinated, would show just how divisive different attitudes to the pandemic could be. Getting vaxxed or not getting vaxxed, from the beginning, was much more than a simple public-health intervention—it had political and indeed almost quasi-religious overtones.

It had medical utility, of course, but it also ended up with much of the utility purity rituals have had for thousands of years, which is to create classes of the pure and the impure. The pure—the vaccinated—would avoid all contact with the unvaccinated impure, again out of a feeling that by avoiding such contact, they would gain agency over the disease. A significant proportion of my Twitter feed felt that avoiding the unvaxxed was only the start: Such people should also suffer punishments up to and including being turned away from hospitals.

Such sentiments were a natural extension of the general feverishness that overcame the United States—and, indeed, much of the rest of the world—as the Covid pandemic combined with the highly elevated rhetorical temperatures associated with Donald Trump's 2020 reelection campaign. It was obvious enough that I didn't even try to start writing this book until after Joe Biden's inauguration: The brain fog caused by Trump was arguably as bad as anything caused by Covid.

When I did start writing the book, I tried to stay true to the epistemic humility I had learned over and over again in the prior months. This book is not going to presume to tell you "the truth" about Covid, or its long-term repercussions. Instead, I've tried to keep in mind something I thought about a lot in the early days of constant handwashing and deep cleaning—the doomed planet Golgafrincham, from Douglas Adams's comic novel *The Restaurant at the End of the Universe*.[6]

The people of Golgafrincham divided the population into three classes. There was Class A, the rulers and thinkers. There was Class C, the people who did the useful work that kept Class A in comfort: the butchers and drivers and people to change your sheets for you. And then there was Class B, the middlemen: "the telephone sanitizers, account executives, hairdressers, tired TV producers, insurance salesmen, personnel officers, security guards, public relations executives, and management consultants."

Class B was persuaded to board a spaceship that eventually crashed into Earth, thereby explaining the abundance of such people on this planet. They believed, falsely, that Class A and Class C would join them in space—whereas in fact the spaceship was a scheme dreamed up by the other two classes to rid Golgafrincham of the Class B types altogether. As for Class A and Class C, they remained on Golgafrincham, but not for long, since the whole population was soon wiped out by a virulent disease contracted from a dirty telephone.

The idea I couldn't shake, at least in the beginning, was not the idea of existential collapse as a consequence of epistemic hubris, it was just the idea that small things like sanitizing telephones could save an enormous number of lives. It was only later that I started thinking about the way in which all pandemics have been characterized by fatal ignorance—indeed, by the way that fatal ignorance is not so much a human failing as a human constant.

Conversely, the biggest successes of the pandemic came by zagging against the broad consensus of the pre-pandemic years. In the world of vaccines, mRNA researchers struggled mightily to be taken seriously before SARS-Cov-2 came along, and the biggest vaccine companies in the world—names like GlaxoSmithKline, Merck, and Sanofi—all tried more traditional routes to building one.

The household-name pharmaceutical companies of the Covid era—BioNTech and Moderna—ended 2019 with valuations of $7.7 billion and $6.6 billion, respectively, barely a rounding error when compared to the $120 billion or so apiece that GlaxoSmithKline and Sanofi were worth. The richest and most technologically sophisticated companies in the world had effectively dismissed mRNA as a workable technology—before it saved the planet.

Equally impressive was the way in which disparate arms of the US government—both parties in both houses of Congress; the White House; the Treasury; and, most importantly, the Federal Reserve—managed to come together to provide a level of economic stimulus that was unprecedented since at least the Marshall Plan if not ever. What's more, the spending worked: By mid-2021, America had more well-paying jobs for those who wanted them, less hunger, less poverty, higher wages, less inequality, and more wealth for everyday Americans than it had pre-crisis. None of those outcomes was expected—economists from across the political spectrum were genuinely surprised at how fast the economy rebounded. Most of them, as a result, were forced to go back and do some serious recalibration to their macroeconomic models.

This particular pandemic, then, should have permanently punctured the hubris of the Google era. But acting against such humility was the tidal wave of money that sloshed across the country, leaving hundreds of millions of Americans richer—sometimes much richer—than they had ever been in their lives. Wealth tends to make most people think they're smart, especially when it comes from against-the-grain speculative bets—something we saw an unprecedented amount of during the pandemic. Crypto assets, in particular, created an untold number of millionaires, none of whom were any good at the whole humility thing.

On some level, of course, everybody's views of the world changed, consciously or otherwise. Think back to March 2020, when we were seeing exponential viral spread with no conception of when that might end—our ignorance on that front was plain to all. Somewhere, a millimeter below the surface, most of us had secretly believed—with no evidence whatsoever—that human knowledge had advanced to the point at which we could deal with a rogue virus just as easily as we could deal with, say, smallpox. But "we," in that construction, never seemed to include "me." Winning a fight against a deadly virus was something for other people to do—the public-health experts, and especially the people at important agencies with three-letter abbreviations like the WHO (the World Health Organization) or the CDC, America's Centers for Disease Control and Prevention.

The first big thing that most folks learned, then, was the way in which collective action—the *real* "we"—was the central, necessary part of any successful attempt to control the virus. It was only when the world came to a standstill, when billions of people just stopped whatever they were doing and stayed at home, that the first, most terrifying phase of the crisis started leveling out.

Many more lessons were to come, although none of them were quite as universal. As a New Yorker, my experience of the pandemic was vastly different from that of my sister, in New Zealand—although of course we had in common the fact that we weren't able to see each other in person for well over two years. The pandemic radically changed almost every aspect of how we understand and live in the world, from the way we think about death and disease to the way we navigate cities, from the utility of trust to the power of governments, from the way we experience the passage of time to the way vast new areas of our lives became intermediated by screens. So it stands to reason that its long-term effects are going to be profound.

Internationally, there were more changes in a couple of months than there had been in decades. More or less overnight, Covid built barriers between countries—and even between internal states—the likes of which hadn't been seen in living memory. It saw the implementation of ultra-hard border controls in formerly open countries like New Zealand and Vietnam, and the creation of vaccine nationalism—the hoarding of excess vaccine domestically, even when the need was desperate elsewhere.

In that sense, the Covid crisis was a small-scale test run for the climate crisis: Could countries cooperate internationally out of collective self-interest? Or would internal political pressures make that impossible? The initial evidence was not good. The COVAX attempt to centralize the production and distribution of vaccines failed miserably, while the early economic success stories in China and the United States happened precisely because they required no international coordination.

All the ingredients are in place, then, for some truly profound world-historical shifts. The first World War—the Great War—destroyed kings and empires. It introduced women into the workforce for the first time. It created whole new countries, including Poland and the

Baltics. It was responsible for major advances in medicine, especially mental health, including the treatment of what is now known as posttraumatic stress and was then known as shell shock.

World War II was even more consequential—an event of such horror that humanity itself came together for the first time as a species to pledge: never again. From that imperative sprang the United Nations, the European Union, and decades' worth of geopolitical consensus, backed by standing armies totaling millions of individuals and trillions of dollars' worth of matériel, all devoted to addressing a hypothetical future emergency.

The pandemic might not turn out to be as consequential, over the long term, as the two world wars—but it could be. Even if it has only a fraction of the long-term ramifications, it could still end up being a dominant force in national and international political economy for decades to come.

It's worth remembering that Covid came at a time when the medium-term consequences of the global financial crisis were creating chaos in the White House, in the form of Donald Trump; it also came at a quite literal do-or-die moment in terms of global coordination to address climate change. We'll never know for sure how the no-Covid counterfactuals would have played out, and specifically whether Trump would have been reelected, but even if the virus didn't change the outcome of the 2020 election, the repercussions of its polarizing shock will echo for many years yet.

Personal interactions were also polarized. The pre-vaccine American crisis was characterized by what I think of as the First Corollary of Weisberg's Law. Weisberg's Law, named after my friend Jacob Weisberg, who came up with it, states that "Any Jew more religious than you are is mentally insane, while any Jew less religious is a self-hater."

Something similar could be said about virus paranoia. Everybody more paranoid than you had gone way overboard, while everybody less paranoid was not only putting themselves at risk but was acting in a deeply socially irresponsible manner.

That spectrum was visible well into the vaxxed era. One of the many things that surprised me about the crisis was the way in which people on the cautious end of the pre-vax spectrum remained very hesitant to do things like dine indoors or take off masks, even after they had recovered from Covid, been vaccinated, or both. On the other hand, one of the things that *didn't* surprise me was the way in which people convinced themselves that the morally correct thing to do was also the self-interested thing to do—that getting vaccinated, in particular, conferred on the recipient of the vaccine a moral superiority over the unvaxxed, or at least over anybody who had access to the vaccine and hadn't availed themselves of it. The tensions between the vaxxed and unvaxxed—with much self-righteousness on both sides— will show up in unexpected places for years to come.

More broadly, all trauma has long-term consequences, and global trauma has global consequences, much of which will take years to become visible. In this book, I'm going to look at what changed through three lenses.

Part 1, "Time and Space," is an examination of how the very dimensions of our lives were fractured, and what the consequences were. Chapter 1, "The New Not Normal," examines the way that time broke during the pandemic, rites of passage, the uncomfortable nature of liminality, and the shift from risk to uncertainty. Chapter 2, "The Great Acceleration," looks at corporate America's fast-twitch response to the crisis. Chapter 3, "From Ladders to Trampolines," looks at the way individual investing changed in profound and gen- erational ways. Chapter 4, "lol nothing matters," is a continuation of Chapter 3 that dives into NFTs and other speculative bubbles. Chapter 5, "Workspace," looks at the transformed physical dimensions of work, and how that has upended relations between employers and employees. And Chapter 6, "The Post-Global World," asks what happens when globalization ends.

Part 2, "Mind and Body," looks at our mental and physical health. Chapter 7, "Arm's-Length Relationships," examines what happened to physical proximity, and wonders what that might mean for the fight against climate change. Chapter 8, "Building Compassion," looks at mental health.

Finally, Part 3, "Business and Pleasure," zooms out to look at the broader economy and its most important drivers. Chapter 9, "The Two-Headed Risk Eagle," looks at the simultaneous rise and fall of risk appetite during the pandemic, and what it portends. Chapter 10, "Shaking the Etch-a-Sketch," examines how the pandemic laid the groundwork for a happier, more productive workforce. Chapter 11, "The Armies of the Public Fisc," looks at the way the US government reacted to the crisis, and what it means for the future. Chapter 12, "Consider the Lobster Roll," tackles inflation. Chapter 13, "New Money," asks what has happened to the dollar. Finally, Chapter 14 examines inequality—both its downsides and its upsides.

I'm going to start with our conception of time. For most of us, the pandemic broke our ability to place events on a neat timeline: Ask yourself where you traveled in 2019, for instance, and see if you can remember the answer without being forced to look it up.

Our forms of subjective time changed, too. Think about how long a two-week lockdown felt in March 2020, versus how acceptable it felt, just one year later, for people wanting to travel to countries with quarantine. Conversely, think about how much time you thought someone would need in order to make a lot of money in the markets. I'll wager that shrank dramatically during the crisis. If that describes you, or if you want to understand why it doesn't, read on!

Part I

Time and Space

1

The New Not Normal

COVID BROKE TIME.

"Time has no meaning anymore" is a phrase I found myself using weekly, sometimes even daily, over much of the course of the pandemic. Recording my podcast at the end of December 2021, I found it almost impossible to distinguish between the events of May 2020 and things that happened a year later, in May 2021—everything had been commingled into a single Covid year that started in March 2020 and would end only with Russia's invasion of Ukraine in February 2022.

When I asked my friends what countries they had gone to in 2019, none of them could answer without looking it up. There were "before times" and there were "Covid times," both of them foreshortened into indistinguishable masses.

One of the mental shortcuts I've been using to think about life since the arrival of Covid has been "the New Not Normal." It's a play on the financial-markets concept of "the new normal" that was popularized by Mohamed El-Erian of PIMCO in May 2009—the idea that the world was entering a long period of low growth.[1] It's also a play on the idea of the normal distribution—the familiar bell-shaped curve where most things are normal, near the center of the curve, and outliers are rare. During the pandemic, by contrast, the Red Queen, who famously believed six impossible things before breakfast,[2] would have felt quite at home.

Our newfound perception of time fits neatly into the New Not Normal framework; it became uncommonly elastic during the pandemic. Normal time works predictably: It ticks by painfully slowly in childhood, accelerates with age, and we always have a pretty clear (if not always accurate) mental chronology of which events happened before which other events. None of that obtained during the pandemic.

For starters, the Covid era saw entire populations experience their fast-paced world doing something they had never seen it do before: It decelerated violently.

The initial resistance to lockdowns, for instance, came not from a position of libertarianism, but rather from a position of "I haven't got time for this." We had places to go, things to do, people to meet. We *couldn't conceive* of the way life might operate, for any period longer than about twenty-four hours, under the strictures of lockdown.

Speaking just for myself, I certainly had a pre-existing intellectual awareness of the fact that a major global pandemic could strike at any time: That was a known risk. But in my mind, the effects were all health-related: They all involved sickness or death. On the occasions I thought about what it might be like to live through a pandemic—admittedly they were hardly frequent—I generally stopped at the first-order effects of getting sick and possibly dying. After all, that's what most plague histories concentrate on: the bubos, the bloody deaths, the murine vectors. Not the people sitting around at home, the social distancing, the postponed weddings. But that of course was the lived experience of the pandemic; with the exception of people suffering from long Covid, sickness was the exception rather than the rule.

The thing that stayed with us daily was not disease, it was the small and large ways in which our regular routines—anything from the commute on the subway to the annual Thanksgiving trip back to visit the parents—were scrambled, making the whole world feel deeply and weirdly unfamiliar.

We all need habits—they're the things that free us up to concentrate on what matters. By their nature, habits are time-based: They're things that happen on a regular, predictable schedule. When those schedules were dismantled overnight in March 2020, it threw the whole world out of kilter. That was one of the reasons why everything felt so febrile, so intense. We don't notice the things we're habituated to, and we pay much more attention to everything strange and new, no matter how inherently banal it might be.

We also tend to choose our habits: If we don't like to do something, it's unlikely we'll make a habit of it. That again changed radically in 2020. Middle-class individuals and families who had carved out their piece of the American dream found themselves living under constraints they would never have chosen for themselves. In other countries, like Australia, it was much worse: Melbourne was under ultra-strict lockdown—much harsher than most Americans ever experienced—for almost nine months in total.

In lockdown, the radius of our world shrank dramatically. "Stuck at home" syndrome kicked in, with all its attendant annoyances and deleterious effects on our mental health. The days stretched out, filled not with the excitement of squeezing multiple activities into a busy day, but rather with cooking, cleaning, childcare—and, of course, endless Zoom meetings. Time flies when you're having fun, which meant that for most of us it slowed to a crawl.

The real problem, however, was not the slowness of time, so much as its liminality. The whole *texture* of time changed: Instead of simply moving forward, at a faster or slower pace, it felt more as though it was taking a circumbendibus via parts unknown. You could follow the "detour" signs in real time, as they were handed down by the authorities or by epidemiological necessity, but there was no map, because no one knew where we were actually headed.

When I was going through the process of getting my green card in 2006, I'd have to go through an odd ritual every time I entered the United States. I would present my papers to the immigration officer, who would study them, and then find someone to escort me to "the room."

The room in question was reasonably large—it probably had a hundred or so seats, most of them empty, all arranged in neat rows, facing a low stage on which sat a handful of customs officers. My escort would take my papers and add them to a pile at one end of the stage, while I'd be instructed to take a seat and wait. Veterans of the process knew to always pack some reading material in their hand baggage, since we weren't allowed to use our phones.

Every so often, one of the officers would call out a name, and a person in a chair would walk up to the stage, have a conversation, and—if all went well—get their passport and other papers back, and be free to go back out to baggage claim and customs. One thing soon became clear: The papers were not being dealt with in a first-come-first-served basis. Sometimes it felt like the opposite was the case, where the escort would place papers on top of the pile and then the officers on the stage would just grab whatever was easiest to hand, resulting in a last-come-first-served system. Every time I went there, I would see people arrive after me and leave before me; I would also leave while other people, who had already been there when I arrived, still waited. None of us ever spoke to each other; there was an eerie silence in the room.

The room caused deep discomfort in everybody who went there—an unease caused by liminality and uncertainty. The room was an in-between space, an airside place of limbo. For the officers on the stage, it was their regular workspace, but for the rest of us it felt a bit like the strange white world at the end of *2001: A Space Odyssey* in terms of its unfamiliarity and our inability to navigate it by using our own wits and abilities. We found ourselves in an opaque system, one we had no individual ability to leave; all of which was up to a faceless system applying rules and procedures whereof we knew nothing.

The worst part of waiting in the room was not having a clue when your name would be called. I probably spent less time waiting in the room, on average, than I spend waiting on line at Di Palo's in Little Italy to buy mozzarella and prosciutto. But at Di Palo's you can see your progress; you can see how many people are ahead of you in line, and you have the feeling that the amount of time you're still going to need to wait before you get served is falling by one minute per minute. Wait for ten minutes, and you're ten minutes closer to getting food.

That's why arrival clocks at subway stations and bus stops are so calming: They reassure commuters that the train or bus is on its way. The same syndrome explains why sitting in traffic is so frustrating: When you come to a grinding halt, you have no idea how long you might be stuck there. There should really be a setting in Google Maps that says "just avoid bad traffic jams; even if the total trip takes longer, I'd rather be moving the whole time, feeling that I'm making progress, rather than having to sit and go nowhere for a significant chunk of the journey." A lot of people would choose that option— and if the immigration authorities at JFK cared about the mental well-being of people coming into the country, they could make a world of difference just by putting up DMV-style signs showing people where they were in the queue.

When the pandemic struck, it put all of us into a JFK-style limbo, with no indication of when we might be able to leave. Dodai Stewart, at the *New York Times*, diagnosed a "collective feeling of joyless aimlessness."[3]

Novelist Ben Dolnick put it differently: "Since March, I (and, more important, the entire human race) have been living inside a set of massive parentheses," he wrote in July 2020.[4] "Our lives as we knew them before the coronavirus—the subjects of our days marching crisply along, the verbs of our every hour thoughtfully chosen—have been suspended." He had no idea how long the limbo would last; all he could do was talk wistfully about the amount of time "until God or Merck blesses us with an end-parenthesis."

That was the big hope—that a vaccine would put an end to the pandemic—and of course it was dashed, since the vaccine did no such thing. The parenthesis remained open; and the feeling of continuous discombobulation continued, for millions, well into 2022.

Some folks decided to close the parenthesis by sheer force of will. From the earliest days of the pandemic there were people saying that "it's just a bad flu," that they had no desire to live in fear of an infectious disease, that it was only really harmful for the elderly and for people with pre-existing conditions, and that they wouldn't change their behavior as a result. People who tested positive for Covid declared that they had "natural immunity" and therefore had no need to live under public-health constraints. Once the vaccine arrived, it became even easier for groups of people to decide that it was time to "get back to normal."

Such decisions can't be made on an entirely unilateral basis, which is precisely why noisy demonstrations against mask mandates and other public-health indicia of the pandemic sprang up across the world, featuring everybody from truckers in Canada to yoga instructors in New Zealand. If you're navigating a world where businesses and potential employers ask you for proof of vaccination, and where you're required in many situations to wear a mask, then the pandemic parenthesis has clearly not been closed—you're still living in limbo. In order for the period of unease to end, you need everybody—or at least a large supermajority of people—to move on with you. Since that won't happen without the government getting involved, the demonstrations invariably targeted lawmakers, for reasons I finally understood after visiting England in the winter of 2021.

Both my wife and I live three thousand miles away from our nearest close family—she's Californian, I'm English, and we live in New York. Between the physical distance and the Delta surge of Covid, there was no way we were going to spend the pre-vaccine 2020 Christmas holidays with relatives. A year later, however, such festivities were possible, if difficult, given the Omicron surge, and we found ourselves in the UK in late December 2021.

When I first moved to New York in the late 1990s, I liked to say that New York had more in common with London than it did with the rest of the US. I wouldn't say that anymore, but still, for my first trip back to the UK since January 2020, I wasn't prepared for what I saw in terms of the public attitude toward Covid, or for the massive disconnect between the stance of the folks I was hanging out with, on the one hand, and the behavior of the everyday Londoners I saw, on the other.

New York was a city of broad adherence to public-health protocols. When you got on the subway, it was generally possible to find travelers who didn't wear a mask covering their mouth and nose—but they were the exception, not the rule. More to the point, the people who *didn't* follow the rules were clearly violating societal norms. Some, like much of the homeless population, had pre-existing mental-health problems; others, like groups of drunk or high kids out on the town for an evening, would revel in their rebelliousness. What you *wouldn't* see would be, say, a middle-class professional commuting to work in a suit on the subway and wearing no mask at all.

One Friday morning in October 2020, for instance, I was on the A train from Brooklyn to Manhattan, coming back from taping my weekly podcast. A disheveled man, clearly homeless, would occasionally stand up and shoot me glances, and eventually he approached me, bearing a piece of paper with the details of city services in downtown Brooklyn and a careful notation that he had to exit the train at Hoyt-Schermerhorn. He wanted to make sure he got off at the right stop; I was happy to oblige. But the interaction was also tinged with discomfort on both sides, thanks to the pandemic—discomfort that was made even more acute by the woman sitting opposite us who started crouching over and coughing into a baseball cap. I was sympathetic, but also horrified, and couldn't wait to get out of that car.

Everybody on the subway was conscious of the way in which they were navigating the pandemic, and while there were certainly many occasions when I wished that certain people would behave differently, I broadly understood that those individuals were simply evincing a very different risk appetite to my own. They knew they were running a risk of contracting Covid or passing it to others, and they were comfortable or at least resigned to living with that risk.

London was very different. Even at the height of the Omicron outbreak, with the local case count hitting new all-time highs daily, the prevailing attitude seemed to be one less of deliberate openness to risk and more of blissful denial. The London Underground had clear rules about wearing masks, for instance, which were broadly ignored. In New York, refusing to wear a mask on the underground was a sign that you were rebelling against prevailing strictures. In London, it didn't feel like that; it just felt that the population broadly had moved on from such things, the epidemiological facts on the ground notwithstanding, and that the people making the rules were behind the curve and would ultimately have little choice but to capitulate to the facts of public behavior.

Even the rules themselves sent very mixed signals about Covid. On the one hand, everybody needed to wear a mask over their mouth and nose—but on the other hand, the official rules listed eleven different groups of people exempt from the mask mandate, including all passengers under the age of eleven. The existence of all those exempt groups had the effect of making the official rule feel like security theater—something that could be ignored on the grounds that if children or "persons providing agreed services to Transport for London" didn't need to comply, then obviously there was no real necessity to mask up.

The overall atmosphere in London was one of "every man for himself." In the absence of broad public-health protections, there was a lot of individual freedom—on New Year's Eve, for instance, we walked to a rather subdued six-person party at a friend's house, after testing for Covid that afternoon, rather than risk a restaurant that, like all other London venues, was not asking for proof of vaccination. On the way there, we passed many long lines of unmasked revelers waiting to get into crowded clubs and bars—while also encountering no shortage of individuals protecting themselves against their compatriots by wearing N95 masks on the street. (Such masks were rarer on the Underground, where the risk-averse generally didn't venture at all.)

It took me a long time to understand what was going on in London. *Why* weren't people doing something as basic as wearing masks in badly ventilated spaces, in the middle of the most virulent outbreak yet? And when they did wear masks, why were they still wearing fabric masks rather than the ones proven to be much more effective? As an Englishman myself, I thought that I ought to be able to work it out, but I couldn't. And my English friends didn't understand it any more than I did.

In the end, I realized that I was looking in the wrong place. I was trying to understand what it was about the *English*, as a people, that would explain their behavior; I kept thinking back to Kate Fox's magnificent book *Watching the English*, in which she unpacks the idiosyncrasies of my compatriots.[5] In fact, however, I suspect that the real reason had nothing to do with Englishness, as distinct from, say, Frenchness, or whatever it is we have in New York. (Assholery?)

What the English had that the New Yorkers lacked—and that nearly everybody else lacked, too, although the Danish would get there soon enough—was an official announcement from the country's government that the parenthesis was closed and that the period of limbo was over.

Prime Minister Boris Johnson called it "Freedom Day," and it arrived on July 19, 2021, when new Covid cases were running at a rate of about 300,000 per week—up from only about 10,000 a couple of months earlier. Johnson famously had effectively declared his own personal Freedom Day many months earlier, participating in illegal parties at his Downing Street residence even as the rest of the country was locked down. Now, he was extending such freedoms nationwide. At a stroke, nearly all Covid restrictions were lifted: Masks no longer needed to be worn in shops, bars and restaurants no longer had capacity limits, and any number of people could socialize together. (The London Underground was one of a small number of places where restrictions remained.)

As a matter of public health, Freedom Day made no sense—restrictions that had been in place when the number of new cases was very low were suddenly lifted when it was high and rising. *Bien-pensant* opinion was overwhelmingly and understandably opposed to the move, and with hindsight it's easy to see why: After Freedom Day, new cases remained at a very high level—much higher than they'd been before it—for well over seven months, while the number of patients hospitalized with the disease only seemed to go up.

As a matter of *fixing time*, however—essentially decreeing that the country could get out of its fugue state and get back to concentrating on its other problems—Freedom Day achieved its goal, at least for a majority of the population. It placed the onus of navigating the pandemic on individuals, which meant it acted as a kind of permission slip for anybody who wanted to escape limbo. Importantly, this permission slip came in the form of an official decree, from the selfsame body that had imposed all the restrictions in the first place. In that sense, it had the same kind of pleasing symmetry as parentheses do.

On the other hand, a personal decision to go back to normal, in the wake of a government decision to impose constraints, is asymmetrical. It lacks the kind of elegance that people (most people, anyway} want in a closing parenthesis.

Because Freedom Day was given a memorable name and came into force dramatically at the stroke of midnight, it had some of the power necessary in a rite of reengagement—the term for the last and in some ways most important part of any rite of passage.

The anthropological concept of the rite of passage dates back to 1909, when thirty-six-year-old French ethnographer Arnold van Gennep published a book, *The Rites of Passage*, that's still in print to this day. Van Gennep, who spoke eighteen languages, looked around the world at things that seemed familiar—birth, puberty, marriage, death—and found something they all had in common: a set of clearly defined rituals marking the transition from one state to another.

Van Gennep studied customs that mark the passage of time and change. Such rituals exist in pretty much all cultures, and van Gennep discovered strong commonalities among them. There's the pre-state before the rite, then there's a rite of disengagement where the old order is ended. That's followed, crucially, by a liminal period—the state of transition from one status to another. Finally comes the catharsis: the all-important rite of reengagement, where the new order begins.

Everything from weddings to graduation ceremonies to Jewish funerary rituals fits this rubric, as do many rites marking important moments in the calendar, such as solstices, equinoxes, or the new year. Consider the bride in a traditional wedding: She is walked down the aisle by her father, who "gives her away" in a rite of disengagement. Then there is a ceremonial liminal period of prayers and incantations. Eventually comes the moment that everybody has been waiting for: the exchanging of rings, the "I now pronounce you man and wife," the kiss, and the walk back up the aisle, arm in arm with her new husband, a new family, forever changed in status.

The rite that was Covid certainly began with disengagement, of a brutally literal form: Billions of people were forced to radically restructure the lives they had chosen and to which they had become accustomed, without having any real notice or choice in the matter.

The initial rite of disengagement was about as intense as such things get. Covid arrived on a planetary scale, with almost no warning. Think of the long period of apprehension and anticipation that precedes any other rite—a wedding, a bar mitzvah, a presidential inauguration. The knowledge that it's coming helps you to prepare yourself for it, and puts you in a certain state of mind when it happens—you know that a very important day is coming up, and at some point you start counting down the days until it happens. Covid, by contrast, happened so quickly that no one was able to mentally prepare for what was about to happen. Entire countries, including local and national leaders, were put on edge.

It's instructive to look back at a viral YouTube video[6] from March 2020 of Italian mayors urging people to stay home and chiding them for venturing outdoors. "Hundreds of students will be graduating," says one. "I hear some want to host a party. We'll send armed police, and we'll send them with flamethrowers." The natural inclination of the students was to mark the important inflection point in their lives with a well-lubricated ritual, whether they were allowed to or not. The pandemic be damned, they had a deep human need to undergo this rite of passage. But the mayor made it clear that he was focused on a much bigger and more important ritual—one that had been invented more or less on the spot, but that still required full obeisance.

Public-health protocols varied wildly between countries and between regions within countries; virologists and epidemiologists had massive debates about optimal policy. There was broad agreement on one thing, though—that once a policy was set, everybody should follow it, even if they thought it was misguided. Scientists advised the government; the government set the rules; and the population followed the rules—that was the only way the requisite degree of collective action could possibly come to pass.

That's why the UK's Freedom Day was so important. It wasn't so much the changes in the rules themselves, which, truth be told, were relatively marginal. Rather, it was the unambiguous signal being sent by the prime minister to the country: This is me getting out of your business; there are no more rules to follow.

A few months later, the same prime minister, Boris Johnson, would even go so far as to say that individuals with Covid no longer had to self-isolate. Most people *did* still self-isolate, of course; there was no rule against it. But such decisions were explicitly being knocked back down to the level of common sense, rather than criminal law—something that only a government is capable of doing.

The reason for the Freedom Day declaration was simple: It was popular. And the reason for its popularity was that the English hated waiting for something to happen, in much the same way that I hated waiting for my name to be called at JFK.

After all, one thing all rites have in common is that the liminal period is bounded and known. "People need to know 'when does it end,'" the Australian anthropologist, technologist, and all-around polymath Genevieve Bell told me at the beginning of the pandemic, "because being liminal is quite unpleasant."

Even when the rite is long or painful, its subject can see the light at the end of the tunnel. Covid was worse, because of its very unpredictability. The virus didn't care about public opinion; wasn't honed and optimized over generations in a Darwinian battle of rites where, ultimately, populations only opted into the rituals they liked and wanted to perpetuate. Instead, we saw our hopes raised by the swift arrival of the vaccines, only to see them dashed by the fact that the simple existence of the vaccines was clearly insufficient to put an end to the pandemic.

The deeply unpleasant situation of knowing that you're in a liminal period, but not knowing when it will end, did differ between countries—but not as much as you might think. Places with more effective Covid suppression strategies—New Zealand or Australia, say, or even Greece—did have a moment of feeling justifiably self-congratulatory about managing to get the virus under control. But sometimes those strategies failed, and sometimes they were so harsh that public opinion broadly started turning in the direction of "some Covid is fine, it can't be as bad as this."[7]

Such attitudes partly came as a result of thought-through risk assessment, but they were also much more primal than that. As the anthropologist Mary Douglas wrote in *Purity and Danger*, a book that in many ways is a follow-up to van Gennep's *Rites of Passage*, we naturally fear liminality, because "danger lies in transitional states."[8] Closing the parenthesis, ending the uncertainty, just in itself made people feel safer, whatever the epidemiological facts on the ground.

Other countries, such as Vietnam or China, took a different tack: Rather than make a big show of freeing their populations from the purgatory of living in a constant state of uncertainty, they doubled down on it and made it an even more central part of their governing philosophy. The pandemic forced all governments to impose unprecedented restrictions on how and where their citizens lived their lives. For authoritarian regimes, it felt like something of a gift.

China's Xi Jinping was already uncomfortable with the degree of freedom and inequality in his country; come the pandemic, he was able to start tracking and tracing every citizen, and even started to mandate things like the maximum amount of time kids were allowed to play video games. That uncomfortable feeling of losing your individual agency was something most of us knew was temporary, even if we didn't know how long it would last. In China, it felt much more permanent.

As for the United States, the main thing that could be said about the way that the nation entered and exited the Covid transition was that there was absolutely nothing united about it. Lockdowns began on the coasts—Seattle, San Francisco, eventually New York City—and were initially imposed not by any federal or even state authorities but by individual municipalities. The federal government, led by a president in a permanent state of denial, mandated nothing, leaving all such decisions to the states—a decision that made no logical sense, given that interstate commerce and travel was never banned in the way it was in Australia and that state borders were entirely porous to Covid.

The result was a whole new axis along which the US could cleave apart—one that was correlated with political divisions, but not exactly aligned with them. Rarely have US state governors had such power, and the fact that it was so unfamiliar to them meant they had very little institutional ability to coordinate and cooperate. Operating in a state of emergency, they naturally put their own states first, except for the governors of Florida and New York, who treated the pandemic as an opportunity to make headlines and raise their national public profile ahead of a possible run for president.

Some governors, mostly Republicans, had the same political instincts as Boris Johnson—that the best thing they could do to make their states happy was to make a loud proclamation that the pandemic was over and that all public-health interventions were scrapped. Such decisions were broadly popular with the Republican base, even as they left the immunosuppressed and other risk-averse individuals feeling increasingly isolated and afraid.

In other states, including my own home of New York, the tendency was to deal with the problem of seemingly unending liminality by recasting it as a new permanent normal. Dan Doctoroff, an urbanist and former New York City deputy mayor, likes to say that his first rule of government was that "anything temporary becomes permanent." There are precious few truly temporary fixes in municipal government: Introducing something new is hard, because there are always existing interests opposed to it, but once it is introduced, changing it becomes equally hard, since the new system now has its own constituency of bought-in stakeholders.

The pandemic, from its very earliest weeks, was greeted in many quarters as a once-in-a-lifetime opportunity to make the kind of fundamental changes that would be almost impossible during normal times. In Europe, cities like Madrid, Rome, Milan, and Paris implemented aggressive attempts to get people out of cars and to use their feet or bikes or mass transit instead, with large chunks of the city center becoming off-limits to private cars entirely. New York didn't go that far, but it did effectively seize a huge quantity of on-street parking, to replace it with outdoor dining. That was necessary to keep restaurants alive when indoor dining was banned, but the temporary became permanent, and the ubiquitous on-street dining sheds became part of the New York streetscape in perpetuity.

Anything unusual, once we've lived with it for long enough, becomes normal: The perceived default switches from one state to another. One of the reasons we canceled our New Year's dinner reservations in London was that a restaurant vaccine mandate was normal and reassuring for us, rather than being a sign of abnormal pandemic-era liminality; in fact the *absence* of a vaccine mandate was the thing that worried us greatly. None of us was remotely qualified to adjudicate the relative riskiness of an indoor dinner with mandates versus one without them, but as New Yorkers we just felt that the kind of "we're looking out for you" reassurance that comes with a vax check was a very important part of the service provided by a restaurant, and we didn't want to go to a restaurant that didn't provide that service.

The great pandemic-era geographical rotation was even more permanent. Once you've taken the plunge of moving house, putting together a home office, recentering your life in a new place—you're emotionally and financially invested in your new life, and don't want to unwind all those investments to return to the *status quo ante*.

Even people who liked outdoor dining and new bike lanes and working from home, however, still had a psychological need for permission to exit the pandemic. Without it came guilt—the idea that if you personally persuaded yourself Covid was no longer something you were going to spend every day actively trying to avoid, then that decision might end up killing someone. Your likelihood of contracting Covid would rise by some small but meaningful amount, and if you multiplied that number by the nonzero probability that you'd then infect someone who might die of it, then, well, congratulations, you're now a potential blithe killer. In order to avoid that guilt, you couldn't just make the decision unilaterally; you needed the governor of your state—or, even better, the president of the whole country—to reassure you that it was okay to go about your life in the way you wanted to. Every day that reassurance didn't come was a day that limbo was extended.

After all, the Covid scolds weren't going anywhere. As early as March 2020, the novelist Leslie Jamison insightfully noted that "getting righteous about other people's inadequate social distancing is how we manage our fear."[9] The self-righteousness evolved over time—it moved on to target incorrect masking, failure to get vaccinated, or even just stating a desire that schools reopen—but it was always present enough, on Twitter and Facebook and in loud public statements from epidemiologists, that any attempt to live a post-Covid lifestyle was always tinged with guilt, or at least occasional bouts of second-guessing.

The guilt was mixed with anger since no one likes a scold. In the early days of the pandemic, there was a spate of essays from various parts of the policy wonk community, all making a variation of the argument that Covid presented a once-in-a-lifetime opportunity to reconfigure our lives in precisely the direction these people had been advocating for years. Lockdown reduced carbon emissions? Let's keep them low even once the pandemic is over! Covid won't be gone anywhere until it's gone everywhere? Let's make sure that everybody on the planet has access to basic healthcare, to make that more likely! Etc.

Much more consequentially, that kind of "never let a crisis go to waste" attitude was rapidly adopted by most of the Democratic Party in America. The idea, as described by former White House chief of staff Rahm Emanuel, is that a serious crisis is "an opportunity to do things that you think you could not do before."[10] The broad-based fiscal stimulus seen in the immediate wake of the pandemic was not only unprecedented in scale and scope; it was also progressive, in that it helped the poor more than the rich, and it even came with the support of most of the Republican Party. What the Republicans saw as an emergency response to an unprecedented crisis, many Democrats saw as exactly the kind of policies they had been agitating for long before the pandemic arrived.

Joe Biden certainly wasn't going to let the crisis go to waste: As soon as he was sworn in as president, he pushed through another $1.9 trillion of fiscal stimulus, including a child tax credit of $3,600 per year for children under six and $3,000 per year for children under eighteen. That tax credit was to continue, at a lower rate, through 2025, a clear indication that this was not an emergency stimulus but rather an attempt to build a new safety net into the American welfare system.

Biden wanted even more spending than that—the next stage of what he called "Build Back Better" was a $1.75 trillion infrastructure plan that sought to dramatically reduce carbon emissions and turn the US into a leader in the fight against global warming. The problem was that, to put it bluntly, America wasn't suffering an economic crisis anymore. The combined might of the country's fiscal and monetary response had got its economy humming again, with unemployment falling faster than at any point in over fifty years and the stock market hitting new record highs seemingly every other day. Democrats, most notably including former Treasury secretary Larry Summers, were warning that all the government stimulus was going to cause the economy to overheat, with the result that the "kill two birds with one stone" argument became much harder to make with a straight face. Sure, the new spending plan would be good for greening the economy and would be a big step toward enacting a broad left-wing agenda. But it wouldn't serve the dual purpose of providing much-needed economic stimulus for a country suffering the privations of the Covid recession, for the simple reason that the recession at that point had been over for more than a year, and the country's economic privations were less severe than they had been even before the pandemic.

The broad public understood this dynamic perfectly well. The crisis was bad, and desperate times call for desperate measures, but those measures must by their nature be temporary. Once the times were no longer economically desperate, the public wanted an indication that the crisis days were over. What they *didn't* want was their president telling them that the bad days were still at hand, and therefore necessitated another $1.75 trillion in fiscal spending that would never get through Congress in a normal year. By pushing his Build Back Better agenda well into 2021 against the backdrop of an ultra-tight labor market and a roaring economy, Biden was essentially sending the message that as far as he was concerned, the Covid emergency would *never* be over as long as he still had an agenda to enact.

The implicit message, therefore, was that the longed-for release from limbo was not going to come from the White House, the one place that had the greatest amount of power in terms of freeing the country from its existential discomfort.

As a matter of public health, the White House had science on its side. The number of people dying of Covid remained stubbornly high well into 2022, the year the total death toll exceeded one million. Morally speaking, the millionth person to die of Covid was just as important, their life just as valuable, as the hundredth, and if a certain course of action was capable of saving lives in 2020, and would continue to save lives in 2022, then that public policy should remain in place.

As a matter of public opinion, however, Americans had a deep desire to move on, to put the pandemic decisively behind them, and to lump Covid deaths alongside all the other tragic, avoidable, and ignored deaths that happen every day in America—deaths from opioids, deaths from guns, deaths from traffic, deaths from poverty and inadequate access to healthcare.

Death by natural causes is, after all, natural; if you're religious, and most Americans are, then it's part of God's plan. It's not pleasant, or desirable, but it's part of the great tapestry of life and death we're all eternally weaving. Covid introduced a new color, a new texture, to that tapestry—one that was shocking at first but, by force of sheer ubiquity, became less so over time.

Consider the so-called Spanish Flu of 1918, which killed roughly 675,000 Americans, compared to 53,402 who died in battle during World War I. It's possible that the influenza pandemic even killed more *soldiers* than combat did, partly because, unlike Covid, the 1918 flu proved especially deadly to men of fighting age, particularly those around twenty-five years old.

There was very little cultural memory of the 1918 flu before the Covid pandemic came along and people started needing to draw parallels. Similarly, there's an extremely high chance that you've never heard of California's Great Flood of 1861–62, a cataclysm that devastated the state to such a degree that communication with the East Coast was cut off entirely after flood waters reached the tops of the telegraph poles. The young state capital, Sacramento, home to the state legislature for just six years, was completely submerged, forcing the government to evacuate. The entire Central Valley— some eleven million acres of prime agricultural land—found itself transformed into a lake almost as big as Lake Superior, with as much as fifteen feet of water. Crops, livestock, and housing were all destroyed—as were the livelihoods of the Mexican rancheros who up until that point had farmed the land.

The most vivid contemporaneous account of the Great Flood comes from a New York botanist named William Brewer who was hired to be the California state geographer. In his letters back home, he not only detailed the enormity of the flood, but also astutely anticipated that it would soon be forgotten:

No people can so stand calamity as this people. They are used to it. Everyone is familiar with the history of fortunes quickly made and as quickly lost. It seems here more than elsewhere the natural order of things.[11]

The same idea explains the relative equanimity with which the Spanish Flu was accepted in 1918. The average American in 1918 was a Victorian, born in the nineteenth century. If you were an American over the age of five, you could count yourself pretty lucky—roughly 20 percent of babies didn't live that long. The world was still a decade away from the invention of penicillin. Death by infectious disease was a fact of life—and most Americans only really paid attention to their local communities, which meant they were largely unaware of the degree to which this particular influenza strain was killing tens of millions of people around the world.

Mass mortality events, then, don't always cause great societal trauma; historically, a plague has had to wipe out a very large percentage of the population before it rises to the level of a politically important event.

Then again, we went a century without a plague of this magnitude—a century during which medical science advanced enormously, infant mortality plunged to less than 1 percent, and a broad complacency set in with regard to infectious diseases broadly. Few of the generation that remembers polio are still alive; instead a new generation grew up, rooted in 1970s environmentalism, blessed with the luxury of being able to free-ride on broad public-health advances while extolling the virtues of nature and eschewing anything that felt artificial, like GMOs or vaccines.

The initial Covid wave hit with visceral force—the death toll in Bergamo or Tehran; the dystopian images of airplane passengers being escorted off planes from China and straight into military quarantine by soldiers in full hazmat suits. The whole world basically just . . . *stopped*, for a few weeks, in an astonishing show of collective action, humanity coming together to try to bend the exponential curve of infection down and to the right. The sheer weight of ignorance, about how fast the virus spread, how it was transmitted, how deadly it was, was genuinely terrifying.

Eventually, the first-wave lines peaked and started coming down, gratifyingly fast in many cases. By the summer of 2020, the societal fear of a deadly new virus had started to be replaced with workarounds and risk assessments; many cities and countries felt almost normal, even if traveling between them could be fraught. Still, there was no official sigh of relief, no celebration after winning localized battles so long as everybody understood that the war was still very much afoot.

The world was still on edge—just in a slightly different way, with less fear and, in many parts, more resentment. From that point on, it was probably impossible to deliver a truly satisfying declaration that the pandemic was over. Every government decision was fraught—mask mandates, school reopenings, vaccine mandates, indoor dining, border controls, you name it. One side would point to the number of lives that could be saved by erring on the side of caution; the other would point to the number of lives hobbled by continuing Covid restrictions. Both sides would get vocal and self-righteous.

One of the big differences between the two sides was precisely whether Covid deaths had become part of what William Brewer, the chronicler of flooded California, called "the natural order of things." At some point in 2021 it became clear to many—but not to all—that Covid would never be eradicated, and that there was a certain inevitability that almost everybody would end up being exposed to it sooner or later. That concept, of Covid becoming endemic to society, was often accompanied by a certain degree of fatalism: the idea that there's not a lot of point in inconveniencing oneself and others if we're all going to end up getting it anyway.

The opposing argument was often couched in terms of deaths, and specifically in terms of how many days it took for America to rack up the same number of deaths as were caused by Osama bin Laden on September 11, 2001. The clear implication: If America was willing to embark upon wars in Afghanistan and Iraq costing hundreds of thousands of lives and trillions of dollars as a result of an event that killed fewer than three thousand people, wouldn't it make sense to spend a fraction of that effort to prevent the deaths of thirty thousand people or more?

The difference—the fallacy—is that all deaths are not equal; deaths from natural causes don't shock the conscience in the way that deliberate murder does. It's not murder to calibrate Covid protocols when there's a statistical certainty that anything short of full lockdown will cause some number of excess deaths. The politicians who made those decisions were often thanked by people who were grateful for permission to take off their masks and start putting the pandemic, and its associated fears, behind them.

There was also hope that the spike in crime that many cities saw during the pandemic might start to come back to pre-pandemic levels once the societal fever had broken. Liminal periods—transitions from one orderly state to another—are often characterized by a lack of rules. In the early days of the pandemic, drivers took advantage of the empty roads by speeding, and then were genuinely surprised when they got speeding tickets. On some level, they had convinced themselves that the speed limit had been suspended due to the pandemic.

Even Nobel Prize–winning economist Paul Romer was happy to embrace the spirit of lawlessness, loudly encouraging companies to start making Covid tests regardless of whether they had FDA approval to do so.[12]

So while there were few areas of the US that managed a quasi-ceremonial official end to Covid limbo in the way that the UK did, the psychological need for such a thing remained, and many people ended up quite consciously picking a point or two in the pandemic and mentally declaring it their own private Freedom Day.

One common such day was the day that vaxxed, and usually boosted, Americans started going back out into the world again after self-isolating with Omicron. They had protected themselves with the vaccine, they had protected themselves even more with the booster, they had contracted the virus, and now it was all over. They faced minimal risk themselves, and even the risk of them inadvertently passing Covid on to someone else was now tiny. The disease itself had the silver lining of acting as an adequate rite of disengagement—a process you could go through and come out the other side a different person. At that point, different rules applied, in much the same way as if a senior politician made a public declaration to that effect.

The alternative was for such journeys to be marked with baby steps, which are much less psychologically satisfying—and which indeed can serve to increase rather than decrease base-level worry and discomfort. I went through many such steps myself. There was the amazing day in April 2020 when a *pizza delivery person* drove up and handed over what I'm pretty sure was the most delicious pizza I've ever eaten, a meal made all the sweeter by the feeling that it represented the first signs of a return to normalcy, complete with (masked, arm's length, outdoor) human contact. There were the subsequent halting steps toward social interaction, from distanced outdoor drinks within a small bubble (bring your own wine bottle) to well-ventilated indoor meals within the same bubble (but still, elbow-bumps only).

The out-of-bubble interactions were more meaningful to me.

Anything planned with friends, even a big event like my wife's fiftieth birthday party in September 2021, could have well-defined ground rules about day-of testing, vaccination status, and the like. But what sticks in my memory is the day in April 2021 when the Centers for Disease Control announced that if you were vaccinated, outdoors, and on your own or in a small group, then you didn't need to wear a mask. I bumped into my downstairs neighbor outside my building, and we had an unmasked conversation, the fact of which was far more significant than anything we actually said.

Something similar happened in early March 2022, while I was holed up in a lovely house on the west coast of Ireland putting together a first draft of this book. I'd arrived at the height of the Omicron wave and had been ultra-cautious in terms of Covid pre-cautions through January and even February, but by March cases were down sharply, and people were beginning to feel much more comfortable around each other. I walked into my local coffee shop, Coffee Cottage, for a long black coffee and a bowl of their excellent soup, to find the owners, Aoife Geary and James Elcock, smiling at me from behind the counter, both of them mask-free. We didn't say anything—we didn't need to—but nothing made me happier than to keep my mask in my pocket as my order was prepared.

Those were the good experiences—the ones where social norms were evolving at roughly the same pace as my own comfort level. There were also bad experiences, where I found myself surrounded by people with a much greater risk appetite than my own. There was that time in Texas where four of us went to a Trombone Shorty concert, for instance, and we were pretty much the only people wearing masks (which, per the venue, were technically mandatory). And there were lots of moments in between, like my *other* favorite coffee shop, Variety Coffee, next to the Axios office on Twenty-Fifth Street and Seventh Avenue in New York, where the baristas quietly stopped wearing masks one day, and on one level I wanted to welcome that as a positive sign, but on another level it did weird me out a bit.

That kind of mixture of optimism and apprehension, arriving in unpredictable doses with uncertain timing, will never be looked upon as an adequate rite of disengagement when faced with a terrifying virus. I'm reminded a bit of the organization MoveOn, created in 1998 as a group devoted to the idea that a censure of President Clinton would provide closure to the impeachment debate, and allow society to move on to more pressing issues. Decades later, the call to "move on" still exists, as does the group bearing its name, but the idea of achieving any kind of closure seems to have disappeared entirely.

The year beginning in March 2020 was the longest year that most of us have ever experienced, in large part because it was so difficult to identify an endpoint for it. That's a real problem: So long as one year doesn't end, the following year can never begin.

For millions of people, their Covid conservatism, relative to the population around them, has become a defining part of who they are. Whether it's because of immune deficiencies in themselves or their loved ones, or just out of a sense of what is sensible and proportional when it comes to a pandemic response, they feel every day a little more distanced from a society seemingly determined to embrace denial and magical thinking.

This is not a small minority, either. When New York City public schools got rid of the mask mandate for students, all but one of the kids in my friend's class down the street kept their masks on—thereby rendering even more acute the feeling that they are out of step with mainstream society. (This was in Chinatown, which at the same time was suffering a terrifying spike in violent crimes against Asian-Americans.) For much of New York, the removal of mask mandates by Mayor Eric Adams was one of those key steps on the way back to normal—but for a substantial minority, it only served to intensify the feeling that they were out of sync with society.

Eventually, the discomfort of limbo erodes with time, while the sense of precarity and contingency becomes normalized. The generation born around 9/11 has spent their entire lives being told *this isn't normal*—with *this* being everything from 9/11 itself to the Iraq war to the financial crisis to the Trump administration to the pandemic to the invasion of Ukraine. They're deeply familiar with the Not Normal; what's lacking is any lived experience of what Normal might be.

In such a world, the strange and unusual can feel no stranger, no more unusual, than anything else, and ideas that were formerly considered outlandish seem positively sensible in comparison to reality. That helps explain everything from the rise of crypto to the demand that local authorities should defund police departments. When august financial institutions are putting out sober research reports placing the twelve-month risk of nuclear armageddon at 10 percent, when a microscopic virus can kill six million people in two years and almost bring the entire global economy to a halt, when *time itself* has become broken and unreliable—that's when the New Not Normal is able to settle in for an extended visit. Don't ask how long it's coming to stay; the answer wouldn't mean anything anyway.

A not-normal world is inherently unpredictable, dominated not by risk—something that can be calculated, hedged, and minimized—but rather by uncertainty. Such a world tends to be buffeted by unknown unknowns; it rewards the agile and resilient more than the farsighted or robust. Rather than seeking to anticipate the future, the successful are more likely to be those who can most nimbly adapt to the unexpected.

An old Yiddish saying, "Der Mensch Tracht, Un Gott Lacht," translates as "man plans, and god laughs." It's a sentiment born of centuries of Jewish persecution and the inability of the Jewish people to control their own destiny. People who grow up in highly volatile situations often are better attuned to the way circumstances can turn on a dime. Nassim Nicholas Taleb, the author of *The Black Swan*, for instance, grew up in the midst of the Lebanese Civil War of the 1970s, and later made his fortune by betting that low-probability events would happen with a significantly higher frequency and amplitude than was priced in by the markets.

The Old Normal can be thought of as the world that made Warren Buffett, for a time, the richest person on the planet. Buffett's wealth-creation vehicle, Berkshire Hathaway, has two main components—the insurance arm, and the investments arm. The investments arm buys strong companies, or shares of strong companies, with a time horizon of decades and a thesis that over the long run, these giants will continue to rise steadily in power and value. The insurance arm provides a lot of the cash that is used to acquire the investments—cash that might be needed at any time to pay out on the low-probability events that the insured are protecting themselves against. Berkshire Hathaway does best in a boring, no-surprises world where big, well-run companies grow steadily and don't blow up, and where unlikely events don't cause billions of dollars in insured losses.

Steve Coll's massive corporate biography of ExxonMobil, *Private Empire*,[13] is a very Old Normal book. Published in 2012, when Exxon-Mobil was the most valuable company in the world, it described an ultra-powerful and far-seeing corporation, an empire unto itself, making decisions on century-long timescales and wielding power akin to that of a major nation-state. By the end of the decade, the former giant was worth less than renewables-heavy competitor NextEra Energy, had been kicked out of the Dow Jones Industrial

Average, and was resorting to financial engineering to try to prop up its nosediving share price.[14]

The New Not Normal is likely to see many more such stories, both on the downside and on the upside. ExxonMobil, for instance, turned out not to be entirely dead after all: It saw its market value double after Russia invaded Ukraine, during a period when it was Facebook, desperately renamed Meta, that took on the mantle of world-beating company plunging in value.

In terms of the more quotidian existence of the rest of us, the comfortable and predictable is likely to become increasingly rare. Tens of trillions of dollars are spent "securing retirement," for instance—trying to move money around and delay consumption in such a way as to make our post-work lives as calm and constant as possible.

That's been a pretty quixotic quest for decades now. First, interest rates fell far enough that it no longer made sense for most people to buy an annuity at retirement—to convert your lump-sum savings into a fixed income for life. Then, medical-cost inflation started spiraling upward, and health insurance failed to keep pace, in such a way that even a generous fixed income could easily be wiped out by a single nasty illness of the type that most of us suffer before we die.

Those known unknowns have been with us for eternity—how long we'll live, how we'll die—and they're harder to hedge than ever. In the New Not Normal, they're going to be layered on top of an increasing number of unknown unknowns, of which Covid was only the first. It's going to be great for people who like surprises.

2

The Great Acceleration

ON AN ECONOMIC level, time sped up during the pandemic, rather than slowing down. The Covid recession of 2020 was so short that it forced economists to tear up the normal definition of a recession, which is two consecutive quarters of negative growth. Two quarters? The Covid recession barely lasted two months. Still, it was so sharp and so deep that no one doubted it was a real recession, one that caused enormous damage.

According to the Business Cycle Dating Committee of the National Bureau of Economic Research (yes, there's a very grand committee devoted just to dating recessions), the peak in US economic activity happened in February 2020, while the trough was in April 2020. That's true when your smallest unit of time is a full calendar month: Total economic activity fell off a cliff in mid-March, causing March's numbers to be lower than February's. But as anybody who lived through the pandemic can tell you, the recession didn't start in February; in reality, it started in mid-March.

The Business Cycle Dating Committee never used to worry about what happened within any given month. Recessions could last for years, after all. Being accurate to within a month either way was perfectly fine. In the Covid era, by contrast, months could contain the kind of seasonal variation that normally economists only see, well, with actual seasons.

Something similar happened in markets. Financial markets don't care much about the Business Cycle Dating Committee—its job is to provide a backward-looking determination, while markets are normally only interested in tomorrow. But that, too, changed during the pandemic: What they really wanted to know was not what was going on tomorrow, so much as what was going on today. The epistemic fog that came down on everybody at the onset of the pandemic didn't spare financial markets: While normally they know where they stand and are trying to work out where they're headed, for most of mid-2020 they didn't even know where they stood. Things didn't become clearer with time, either: In July 2022, there was significant disagreement as to whether the US had been in a recession six months earlier. The economic data, on some deep level, had just stopped making sense.[1]

Consider the most important economic report in the world. It isn't anything from the National Bureau of Economic Research; it's not even the quarterly GDP report. Rather, it's the monthly jobs report, which comes out on the first Friday of every month and which tells markets just how many people had jobs the prior month.

The prior month? *When* during the prior month? The jobs report is based on two surveys—one of households, and the other of employers—and each survey takes place during a certain week. Economists found themselves, well into the Covid crisis, looking very closely at *which week* the surveys were being taken, and even trying to work out which *days* of that week saw the most responses and would therefore move the needle the most. That's because the survey for December 2021, say, would show very different results depending on whether it was taken just before the Omicron wave hit, or while the wave was hitting, or after the wave was in full force—a process that took about two weeks in total.

The Bureau of Labor Statistics, which compiles the report, always adjusts for seasonal variations. Jobs, like tides, come and go with predictable seasonality. But during Covid, seasonal variations were swamped by Covid-variant variations. Covid was the signal people were trying to discern in the jobs numbers—everybody wanted to know what effect the pandemic was having on employment. But it was also the noise that made those jobs numbers incredibly hard to read.

When strong signals did emerge, they could flip polarity with dizzying speed. Consider Zoom and Slack, for instance, two remote-work companies that went public in the spring of 2019, less than a year before the pandemic hit. If there was one pair of companies that epitomized the ability to be in the right place at the right time when Covid arrived, it was these.

Zoom, the cross-platform videoconferencing platform, became a generic verb within weeks of lockdown. A stock-market darling since its IPO in 2019, the company surged to a capitalization of more than $150 billion by October 2020, fueled by the evangelism of users who had downloaded the product for free and persuaded their employers to use it across the organization.

That was a model Zoom had already seen perfected by Slack. Instead of spending years trying to get a meeting with a company's CTO to show off your software and try to make a big sale, just make your software available for free to all of the company's employees and let them get so used to it—become so reliant on it—that they'll object if senior management asks them to use anything else. Eventually, managers, knowing the value of a happy workforce, will buy a big corporate license and the software company can make the sale with a fraction of the time and effort that normally goes into such things.

The early weeks of the pandemic accelerated the already-astonishing growth rates seen by Zoom and Slack, and they became the twin exemplars of what investors saw as the post-office, post-city, post-pandemic world of distributed knowledge workers.

Then, as fast as they rose, the magic wore off. Not because workers were back in their offices faster than expected, communicating face-to-face, but rather because the new forms of communication became so central to how everybody worked, such an obviously permanent part of the future, that large corporations decided it wasn't wise to try to fix the problem by using one company's video tech, another company's group-chat tech, and so on.

When technologies like those underpinning Zoom and Slack were new and were exciting the early adopters within large enterprises, senior decision-makers were happy to give those groups the tools they wanted to improve their efficiency and productivity. When it came time to bake in a solution for *everybody* to use on a daily basis, however, the cool tech kids found it harder to influence their employers. They're the kind of people who love to talk about the relative merits of different software products, and who spend a lot of time trying to pick the very best one. If Google Docs becomes a better authoring tool than Microsoft Word, these are the people who will switch to Google Docs almost overnight, even as normal people just keep on using Microsoft Word because, frankly, they don't really care very much about software and have more important things to worry about.

With work-from-home software, the normies ended up handily winning the war. Zoom and Slack didn't disappear; in fact they kept on growing. But at large organizations where everybody already used

Microsoft Office, the path of least resistance—and also the cheapest option—was to just use Microsoft Teams for such things. It came at a marginal cost of zero, it was supported by a trillion-dollar tech giant, and—best of all—the great mass of normal employees running Office 365 on their Windows computers *already had it*.

Thus did Slack disappear into the maw of Oracle, and Zoom retrace its stock-market steps so that, just like that other pandemic darling Peloton, its stock price ended up at pre-pandemic levels.

In the end, there's a case to be made that the pandemic was something of a poisoned chalice for many companies that seemed initially to benefit from it. Absent Covid, Zoom and Slack would not have grown nearly as fast as they did in 2020. But by growing slowly, they could have crept deeper into the enterprise and become an institutional habit before Microsoft really woke up to their competitive threat. We'll never know. What we *do* know, however, is that once Microsoft realized the size of the opportunity and the quality of the competition, it moved with astonishing speed to build a product that in many ways soon surpassed the upstarts—a speed that few anticipated, especially from a company that was notorious just a few years previously for its endless development cycles.

One of the most popular pastimes of the pandemic was Beat Saber, a workout rhythm game designed for virtual reality headsets like Facebook's Oculus. You strap on the headset and arm yourself with a pair of lightsabers—one red, one blue—that are used to slash at Tron-style blocks that come at you in sync with various songs. It starts out hard and gets exponentially harder, and accomplished players of the game post videos that rack up millions of views on YouTube or TikTok, showing off a degree of dexterity and speed that barely seems possible.

Sometimes, the pandemic itself felt a bit like Expert Mode in Beat Saber, with business and finance and economics just moving *faster* than sometimes seemed possible. Entire business cycles got compressed into a period of months; industries could rise and fall before the pandemic was even over. To keep up required a constant recalibration of priors—a willingness to jettison everything you'd just laboriously learned, whether it was about the virus, the economy, or the way the two interacted.

On some level, that's just the modern condition—everything is always fast and new. But what we saw during the pandemic constituted a step change even by the standards of digital natives, and it left a lot of people behind. Even when the economy was clearly roaring ahead, for instance, I would frequently be told by very smart people that it was in a crisis. After all, pundits like myself had confidently declared in the early days of the pandemic that the only way to get the economy back on track was to get the virus under control. The syllogism was therefore simple: Since the virus wasn't remotely under control, surely the economy couldn't be back on track. The only problem was that I had been completely wrong. I was right that we couldn't get our old economy back without solving Covid; what I failed to anticipate, even as I was pitching a book entitled *The Phoenix Economy*, was just how quickly we could build a whole new economy that worked around the virus and could operate at even higher velocity.

Once things speed up, they rarely slow down for very long. Records are made to be broken; Beat Saber performances that dazzled in 2020 were commonplace in 2022. Pandemic conditions laid the groundwork for the unprecedented speed seen in everything from corporate hiring to Microsoft development cycles—but once those precedents were set, they became achievable and even predictable.

Companies across the economy realized that, pre-pandemic, they didn't know their own strength—how fast they could hire, how aggressively they could raise their prices, how quickly they could develop new software. Now that they have that knowledge, they're not going to be content to relax back into the kind of performance they might previously have found acceptable.

A major component of the rocket fuel propelling the phoenix out of the ashes for years to come is going to be just the newly acquired knowledge of what is possible. We won't always have the fiscal and monetary tailwinds that we saw during the pandemic. But executives are going to remember what they managed in the early 2020s, and are always going to want to surpass that mark.

3

From Ladders to Trampolines

OVER THE COURSE of the pandemic, time shortened dramatically in one area in particular: investing.

When someone makes money, that income generally comes from one of two sources: Either they worked for it, trading their labor for cash, or else it was investment income, where their wealth was being put to work.

The distinction between the two is not always clear-cut. Almost anybody who makes a lot of money from investments puts some significant amount of work into determining what they invest in and when. But for most folks it's pretty obvious which is which. Broadly, money earned (or inherited) but not spent gets moved into savings, where it then gets invested, often in stocks. When those investments rise, wealth grows.

Both earnings and investments are time-based. Labor is denominated in time-based units: You get paid so much per hour, or per year. When it comes to labor, annual salaries are higher-status things than hourly wages. Investment is similar. You can make bets on short-term price movements, but the high-status move is to float above such concerns and have a decades-long time horizon, where you worry about things like retirement income or your grandchildren's college fund.

During the pandemic, those investing timeframes changed dramatically. Labor timeframes didn't: The amount of time it took to do a certain thing at a certain job was broadly unchanged. But when people invested the financial proceeds of those jobs, their attitudes—and the potential returns to short-termism—were something that markets hadn't seen since possibly the 1920s.

For most of my career, the received opinion when it came to investments was clear and unambiguous—that it's one of the few areas of life where there really is such a thing as a free lunch. Investing is also one of the areas where it's possible to see a clear dividing line between Gen X—my generation—and the Boomers. Post-pandemic, a new dividing line has started to emerge, between Gen X and the Millennials. Think of it as the difference between a generation that *lost* a lot of money when the stock market crashed in 2000 versus a generation that *made* a lot of money when the stock market crashed in 2020.

The first big investing generation, however, were the Boomers; in fact, they still control most invested money to this day.

When the Boomers were entering the workforce, the standard way to save for retirement was to belong to some kind of corporate pension plan. A steady and predictable retirement income would come from your employer, and it was up to the company whether to put money away against that future liability, and if so how much. Largely as a result, direct investing in the stock market was mostly a pastime for the rich.

For them, investing generally involved picking a portfolio of individual stocks and bonds, many of which would have been recommended by a golf buddy or some other social contact. Alternatively, you could sign up as a client of one of the professionals—investment managers who would give you investment advice for a hefty fee. As early as 1955, the wonderfully named Fred Schwed published *Where Are the Customers' Yachts?*,[1] a classic investment book predicated on the tale of a man who came to New York and admired the magnificent vessels of the bankers and brokers of Wall Street. The punchline was that the customers had no yachts: Dutifully following the advice of the Wall Street elite would make the brokers more money than it would the investor, in much the same way that modern-day hedge-fund managers and private-equity titans make much more money than their investors do. (Or, for that matter, in much the same way that the founders of Robinhood, the stock-trading app beloved of Millennials, became billionaires even as the size of the median Robinhood brokerage account remained stuck at about $240.)

Pre-internet, people would find out stock prices by looking them up in agate print or by phoning up their broker. (Or, often, by their broker phoning them.) Stock-market indices existed, but index *funds* were expensive and hard to find, and certainly weren't accessible to most individual investors. The Boomer conception of stock-market investing, therefore, became one in which it was an expensive and somewhat mysterious upper-middle-class hobby. That's a conception which lives on to this day among graying *Barron's* subscribers and retirees who might mistrust email but are happy to log on to their online brokerage accounts to trade in and out of their favorite stocks. Such investors have a wealth of hard-earned experience that they put to use in their stock-market strategies, and generally believe that their experience gives them some kind of an edge. After all, they've been exploring the recondite mysteries of the market for decades.

Thanks to the fact that there was a strong bull market over those decades, most of those Boomers have done pretty well for themselves. Lucky to be entering adulthood when houses and housing were cheap, they could afford to put excess savings into the market; their houses simultaneously soared in value, which also helped.

Human psychology being what it is, few if any of them beat themselves up for failing to have kept pace with a hypothetical market portfolio; instead, they congratulate themselves on their winners and console themselves about their losers, often over drinks with friends. As hobbies go, there are many that are more expensive, and few that are so good at giving monied men something exciting yet uncontroversial that they can argue about. (Sports can't be the *only* topic of conversation.)

Boomer-style investing has the side effect of turning your entire portfolio, implicitly or explicitly, into a trade: Whatever you own, it's always in a temporary state between being bought and being sold. If you manage to consistently buy low and sell high, that makes you a great investor.

The dream is to invest like Ted Weschler, one of the two men tapped by Warren Buffett as being able to take over his stock-investing job once the Oracle of Omaha dies or (less likely) retires. Weschler had a $70,000 retirement account in 1989, which he held at Charles Schwab; he used that account to buy and sell publicly traded securities. By 2012, it was worth $131 million—more than he could have made, with perfect foresight, by investing in *any* individual stock.

Don't ask me how it's possible to see the future and know which stocks are going to go up, and therefore should be bought, and which ones are going to go down—or have stopped going up as fast as other stocks—and therefore should be sold. That skill has always seemed somewhat alchemical to me, but in any case, it's a skill that millions of investors aspire to. And the key to doing it well is that you have to get two things right, for every trade: not only which stock to buy, but also how long to hold it for.

The genius of securities markets, after all, is that they create an infinite range of possibilities around the amount of time it takes to make money. If my bank extends to me a five-year loan, then, assuming the bank doesn't enter into some elaborate contract to sell that loan, it will make money only after five years, once I've repaid the principal. That's because a loan isn't a security. On the other hand, if my employer issues a five-year bond, which *is* a security, then bond-market traders and speculators can hold that security for any period of time from minutes to years, and no one needs to wait until the maturity date to make money.

Again, this is a big difference between labor and capital. If you want to get rich from working—if you want to be a successful entrepreneur—then you have to be able to build a company capable of sealing off all real and potential competition and that survives—indeed, thrives—for decades. You're not only invested in your company, you're committed to it.

In order to be a successful investor, on the other hand, you only need to ride any upswing for as long as it lasts. Then you can transfer your investments elsewhere—or, if you're playing in Expert Mode, you can even go short and get paid when stocks fall rather than rise. Markets, in other words, transform investments into trades.

This, at heart, is the genius of markets. A company like General Electric can issue stock in 1889, invest the proceeds into internal growth, and never have any obligation to pay it back. (In finance-speak, stock is "permanent capital.") If things go well, then GE has the *option* to return money to shareholders, via dividends and share buybacks. The more it does that, over time, the more the stock tends to be worth. But the way to make real money on GE stock isn't to sit back and cash dividend checks. It's to stay out of the stock entirely for the long periods when it's flat or declining, and instead buy it when it's about to rise—in the early 1990s, perhaps, just before it went on a tear and rose tenfold in less than a decade. Then, of course, you need to sell it before it gives back most of those gains.

Alternatively, instead of holding for ten years, you could hold for one ten-millionth of a second. That, too, is possible in today's markets. So-called high frequency traders take advantage of the fact that there isn't one price per stock, there's two. There's the "best bid"—the highest price anybody is willing to pay—and there's also the "best offer," which is the lowest price at which anybody is willing to sell. The gap between them is small: For GE it might be just one cent. But when you place an order to buy GE stock, the price you pay is the "best offer" price. Call it $12.72. And when your golfing buddy places an order to sell GE stock, the price she gets is the "best bid" price of $12.71. For any normal holding period, the difference between those two prices is not going to make a significant difference to your total return. But if a high-frequency trading (HFT) shop like Citadel or Knight is the counterparty for both of you, and does all of the selling and all of the buying, selling at $12.72 and buying at $12.71 thousands of times a minute, then it can make real money with surprisingly little risk. Those profits then get divvied up between the owners and employees of the HFT shop; a kickback (so-called payment for order flow) goes to the brokers sending that shop all the trades; and even, sometimes, a bit of money goes to the actual original investor, which is known as "price improvement."

We'll come back to the implications of high-frequency trading in a minute. But the bigger point is just the magic of securities markets: By allowing stock to be traded painlessly at any time, without the knowledge or consent of the company that issued it, markets allow investors to buy and sell according to their own needs and desires, rather than according to the needs of the issuer. That's incredibly valuable and is one of the great inventions of modern capitalism.

It allows companies to fund themselves in perpetuity, for instance, by selling stock to a trading desk that might only hold it for one day or less. (In the biggest and most liquid market in the world, that for US Treasury bonds, the government regularly sells billions of dollars' worth of bonds to so-called primary dealers whose *job* is to sit on them for as short a time as possible before selling them into the market. Treasuries might be owned by the broadest conceivable cross-section of international investors, but as far as the government is concerned, it only actually borrows money from a couple dozen big banks like Goldman Sachs or BNP Paribas.)

The issuer's counterparty is the investor. The interests of the two parties are rarely perfectly aligned; while the issuer is generally a real-world business dealing with real-world problems, the investor is someone with a dream of turning money into profit—something which, in the world of securities, is achieved by buying low and selling high. That's two separate transactions, both of which need to be timed correctly. The result is a kind of investing, for Boomers, that's a difficult discipline, one where expertise is necessary and rewarded, and where people capable of successfully timing the market achieve the status of demigods.

There's a lot of value in markets, then, and in the way they transform stodgy corporations into fast-moving fungible and liquid securities. But there are downsides, too. For one thing, they offer such outsized financial rewards that they tend to attract some of the most talented human capital in the country, all of which gets devoted to the service of what Adair Turner, the former investment banker and British establishment grandee, has identified as "socially useless" activity.

More subtly, the message from much of the financial media, certainly during the Boomers' prime earning years and even to this day, is that there are enormous potential rewards from successfully picking stocks and timing the market, and that the effort needed to reap those rewards can be relatively small. Just being fortunate enough to buy Berkshire Hathaway stock in the 1960s, and then having the discipline not to sell it, would suffice. Anyone can do it—which means that millions of people give it a go, and/or kick themselves for not having bought Berkshire or bitcoin or even Domino's Pizza stock when they had the chance.

That message was turbocharged during the dot-com boom of the late 1990s, when stock-market information flooded the internet and created what seemed like a level playing field for a new generation of investors armed with online brokerage accounts and the desire to dive into a frenzy of wealth creation. Trading was tougher back then—stocks still traded in eighths of a dollar, rather than cents, and discount brokerages charged $15 or so per trade, a price that has since fallen to zero. Still, a lot of individuals made a lot of money buying high-flying technology stocks. I moved to New York in 1997 and saw the dot-com frenzy happen before my eyes; one of my colleagues at Bridge News even maintained a spreadsheet of his portfolio that was dynamically updated to show his profit and loss on a real-time basis. Every time I looked at it, it was showing a very healthy profit—until, of course, it wasn't, after the market crashed in 2000. The stocks that had risen the most also fell the most, disabusing the late-nineties generation of stock-pickers of any illusion that they had any real skill at the game.

That sobering experience helped to turn Gen X—the "Slacker" generation—into the first and possibly the only generation to really embrace the passive-investing revolution. Those of us who read the literature had all manner of empirical data to back up our justified true belief that simply investing in index funds, and then doing absolutely nothing, would almost certainly, statistically, outperform any attempt we made to outperform the market. Those of us who rode

the ups and downs of the dot-com boom had an early and visceral
real-world lesson in how that was true. Most importantly, all of us
had a degree of *access* to index funds that our parents never had at
our age. Passive investing wasn't just strategically optimal, it was
also *easy*.

Index funds didn't start life as the cheap and easy way to invest.
As Robin Wigglesworth details in his book *Trillions*,[2] they were initially laboriously constructed as an expensive but effective way of
beating rival fund managers. They remained inaccessible to individual investors for decades and were such a strange beast even
after they arrived on the retail market that they took many more
years to become entrenched as the default option for anybody who
understood the realities of the market and who had no particular
reason to believe that they were smarter and faster than the smart-
est hedge-funders out there.

The strangeness didn't just come from the fact that index funds
were offering the proverbial free lunch—outperforming the vast
majority of hardworking fund managers while doing basically no
work. It also came from the fact that the way index-fund investing
works is by completely discarding the wondrous fact that markets
allow investors to enter and exit positions at will. The archetypal
index investor buys the index—and then never exits, until such time
as they want to actually spend their money.

Gen X needed to make two mental leaps in order to fully embrace index investing. The first was to eschew all dreams of making
money by timing the market—which is to say, all dreams that can
be summarized by saying "I wish I'd bought X in (insert year)."
Those dreams are hard to eschew! Especially when so much of the
media is devoted to extolling people who have made lots of money
after buying something that subsequently went up in value enormously.

The second leap is to jettison the idea of any kind of exit strategy and to embrace the concept of the roach motel. After you enter the index, you stay there until you actually need to spend the money. (This is especially true of so-called target-date funds, which automatically tweak your asset allocation according to your age.) In your retirement—or maybe earlier—you might need some cash, and when you do, you spend some of the money you've accumulated up to that point. But needing cash is pretty much the only reason to sell. You don't sell because you're worried that the market is going to fall, and you *certainly* don't sell because the market has already fallen.

It's unnatural to think this way, especially when the media constantly bombards investors with forecasts and analyses. Doesn't it make sense to sell when stocks are expensive and the economy is about to shrink? The empirical answer is: not really. Most people who do that end up missing out on substantial future gains, since almost no one can successfully time both their exit from the market and their subsequent reentry. But the *story* is compelling, and storytelling drives many more investment decisions than most Wall Streeters would like to admit.

When I briefly worked for the short-lived *Condé Nast Portfolio* magazine, my colleague Michael Lewis—the best financial journalist of his generation—took it upon himself to turn passive investing into a compelling story, complete with a sympathetic protagonist. He ended up alighting on Blaine Lourd, a multimillionaire Wall Street stockbroker charging Hollywood clients very high fees for putting their money into index funds.

There was enough human drama in the piece to keep you turning the page—Lewis is nothing if not a natural storyteller. But there was also something, dare I say it, *Boomerish* about it. (Lewis, born in 1960, is a young Boomer, but a Boomer all the same.) Lourd is very open about the fact that he's not earning money for his stock-picking prowess, and that his clients could get exactly the same returns at a much lower cost by just putting their money into index funds directly. What's interesting is the way he told Lewis that he keeps his clients: "I say, 'Howard, be careful or I'm going to send you back to Smith Barney.' And they laugh. But they know exactly what I mean."

Boomers knew exactly what Lourd meant; Gen X would have no idea. The reason Boomers needed Lourd to hold their hands and tell them that they were doing great by doing nothing at all was that they were prone to regret the investment decisions not taken, given how enormous the rewards to taking them could have been. Very few Boomers were fortunate enough to invest in Berkshire Hathaway, for instance, but those who did often made a *lot* of money, while those who didn't generally had a niggling feeling, thanks to the financial media, that somehow they could or should have managed to do so.

They might look with envy at the story of Stewart Horejsi, who had one great idea when he took over his family's underperforming welding-supply company in 1980. He could manage it for the long term, reinvest all of the firm's profits, try to grow it back to its former glory with the goal of seeing off its new domestic and foreign competitors. Or, he could manage it for the short term, maximize cash profits, and reinvest those profits in a better business instead.

That's kind of what Warren Buffett did—he used the profits from a small textile company, Berkshire Hathaway, to invest in a vast array of other businesses, from insurance to his beloved Coca-Cola Company. Horejsi, on the other hand, saw no need to reinvent the wheel—he just took his company's profits and invested them in Berkshire Hathaway stock. His welding-supply company never grew much in value, but his Berkshire stake eventually made him a multi-billionaire.

The dream of emulating Horejsi and turning a modest fortune into a large fortune was what prompted Boomers with time or money to spare to avidly consume publications like *Barron's*, devoted to helping them pick the stocks that would outperform, and spend billions of dollars on financial advice of various forms, much of it bundled into "management fees" at brokerages like Smith Barney.

For Gen X, on the other hand, getting pressured by a stockbroker into buying shares in some company they've never heard of is not a base-case expectation they need a hero like Blaine Lourd to save them from. Rather, it's something they've never experienced and would react very badly to if it ever happened.

The reason is largely generational. Most Gen Xers never had a modest fortune to begin with, since the Boomers and what's left of the Silent Generation, before them, have done a fantastic job of keeping hold of most of the wealth in America. They might only be about 28 percent of the population, but they control over 70 percent of the country's assets.

Partly as a result, Gen X has a level of cynicism about the economy and markets that is hard to find outside Boomers who aren't active in left-wing politics. In terms of wealth accumulation, we Gen Xers might be doing better than the Millennials, on average, since we were in a bull market for substantially all of our professional lives and we missed out on some of the most egregious increases in college tuition fees. But when we look at the effortless single-income middle-class lifestyle afforded many of our parents, we don't feel particularly fortunate. We tend to spend much more than they did and save much less, thanks in large part to soaring housing prices and diminished bargaining power when it comes to wages.

I might be overextrapolating here from my own experience and that of my friends, but hell, this is my book, so I'll just say that as a generation, we're pleasantly surprised when the economy does well, while generally expecting it to be mediocre going forward. That, of course, is a *terrible* attitude to have from the point of view of an investor cohort. When the economy does well, Boomers and other investors bid stock prices up on the (generally true) expectation that the good times will continue. A Gen Xer, on the other hand, looks at high stock prices and remembers what happened in 2000: What goes up must come down. Emotionally, we think that the healthy economy is something of an aberration, which means we have no desire to pay top dollar today for future earnings that aren't going to materialize tomorrow. That tilts us constitutionally toward the conservative/bearish end of the investment spectrum, where returns are relatively low.

Such decisions aren't necessarily made consciously. More common is a broad disinterest when it comes to financial matters—a feeling that you're not the kind of person who understands money and investments and stuff like that. While the investing game might be a fun hobby for Boomers, it's just not something we Gen Xers ever really got interested in. The best we can hope for is that we were somehow nudged into some kind of automatic savings vehicle— a target-date 401(k) plan, say, or even a mortgage—that saw us putting a bit of money away every month in a way that slowly but surely paid off over time.

After all, there's a strong case to be made that *any* attempt to understand the state of the economy, as a guide to where to put your money, seems ill advised. Legendary investor Howard Marks has a great question: "If you invest on the basis of your macro views, how often have they helped?"[3]

The answer, for most normal humans, is that our subjective opinions tend to work against us rather than for us when it comes to investment returns. For one thing, our personal, idiosyncratic economic analysis is inevitably wrapped up in an inseverable Gordian knot with our political beliefs. Republicans always think the economy is doing badly whenever there's a Democrat in the White House; Democrats feel squeamish about profiting from Republican attempts to rig the system in favor of capital and against workers, or the planet.

In any case, going to cash in anticipation of a foreseen downturn is an even more common error among retail investors than the one that financial advisers always warn of, which is selling after markets have already fallen. Both are attempts to time the market—to sell before a fall—and therefore imply a plan to buy if and when the fall actually happens. Most of the time the fall never materializes, but even when it does, precious few of the market timers are good at getting back in below the level where they sold.

Meanwhile, for the massive Millennial generation, such concerns are laughably theoretical. While Gen X might have lacked a modest seed fortune to get started in the markets, the Millennials mostly lacked any kind of investable positive net worth at all. Either they were college-educated, in which case they had massive student loans, or they weren't, in which case their chances were slim of ever earning enough money to become part of Wall Street's target investor class.

Where Gen X had the dot-com crash of 2000 as their salutary moment, the Millennials had something much, much worse: the global financial crisis of 2008. It wasn't Millennials who were flipping houses in the mid-2000s and taking out mortgages they had no ability to service. It wasn't Millennials who suffered when the stock market fell, since they had negligible investments in the market to begin with. But it was Millennials who bore the brunt of the broad economic implosion that followed. Millions of them attempted to enter the workforce—Millennials are significantly more numerous than Gen X—only to find that the number of jobs was rising slowly if at all, that very few people were voluntarily leaving the workforce, and that therefore there was really no place for them to find good jobs. Never mind getting rich slowly, they weren't going to get rich at all.

If the Gen X attitude to Boomers' investment techniques was an eye roll and a move to something much simpler and easier, then Millennials were broadly disillusioned with—and excluded by sheer lack of cash from—the whole concept of investing in the first place. In the wake of the financial crisis, the idea of long-term savings and asset accumulation as a road to wealth was something that lost credibility with an entire generation.

The 2008 crisis was legitimately traumatic: Home values cratered into negative-equity territory; the stock market crashed. The idea of slow and methodical wealth accumulation started to look like a sick joke played by Wall Street on unwitting chumps—one that came with enormous negative externalities. It wasn't just normal folks who had been suckered into the financialized economy who were harmed. It was everybody, and especially the young and the poor.

Even once the Millennials started to find salaried employment, they found themselves operating in a ZIRP world that vaporized financial assumptions underpinning centuries' worth of investing truisms. ZIRP, which stands for "zero interest-rate policy," was global central banks' desperate attempt first to prevent the global economy from imploding and then to try to restart economic growth in the wake of a crisis that had given the entire world an entirely rational fear of taking on debt.

Debt, or leverage, as it's also known, has historically been the main engine of growth in capitalism. It's a way of matching two groups. On one side are people with savings—money they don't need today but would love to be able to spend tomorrow. On the other are people who want to invest in the future by borrowing money in such a way that they will be better off tomorrow than they would have been without the loan, even after paying the loan back in full and with interest.

Central banks regulate the temperature of the economy by setting the price of debt—the amount of interest you have to pay in order to borrow money. The idea is simple: Some debts are a bad idea and should never be taken on. Others are a good idea if you need to pay them back with minimal interest, but are a terrible idea if you need to pay them back with a lot of interest. Getting a Small Business Administration (SBA) loan to start up a laundromat, for instance, might make a lot of sense—while borrowing the same amount of money from the local loan shark, or even just racking up debts on a credit card charging a 29.99 percent interest rate, would never be worth it.

According to standard economic theory, if the central bank raises interest rates then a bunch of debts that would make sense in a low-rate environment start becoming uneconomic. As a result, people borrow less money, there's less overall economic activity than there would have been without the rate hike, and the economy grows less quickly than it would have done otherwise. Conversely, if interest rates are low then that makes many investment ideas economically attractive, so there's more risk-taking, more activity, and more growth—unless, of course, the risk-taking takes the form of subprime mortgages.

After the financial crisis, the whole world was debt-averse, which made central banks' jobs very difficult. They cut interest rates all the way to zero, but even at zero percent interest, people just didn't want more debt. Indeed, after accounting for inflation, central banks made sure that interest rates were *negative*—that many creditworthy borrowers had to pay back less than they were borrowing, in real terms. And still, outside the ranks of Wall Street financial engineers, there were very few takers.

Normally, the problem with low interest rates is that they risk overheating the economy and creating inflationary pressures. That wasn't the case after the financial crisis. Still, there's no such thing as a free lunch, and the people most hurt by ZIRP were the kind of savers who lend out money—creditors, or bond investors, as they're also known.

Most importantly, the financial crisis effectively killed compound interest. Taking a modest nest egg and watching it grow as it earns interest, year in and year out, used to work fantastically back in the Boomers' prime earning years. Some people called compound interest the eighth wonder of the world, and not just because it helped the rich get richer. They would lend their savings out to borrowers either directly or via banks, thereby helping the economy as a whole while earning so much interest income they could sometimes live just on the interest generated by their assets.

In a world of ZIRP, the dream of becoming a rentier—of living on the income generated by your assets—is out of reach for all but a fraction of the top 1 percent. When the Fed sets interest rates at zero and uses "forward guidance" (press conferences) to make it clear that it fully intends rates to remain at zero in a year's time, then the amount of interest you can earn from lending money to a safe borrower like the US government is going to be very close to zero.

Let's say that the one-year interest rate was 0.08 percent, which was about normal for most of the ZIRP period. If a millionaire invested $1 million in one-year Treasury bills paying 0.08 percent, that would give her a princely income of about $65 per month. To obtain an annual income of $60,000, she'd need to invest $75 million.

By contrast, in March 1989, one-year Treasury bills yielded 9.64 percent. One million dollars in those bills would throw off $8,000 per month, and an annual income of $60,000 required just $622,000 invested in T-bills.

There were two big consequences, to Millennials, of living in a zero-interest world. The first was just that they couldn't hope to see their assets accumulate slowly through the magic of compound interest, as previous generations had been able to do. The big advantage of being a young investor—that you have decades ahead of you with which to compound your wealth—had evaporated before their eyes.

If you can't get rich slowly, then there's only one other way to get rich, which is to get rich quick. Getting rich quick has other advantages: For one thing, it's much more gratifying, and allows you to do wonderful things like call in rich to your job. "Sorry, I won't be coming in today, or ever again, I'm too rich to care about your paycheck." For another, it doesn't require a small fortune to begin with. You can start with just a few bucks, invest them in some highly risky proposition, and next thing you know you're a millionaire.

The downside of trying to get rich quick is obvious: It generally doesn't work, and you end up with nothing. Then again, ending up with nothing was pretty much the expected outcome anyway, for many Millennials.

My former colleague Kevin Roose explains the gap between Gen X and Millennials as the difference between ladders and trampolines.[4] Gen X was broadly still capable of climbing ladders—the career ladder, the housing ladder. Get in on the bottom rung and then, with some mixture of hard work and good fortune, work your way up the ladder to wealth and success. That vision is increasingly hollow to Millennials, who often spent decades getting nowhere, barely hanging on to the bottom rung of the career ladder and not even coming close to the bottom rung of the housing ladder.

Instead, what Millennials found themselves looking for, especially in the wake of the pandemic, were trampolines—defined by Roose as risky, volatile investments that could result in a life-changing windfall. The odds are stacked against you either way, but if you get a lucky bounce on the trampoline then you can clear the top of the ladder in a single bound.

Another word for trampolines is lottery tickets. The broad way lottery tickets work is that if you have a small or negative net worth, you're much more likely to invest in them, either literally or meta-phorically. This is perfectly rational: Lottery tickets are cheap, while investments are expensive. Lottery tickets are also fun and make sense as a consumption expenditure—it's often useful to think of them not as throwing money down the drain, so much as buying a dream. (No one has ever bought a lottery ticket without thinking about what they'd do with the money if they won.) Indeed, good Gen Xer that I am, I even encourage my friends to buy lottery tickets—because by spending a modest amount of money on dreams of untold riches, they will then be much less likely to take silly risks with their real savings. You're likely to lose a lot less money buying actual lottery tickets than you would buying shitcoins or meme stocks or specu-lative NFTs (new-fangled tulips). We'll go into more detail about what these assets are and how they work in the next chapter.

When it comes to folks whose real savings are in the slim-to-none category to begin with, then tut-tutting about the Kids These Days spending their money on <insert something you wouldn't spend your own money on here> is nearly always a bad look. I think of it as the Avocado Toast Fallacy—the argument, generally made by Boomers, that if people just spent less money on avocado toast, or Starbucks lattes, or restaurant food delivery, or $200 sneakers, or lottery tickets, or trampolines, then they would no longer be in the slim-to-none savings category, and they could slowly but surely save their way into wealth in much the same way as the Boomers did.

That's an argument that comes from a position of privilege and ignorance, one that doesn't seek to understand *why* the younger generation is spending money on relatively ephemeral pleasures, and one that's rooted in a weird nostalgia for a time when the opportunity space of things to spend money on was much narrower, and when spending on food was a bigger part of household budgets than spending on housing. When Boomers were teenagers, for instance, internalizing their parents' money worries, food accounted for more than 20 percent of household consumption, while spending on housing was less than 14 percent. Fifty years later, when the Millennials were teenagers, their parents were spending 16 percent of their money on housing—a smaller increase than you might imagine, thanks to falling mortgage rates—but less than 8 percent on food.

Economists will tell you that Millennials are spending money on experiences *precisely because* the opportunity cost of doing so—the amount of wealth they can reasonably expect to accumulate by saving it rather than spending it—is so much smaller than it used to be.

The savings will also have less immediate utility. The first reason why people want to save money—and certainly the first thing that Boomers and Gen X tended to do once they accumulated a decent nest egg—is to buy a place to live. But if you live in most major cities and earn anything near the median wage for Millennials, you have no real chance of being able to save up for a house down payment without taking extraordinary and probably unwise risks with your money.

Or consider the rare and fortunate Millennial who starts earning significantly more than the median wage and begins to see a possible path to homeownership. Even then, putting some spare cash into the stock market made very little sense, given that stocks were broadly considered to be overvalued for the entire time that Millennials have been in the workforce.

Any financial adviser will tell you that if you invest money in the stock market you have to be prepared for it to shrink by at least 30 percent at some unknowable point in the future. The last thing you want, if you're a member of a generation of non-homeowners with aspirations to one day perhaps be able to buy a place to live, is to see a third of your down payment evaporate just when you're about to need it.

The stock market therefore simply doesn't have the same relevance or significance to most Millennials as it did to prior generations. The Boomers thought of it as a mysterious cryptogram whose secrets could be mastered; Gen X thought of it as a place to park money in index funds, in the hope that it would grow over time. (Wonderfully for us, it did.) The Millennials largely avoided it entirely. Perhaps, if they had an enlightened employer, they would put some money aside for retirement in order to get their 401(k) match; perhaps they had some fun with a free Robinhood account. But in general you only really get into the stock market once you've paid off all your debts *and* bought a house—and that, for the most indebted generation in American history, surrounded by eye-wateringly expensive house prices, took much longer for Millennials than it did for their forebears.

Then the pandemic happened, and everything changed. In the first instance, stocks plunged—which was worrying for people invested in the market, since they were losing a lot of money, and also worrying for people not invested in the market, since it indicated that the entire economy had come to a screeching halt, with no real visibility into when or whether it might be able to recover. The market can cope with catastrophe, so long as it's short-lived; the market plunge implied that the catastrophic economic consequences of the pandemic would be anything but.

Those were the days that stretched out like years. "There are decades where nothing happens; and there are weeks where decades happen." That quote, from Vladimir Ilyich Lenin, topped my weekly newsletter on March 12, 2020, the week when the World Health Organization officially declared Covid to be a pandemic in an all-caps tweet with two siren emoji,[5] when the Dow dropped into bear-market territory, and when oil prices plunged after Russia and Saudi Arabia decided to increase the amount they were pumping even as the world stopped moving (and therefore stopped needing oil).

The fear of being infected by a deadly disease was new, and all the more terrifying for being full of unknowns, and it was itself contagious. It fed into apocalyptic exponential extrapolations—simple mathematical exercises that spat out numbers that, just a couple of weeks earlier, would barely have been conceivable.

On March 22, for instance, the president of the Federal Reserve Bank of St. Louis, Jim Bullard, took a call from Bloomberg reporter Steve Matthews. Bullard is not one of those Fed presidents drawn from the ranks of colorful local businessmen, an attempt to keep the Fed firmly rooted in the heartland rather than in academia. Rather, he's a highly respected career Federal Reserve economist, a central banker to his bones—which is to say, in most states of the world, he would be another gray man in a gray suit writing academic papers with titles like "Learning and Structural Change in Macroeconomic Data."[6]

That Sunday, however, a very different Bullard appeared—one with his hair very much on fire. He told Matthews he was forecasting that the unemployment rate would hit a staggering 30 percent in the second quarter, and that the headline GDP figure would show a drop of—wait for it—50 percent. That would be an annualized figure from a single quarter's fall, but even so, both numbers were so much worse than anything seen during the global financial crisis that they barely felt real.

To put those numbers in context, at the very worst point of the financial crisis, in the fourth quarter of 2008, the GDP growth rate was -8.5 percent. The peak level of unemployment came a year later, in October 2009, when it hit 10.0 percent. Bullard was forecasting unemployment three times worse than the lowest point of the global financial crisis, and GDP shrinkage almost *six* times worse.

Had these numbers come from anybody else—a permabear CNBC talking head, for instance—they could have been discounted a little. Bullard, however, while on the dovish end of the central bank spectrum, is no extremist. Perhaps he was trying to shock Washington's politicians into action: He told Matthews that the government should implement an immediate program covering all workers' lost income.

Bullard's forecasts were genuinely held, and in fact he was right that the economy was going to shrink much more rapidly than anybody on Wall Street seemed to be expecting. Bank of America thought second-quarter GDP would fall by 12 percent; the most bearish Wall Street forecast came from Goldman Sachs, which forecast a 24 percent drop. In reality, the final number came in at -31.2 percent. America—and the world—was going to experience an economic tailspin that came harder and faster than even the Great Depression.

As we all know now, both stocks and the broader economy bounced back almost immediately, in economic time. In just one month the S&P 500 fell 34 percent—just as the financial advisers always warned it could. Consider a Gen Xer on February 19 who had managed over the course of a lifetime of saving to accumulate $100,000 in index funds. On March 23, that nest egg had suddenly become worth just $66,075. And of *course* she was checking her brokerage account statements online, because every news outlet was screaming headlines about bloodbaths on Wall Street. She had no way of knowing—none of us did—that the February high would be regained within five months, and that the market would just keep on rising steadily from there. She felt bad about the pandemic, bad about the economy, bad about her savings, and bad about the job she had either just lost or was worried about losing.

For many Millennials, on the other hand, the experience was markedly different. Of course they felt bad about the pandemic. But they had never really felt good about the economy, they had never really built up much in the way of savings, and they had never had a real career. Instead they had moved through a series of less than pleasant jobs and gigs that (under)paid by the hour. On top of that, while they were hardly immune to Covid, they—and especially their children—were young enough that statistically speaking it probably wouldn't harm them too badly.

Getting their bearings after the first few weeks, they found themselves at home with a lot of unexpected time on their hands and a series of stimulus checks in their pockets, while watching the stock market rise quite rapidly from its lows. It took no more than a few iPhone taps to set up a Robinhood account and put that money into the stock market to see what might happen. After all, stuck at home in a pandemic with nothing better to do, what else were they going to do with their money? Robinhood made investing fun, Reddit made it social, the media made it germane, and the market—which, after the first month, started going up and to the right in almost a straight line—made it surprisingly profitable.

All those ingredients combined to reinforce each other, making it extremely easy to get caught up in the excitement. I started corresponding with one teenager who styled himself a hedge-fund manager; he was too young to be allowed to have a Robinhood account (or even a checking account) in his own name, but his mother seeded a Robinhood account for him with a few dollars, and then he did a fantastic job of persuading other grown-ups to give him their money. What can I say, the kid grew up in Brooklyn.

This kid—let's call him Ben, because that's his name—soon started posting very impressive returns, not only in stocks but also in crypto. Like much of the rest of his generation, he was Extremely Online, but he was more focused than most: He had no social media, barely used email, and spent a huge amount of time on Reddit—much more time than any professional money manager at a hedge fund would be able to.

As a result, Ben developed the ability to notice which assets were accumulating buzz long before they attracted the attention of media oldies like myself.

For a long time I thought of what he was doing as a momentum trade—seeing which stocks were going to the moon, and then jumping on them to join the ride. Momentum trading has a long history in the stock market because stocks don't follow a true random walk. Stocks that are going up tend to go up, and stocks that are going down tend to go down. As a result, if you follow the *opposite* of a "buy low, sell high" strategy, you can make a lot of money. If a stock is rising and keeps on setting new highs, then buy it; a higher-risk strategy is to look for a stock that's falling and keeps on setting new lows, and short it. Value investors hate this strategy, because you're buying companies that are expensive and selling assets that are cheap. But if you compare the results of professional momentum investors to those of professional value investors, the momentum investors tend to outperform, at least in the short term.

What Ben was doing, however, wasn't the classic momentum trade, which is based on looking at securities prices and buying the ones that are going up. Instead, his investing thesis was based on what you might call buzz momentum. Buy the assets that people are talking a lot about, ideally before the price rises, and then hold on to them for as long as the volume of the conversation keeps on getting louder, amplified by any upward price moves. Sell when the conversation starts winding down; rinse and repeat.

Ben's strategy aligns with what critic Kyle Chayka calls the

Ragnarok Santa Hat Theory of Digital Capitalism, named after a dumb item in an early-2000s multiplayer video game. "Money is made not from salary or even slow index-fund gains," he writes, "but identifying the right scarce digital meme at the right time."[7] The more Extremely Online you are, the better placed you are in terms of being able to identify what's going to be the new hotness, to be able to jump on the pump and exit before the dump.

That kind of strategy can last for anything from days to months— the kind of time horizon that stock-market graybeards would dismiss as "churn." The great economist Fischer Black invented the idea of the "noise trader"—someone who trades a lot even though she has no particular edge or inside information. In response, Harvard economist Larry Summers, being Larry Summers, decided he had a better name for such traders: idiots.

Summers had (and has) no respect for idiots. (He also has a tendency to assume that almost everybody he's talking to is an idiot, but that's a subject for another book.) In an insightful unpublished paper entitled "Finance and Idiots," Summers began with a now legendary observation: "There are idiots. Look around." He then asked, let's imagine a stock market dominated not by intelligent rational actors, but rather by idiots. What would it look like? Would rational actors like finance professors end up outsmarting the idiots and making all the money?

Summers's conclusion was that they would not:

> Markets reward risk taking. Fools venture where others dare not . . . This leads fools to undertake more risks than finance professors . . . Taking more risk, fools are likely to receive higher returns. Expecting higher returns and less risk, they will save more than rational investors. This will lead their wealth to increase more rapidly than that of smart investors.

Any given idiot, in Summers's market, is playing a losing game. But as a group, the idiots earn just as much money as the finance professors. That's because they misjudge the actual amount of risk in the market, resulting in them putting more money at risk, and taking bigger risks, than a rational actor would. Many idiots end up with nothing, but some end up with billions. "How many finance professors are in the Forbes 400?" asks Summers, pointedly. Markets by their nature are unpredictable, he says, and "risk aversion will prevent smart traders from wiping out the idiots."

Summers concludes, of his hypothetical "idiot-dominated market," or IDM:

> Fools will earn at least the same return in aggregate that others do. Their wealth will come to be concentrated in a dwindling band of ever richer, ever more confident, and therefore aggressive, investors. Greater confidence among the fools who still have positive wealth will reinforce the tendency of fools to take over all the wealth . . .
>
> We might all be better off without a stock market. Letting our terms of trade be determined by an IDM is probably not a very good idea.

The most provocative part of Summers's paper is where he shows how very hard it would be to determine whether or not you were in an idiot-dominated market. Yes, smart traders would do better, over the long term, than most of the idiots—but then again, so would many idiots. "Informed traders would slightly outperform the market but would find it hard to prove to themselves or others that they were informed."

I have more respect for so-called idiots than Summers does,

especially once you zoom out and realize that they're playing a very different game than the finance professors, with different win states and lose states. Think of the kind of risks that all videogamers take, for instance: Hour after hour of losing all your lives, game over, start again from the beginning, all in the service of learning from your mistakes, getting huge amounts of practice, and becoming better over time. Or think of the ways in which gamers glory in ways to try to cheat the system, or put together elaborate compilations of flame-outs and fails. Apply that kind of attitude to the stock market, and the meme stock phenomenon starts to make a lot more sense.

During the pandemic, everything was short term. Investors like Ben weren't looking for blue-chip stocks that they could sit on and hold until retirement; they were looking for quick gains that they could then turn around and reinvest in the next moon rocket. Instead of trying to make 10 percent a year, why not try to make 10 percent a day, or at least every few days. If you can increase your $1,000 nest egg by 25 percent a week, then in one year you'll have over $100 million. That would be awesome! But even failing can be fun, if you're playing this new fast-twitch game with the requisite degree of irony and detachment.

The media, of course, jumped at any opportunity to tell the outrageous stories of the new investor class, and especially the unofficial ringleader of the meme stock crowd, a thirty-four-year-old "financial-wellness education director" at the Massachusetts Mutual Life Insurance Company named Keith Gill. Gill was better known by his screen names—he was DeepFuckingValue on Reddit and Roaring Kitty on YouTube, where he would celebrate big wins with chicken tenders and champagne.

Gill was obsessed with one stock in particular—GameStop, a struggling videogame retailer—and invested $53,000 into it, in both stock and options, which at one point became worth almost $50 million. By documenting his trading thesis and activity in extreme granular detail on both YouTube and Reddit, Gill became something of a legend, representing the triumph of the little guy over evil hedge-fund managers with the temerity to have shorted the stock. Gill ended up testifying before a congressional committee, ending his prepared statement with the simple words: "In short, I like the stock."

As Summers had anticipated many years previously, it turned out to be impossible, in practice, to be able to determine whether Gill was a smart trader or an "idiot"—both theses were entirely consistent with his posted returns. Broadly speaking, stock-market veterans tended to think he had just gotten lucky, while the younger generation treated him as a hero.

An even more polarizing figure was Chamath Palihapitiya, the billionaire investor, financier, and semi-professional troll, who became an expert at using his own notoriety as a profit-making tool. Just like Gill, Chamath would paint himself as the underdog trying to upend an entrenched financial order that overwhelmingly worked to the benefit of old white men.

By bragging about his wealth to his 1.5 million Twitter followers and then creating publicly listed vehicles for those followers to invest in, Chamath—who in reality is a Gen Xer—became both the inspiration and the poster child for Millennial stock-market speculation. Even more than memelord Elon Musk, Chamath could singlehandedly create the kind of online buzz that Redditors like Ben were on the lookout for. As one investor explained to the *New Yorker*'s Charles Duhigg for the Chamath profile he wrote in May 2021, polarization gets attention, and "attention *is* money."[8] Smart institutional investors would buy into Chamath's deals not because they believed in the underlying economics, but just because they believed in Chamath's

Pied Piper–like ability to attract price-insensitive speculators. With hindsight, that was probably the point at which attempting to separate the idiots from the sophisticates became utterly futile: The sophisticates were following the idiots because doing so would give them an edge.

Chamath was such a braggart that it was effectively impossible to write puff pieces about him. When it came to less high-profile participants in the market, however, the default mode, even within the more conservative parts of the media, was one of admiration. Ben appeared on a reasonably popular podcast as an expert on money— at the age of fourteen!—and every other week saw a new inspirational rags-to-riches tale of some impoverished photographer striking it rich in this brave new world.

One BBC story about "Birmingham's self-made crypto-millionaire" told the tale of how twenty-year-old Somali immigrant Hanad Hassan had turned $50 into $500 in three days, turned the $500 into $5,000 in another two days, and then saw that $5,000 double to $10,000 just over the course of a thirty-minute conversation with his parents about what he should do with the money. The mini-documentary talked of his $8 million fortune and the $250,000 he'd given to local charities—before it was rapidly taken down when it became clear that the money had come from a classic rug-pull, where he'd launched his own coin with a high-profile marketing push and then simply absconded with the money, leaving the cryptocurrency unsupported and worthless.

Such tales were the Gen Z equivalent of *Liar's Poker*, by Michael Lewis,[9] or *Wall Street*, the 1987 Oliver Stone movie that lodged the phrase "greed is good" into the national consciousness. Those works were designed as cautionary tales of avarice and excess—but were *received* as aspirational narratives showing just how lucrative the burgeoning world of finance could be. Chamath was the 2020 version of Gordon Gekko, the corporate raider played by Michael Douglas in full 1980s regalia of Winchester shirts, suspenders, fine cigars, and brick-sized cell phones. (Chamath's updated version was the shirtless mirror selfie showing off a hard-earned six-pack and a crotch tattoo peeking out from his Nike workout shorts.)

To put it another way: All publicity was good publicity, in terms of bringing new investors into new asset classes. The crypto true believers would react with fury to the "fear, uncertainty, and doubt" they saw being sewn by more skeptical journalists and analysts, but the broad trends were undeniable: There was no evidence that such stories were slowing the torrid pace of growth in the crypto market, and decent evidence that they were actually accelerating it.

Crypto in particular presented an irresistible subject matter for journalists, since their articles didn't even need to match a name to the fortune. Because of the transparency inherent to blockchain technology, it was easy to identify, for instance, a single wallet that spent $8,000 in August 2020 on a new cryptocurrency called Shiba Inu (not to be confused with Dogecoin, which launched years earlier, in 2013). The cryptocurrency then just sat in that wallet for about fourteen months, during which it appreciated so much that the $8,000 had become worth $5.6 billion. No one knew *who* was the beneficial owner of all those coins, but it was obvious that *someone* was—and that, in theory, anybody capable of scraping together a few thousand dollars could similarly become a billionaire within a year.

It's impossible to overstate the ubiquity of such stories for an entire generation that was living almost entirely online. One piece of hoary Wall Street lore has it that J. P. Morgan—or perhaps it was Joseph Kennedy—got out of the market just before the crash in 1929 after receiving a stock tip from his shoeshine boy. The adage has it that a smart investor should be "greedy when others are fearful and fearful when others are greedy"—and that when shoeshine boys are getting greedy and passing along stock tips, that's a flashing-red sell signal.

During the bull market of 2020–21, there was no shortage of armchair market strategists saying that the self-described "apes" piling into the stock of AMC, a movie-theater chain, were effectively the twenty-first-century version of that 1929 shoeshine boy, and that the smart move, when it came to stocks, was to be fearful rather than greedy. Certainly the second half of the adage had proved itself correct—when the world was at maximum fearfulness, in March 2020, that was in hindsight a spectacularly good time to buy. But a century is a long time, and the post-pandemic rise of the retail trader is more of a secular generational shift than it is a cyclical indicator that the smart money should get out of stocks.

Think about that apocryphal shoeshine boy, for instance. He would have spent a lot of hours shining shoes, and the rest of his time at home, with his family, or out on the streets, playing with his friends. Over the course of any given week, he might have had a few customers who he overheard or talked to about the stock market. Two minutes here, ten minutes there—maybe it might add up to a couple of hours a week during a period when the stock market was top of mind for the customers passing through Grand Central Terminal and stopping off before catching their train or heading into the office. In comparison to someone like Ben, the fourteen-year-old self-described hedge-fund manager, that's nothing.

In our new always-online world, the number of hours available to Millennials and Zoomers who are interested in the more outré corners of the stock market is enormous—and the signal-to-noise ratio of the information consumed in those hours is also exponentially higher than anything available to a Gilded Age shoeshine boy.

During the endless months that stretched from April 2020 through January 2022, with maybe a short reprieve during the "hot vax summer" of 2021, staying at home and dropping into internet rabbit holes became a nationwide pastime. For most of us, the rabbit holes were shallow, if broad—TikTok being a prime example. Others spent eight or more hours per day playing single- or multiplayer videogames. But there was also never a better time to get into stocks or options or crypto—the biggest and most potentially lucrative multiplayer games of all. The broad market was going up, giving everybody a healthy tailwind. The online community was both large and very supportive, understanding that losses are part of the game and voting up posts that were honest about huge financial mistakes that were made. The level of sophistication was lower than what you might find if you did a finance PhD, but was vastly higher than you'd find if you gave a bunch of rich Boomers a financial-literacy test. No one was alone, and everybody was open to learning more about a market that wasn't playing by any historical rules.

That combination of information and community helped accelerate the gold rush, and gave its participants the justified belief—which was true at least in the short term—that they understood the new rules of the market better than the grumpy uncles on CNBC who simply rejected all meme-stock theses out of hand without doing any real work to try to understand the underlying mechanisms, and how they might have changed the entire market in interesting and important ways.

In any case, there was no way that investors like Ben were going to start listening to those grumpy uncles. You can't argue someone out of a position that they weren't argued into, which made it extremely easy for Ben and his Reddit friends to ignore the humorless ratiocinations of Boomers and Gen Xers in favor of anything that confirmed the eternal thesis, the one that millions of people have always wanted to hear, which is that now is the best time ever to get rich quick.

I could make a world-weary case, for instance, that at any point in time, there will be some security or artwork or cryptocurrency or similar that is worth vastly more than it was some years ago. I could raise myself up upon my decades of experience in the news business and sonorously intone words to the effect that journalists will always be tempted to find the people who bought that item back in the day, when it was relatively cheap, because that's a very easy story to write that people are always going to want to read. I could point out that those journalists rarely ask what else that person was buying at the time, or even whether they had any desire to make money from it, and that there is no way that such stories, fun as they are to consume, should be taken as some kind of template for making money.

But nobody wants to read a killjoy grinch except for other killjoy grinches. As Summers said, the world is driven by daring people who ignore finance professors. And in the months after the 2020 stock-market crash, the people having heedless fun found themselves not only winning and making money, but doing so *at the expense of* the concern trolls who had so frequently and loudly told them that they shouldn't play with sharp sticks because they'd end up losing an eye, and when that happens don't come running to me for sympathy.

Glauber Contessoto, a Dogecoin millionaire, explained it to Kevin Roose by saying: "Those experts on TV, the older generation of old money and wealth, they try to scare people into staying safe so nobody gets too rich." His own motto: "Scared money don't make money."

The pandemic only served to reinforce such YOLO ("you only live once") tendencies. Millennials weren't particularly dying of Covid—unlike the 1918 flu, the young were mostly pretty safe in 2020—but they took the opportunity to reexamine their lives all the same, and to decide that a bold attempt to strike it rich made more sense than playing a menial role in a game that had been carefully rigged in favor of uncaring corporations and Boomers.

To our credit, we Gen Xers tended not to get particularly judgmental about the Millennials and Zoomers who were learning about stock-market volatility by being the main cause of it. What we understood was that losing 100 percent of your life savings is a lot less painful and is a lot easier to recover from if you start from $1,000 and you're thirty than if you start from $1 million and you're sixty. People *should* become more risk averse as they get older, and they do. The important thing, when you witness foolish behavior, is to fall back on the epistemic humility that came in so handy across the pandemic. Those who would judge the young just need to remember that they're old, that the young have never listened to the old, and that overall that seems to have worked out okay for the world.

lol nothing matters

THERE WERE A lot of Boomers who took the speculative frenzy of 2020 and 2021 as a personal affront, especially the talking heads on CNBC, many of whom were quite explicitly being targeted by the Reddit crowd. Many predictions were made about an inevitable wave of massive losses that would cause huge harm to people with very little money to lose—and nearly all those predictions proved to be false.

The massive losses never materialized: While volatile stocks were certainly volatile, there wasn't some kind of mass extinction event like the dot-com crash of 2000 where almost everybody lost a huge sum in a short amount of time. More importantly, when people *did* suffer massive losses, they weren't particularly hurt by them. Most had no dependents; people like Ben weren't even investing their own money; almost all of them turned out to be only playing with money they could afford to lose.

In reality, what happened when the stock market came off the boil in 2022—when the Fed started hiking interest rates and the ZIRP game was put on pause—was that Millennials just stopped playing. Volumes at places like Robinhood and Coinbase fell sharply—and their share prices went down dramatically—and the caravan moved on. Some of the players ended with less money than they invested and others with more, but most of them weren't even keeping score. They'd had fun, they'd had a few shots at making millions, and they could bide their time waiting for the next opportunity to present itself.

The real surprise was on the profit side of the ledger, rather than in any losses incurred. A surprising amount of what went up remained much higher than the pre-pandemic normal, whether it was GameStop shares or CryptoPunk NFTs. Sports betting became a positive-expectation game, thanks to the thousands of dollars that online gaming companies were offering individuals to sign up. A new investing paradigm had emerged, one based not on economic fundamentals but rather on social ones. The trick was just to follow the flow of buzz across the internet, much as a meteorologist might follow the movement of a low-pressure front to predict the weather in St. Louis tomorrow.

You didn't *need* to be Extremely Online in order to play this game. Individuals who wanted to fully YOLO their savings usually had some kind of investment thesis—that a certain meme or community would start snowballing and rising in value. But there were millions more with Robinhood accounts who could just join in on the fun by loading up on Elon Musk's Tesla (TSLA) or Cathie Wood's high-buzz investment fund, ARKK. These investments easily fulfilled the main criterion, in that they had the potential to rise a lot in a short period of time. Even after they had risen, they had almost unlimited potential to rise even further if you were an investor with the cojones to hold, or "hodl" as the vernacular had it. And of course after they had fallen, that was the best time to BTFD: buy the fucking dip.

Zooming out, the big picture is of an online generation with an entirely new attitude to risk. Historically, the risk spectrum was understood quite clearly. On one end you had risk-averse individuals and institutions who tried hard to avoid as much risk as possible and who gravitated toward risk-free assets like Treasury bonds. In many ways, these were precisely the investors who caused the 2008 financial crisis. Demand for risk-free assets was so high that banks had to start manufacturing them out of thin air, through the magic of securitization and overcollateralization. By their nature, risk-averse investors tend to break quite quickly when they're forced to take losses—that's why they're risk averse in the first place. So when their AAA-rated bonds ended up plunging in value, that precipitated a major crisis.

At the other end of the risk spectrum are entrepreneurs or hedge funds or venture capitalists—people who are *willing* to take high risks in the service of trying to generate massive outcomes. The risk isn't pleasant, and the inevitable downswings along the way are painful, but ultimately the hope is that the bad thing (risk) will be more than made up for by the good thing (profit).

The predisposition of analysts with any kind of economics or finance background is to try to understand and explain retail-investor activity during the pandemic as a move along that spectrum—an increase in classical risk appetite. That's more or less what Summers did in his paper, although he did so in a very patronizing manner. But I'm not at all convinced that the new class of investors falls anywhere on that spectrum at all. They don't *begrudgingly accept* risk as the necessary price they need to pay in order to generate high returns, so much as they *actively seek out* risky investments, partly because of the potential returns but also in large part because the risk itself is what makes investing fun.

On Reddit message boards, the type of content most likely to get tens of thousands of upvotes is "loss porn"—screenshots of losses that can be multiples of the poster's annual salary. Losing money is a central means of becoming part of the community, and posting your losses is a way of showing that you can laugh at what one massively popular post on Reddit's r/wallstreetbets message board called "the sadomasochistic part of the capitalistic system we are living in."

The post is worth quoting a bit more of:

> You realize what you are doing here—you true fuck—
> don't you? This is a community of full blown first class
> true tits up degenerates which take pleasure in posting
> losses accumulating into the millions every fucking
> month and you are putting your money into a BET—
> yes my dear it is written out in the name of this very
> fucking sub Wallstreet-B-E-T-S!!!—and follow due
> diligence posted by people with names like "SHOW_
> ME_YOUR_ANAL_TITS"?

As the poster says, "This is not r/investing!"—and neither is it investing, as finance professors and CNBC analysts understand it. It's something else, something much more anarchic; to a certain extent it's something closer to the way in which the pop group KLF burned £1 million in cash for no particular reason. There's an important sense in which people were buying dumb assets like penny stocks or NFT pictures of cartoon rocks or joke cryptocurrencies based on Japanese dogs not because they were good investments but *precisely because* they were terrible investments. Ironic nihilism has real bite when there's real money on the line—just look at those morally offended finance Boomers—making it all the funnier when the trades work out and turn shitposters into millionaires.

The 2008 financial crisis launched its own cohort of nihilists, most famously Dan Ivandjiiski, a former hedge-fund analyst who started the financial blog Zero Hedge and wrote under the pen name "Tyler Durden." Durden is Brad Pitt's character in *Fight Club*, hell-bent on reducing society to fistfights and bringing capitalism to its knees by effectively destroying most of its assets. (A bank's assets are its loans; Durden's plot was to blow up all records of those loans, rendering the debts uncollectible and the banks insolvent.) To this day, atop every Zero Hedge page sits a *Fight Club* quote: "On a long enough timeline, the survival rate for everyone drops to zero."

A similar spirit of anti-capitalist anarchism could be seen at the Occupy Wall Street (OWS) protests in Manhattan's Zuccotti Park in 2011—protests explicitly designed to topple the power structures embedded in the likes of nearby institutions like Goldman Sachs and the Federal Reserve Bank of New York.

Those structures were also very much in the crosshairs of the pseudonymous Satoshi Nakamoto, the inventor of bitcoin, when he published his famous original white paper in 2008. The paper begins by laying out the problem that needs to be solved: "Commerce on the Internet has come to rely almost exclusively on financial institutions serving as trusted third parties," wrote Satoshi. "While the system works well enough for most transactions, it still suffers from the inherent weaknesses of the trust based model." In other words, any system that requires trusting institutions like Goldman Sachs or the New York Fed is inherently flawed, because those institutions are not inherently trustworthy. That thesis was an easy sell, when the bitcoin protocol was developed in the years following 2008.

What bitcoin and OWS lacked was a sense of humor. They were—are—earnest attempts to replace the existing system with something better. One of the defining features of bitcoin maximalists is a sincere belief in the fundamental superiority of bitcoin over existing fiat currencies, while OWS similarly believed in revolutionary change. The financial crisis was evidence of a broken system; that system needed to be, and could be, fixed only by completely reconfiguring the fundamental building blocks upon which capitalism is based.

By the time the pandemic hit, however, online discourse had become increasingly centered on memes and in-jokes. Cruel memes helped Trump ascend to the presidency in 2016; they were based in ugly humor, but humor nonetheless. Online communities, like all communities, built in-groups and defined out-groups; one of the jobs of memes was to needle the out-groups and provoke an angry and annoyed reaction from their members. The "OK, Boomer" meme is a great example: It effortlessly laughs at and defangs any kind of earnest criticism in a way that's exquisitely designed to calibrate the degree of annoyance elicited in the targeted Boomer to the degree of condescension that Boomer originally displayed.

Even the unofficial motto of the Extremely Online crowd—"lol nothing matters"—is itself designed to skewer the sincere and heartfelt. In the crypto world especially, a whole vocabulary emerged to ironize the prevailing discourse around saving and investing; to create a space where "full blown first class true tits up degenerates" is a term of approbation rather than any kind of disapproval.

There was in-group solidarity—WAGMI, for example, stands for "we're all gonna make it," and fellow posters were often addressed as "fren," which is meme-speak for friend. A "degen ape" is a high-risk gambler piling into a crypto project—the kind of behavior that in and of itself helps accrue reputational capital, whatever happens to the investment. NGMI—"Not gonna make it"—is a way to bond over losses, while YOLO and FOMO ("fear of missing out") are terms that basically say "I'm fully aware my actions are irrational, but hey, we're all irrational."

It's weirdly rational to put on heavy armor made of solid irony before heading into the meme trenches, because it's a world where nothing is real, where having your feet placed solidly on terra firma is a surefire way to miss out on almost everything that's fun or lucrative.

Remember the importance of ZIRP. When interest rates are at zero, assets that generate income—bonds, houses, dividend stocks—are doubly unattractive to new investors. Prices move in inverse relation to yields, which means that the price you need to pay for a pathetically tiny income is enormous. To put it another way, the income you get from such assets is so pathetically tiny anyway that there's no real point in buying them.

The natural conclusion is to forget all those income-generating assets. Leave them to the Boomers. What remains is the world of capital appreciation: Acquire something, watch it go up in value, sell it at a massive profit. The faster it appreciates, the richer you get. This is the realm of SWAG.

Investment advisers have always struggled to understand assets that don't have any kind of income associated with them. They gave them a catch-all acronym—SWAG. It stands for "silver, wine, art, gold"—because those were the assets that Boomers would invest in, mostly with very modest success. But the SWAG of the pandemic was very different. It was cryptocurrency or NFTs or Supreme skate decks or Yeezy sneakers. It was baseball or basketball cards, be they physical or virtual. It was prints from the hot Brooklyn artist Brian Donnelly, better known as KAWS, or rare bourbon, or obscure vinyl.

The common denominator is artificial quasi-scarcity—a difficult concept to understand but also a very important one. Quasi-scarcity is the underpinning of all SWAG markets: Items are desirable because they're rare, even though there is always some mechanism to create new versions of them.

Silver and gold, for instance, are mined—about 25,000 tons of silver per year, and roughly 3,000 tons a year of gold. Gold's scarcity gives it value, its value makes it economic to mine, and its continued new supply allows the global supply of the precious metal to expand appreciably every year.

Wine is a bit different—it is constantly being produced, but it is also constantly being drunk. No one will ever make another genuine bottle of 1953 Chateau Margaux,[1] but then again, even a '53 Margaux's best years are behind it, and its value, at least in terms of how it tastes, is inexorably declining. Against that are thousands of vineyards, Margaux included, producing large quantities of first-rate new wine that will live on for decades. Importantly, those vineyards aren't fixed in number. In 1953, a self-respecting oenophile would rarely venture away from Burgundy and Bordeaux; today, a typical wine lover is thrilled to find great producers from other regions and even—yes—other countries, including the US. To collect wine, or even to invest in wine, is in large part to constantly be seeking out the newest wines with the best potential—and there's no shortage of contenders.

Art is the most instructive of the classic SWAG asset classes, because almost all of the world's greatest artworks are in museums and galleries that will never sell them, rendering them literally priceless. There's no dollar value that can be put on Pablo Picasso's *Demoiselles d'Avignon*, or Diego Velázquez's portrait of Pope Innocent X. But the art-collecting bug is eternal, and if there's no market in masterpieces by Rembrandt or Vermeer, the rich will happily bid up something else instead. The demand for fresh new supply is so great that by 2021, the aggregate proceeds of Old Masters sold at auction—art covering more than six centuries—was roughly the same as the aggregate proceeds from resales of works by artists born after 1975.

Silver, wine, and gold all have natural scarcity—there are physical limits to how much can be produced. Unique art objects have it, too, but for centuries artists have also trafficked in artificial scarcity, by creating limited-edition works. Historically, a print edition would be limited by destroying the plates after making a certain number of prints, creating an artificial physical scarcity, but nowadays, in the era of photography, no one destroys negatives or computer files after printing out a certain number of copies of a shot. Indeed, many artists regularly create "exhibition copies"—brand-new prints—of certain works, which are then supposed to be destroyed when the exhibition ends.

For an online generation immersed in irony and fast-moving attention swarms, the SWAG of choice is naturally digital—or, if it isn't purely digital, it still has to be something that can accumulate cultural cachet in the digital realm of Instagram selfies and Reddit flexes. For that, you need community, and for community, you need a critical mass of participants.

That's why the Extremely Online generation tends not to chase the "best" items of SWAG, in terms of connoisseurship. Or if there is connoisseurship, it's mostly of brands that are judged by their ability to create desirability with nothing but a logo. (The American hype-beast retailer Supreme famously proved this thesis by putting its logo on a standard red clay brick and selling out in a matter of minutes at $30 each.) The collecting fervor comes not from genuine love of the brand so much as it comes from avarice with a dash of self-loathing—a disgust born of the fact that any profits from buying and flipping products will be a tiny fraction of the profits accruing to the corporation manufacturing demand. (Supreme was sold by its private-equity investors to VF Corp in November 2020 for $2.1 billion, or $175 million per retail store.)

The phenomenon of time speeding up during the pandemic didn't just apply to investment time horizons, it also applied to the life cycle of brands, which are the main engine underlying almost all collectibles. Consider fine watches, for instance: The biggest and most valuable brands in the world, like Rolex and Omega, trade heavily on their long histories—as do the world's most storied and valuable vineyards. Artists are brands, too; that's why a genuine artwork is much more valuable than a perfect facsimile. As brands survive and thrive over the course of generations, they generally increase in value and in pricing power.

If you're collecting objects with an eye to price appreciation, then by definition you're not just buying the objects you like the most; instead, you have at least one eye on the objects that you think *other* collectors are going to most covet. In a Keynesian beauty contest, judges are rewarded not for their ability to pick out the most beautiful contestant, or the one they admire the most, but rather for their ability to pick out the contestant who's most popular with judges as a group. The analogy was designed to describe the stock market, but it describes markets in collectibles just as well.

During the feverish days of the pandemic, the value of connoisseurship in determining the most desirable digital collectibles declined effectively to zero. A keen eye, a sharp intelligence—these things started to become outright disadvantages for anybody trying to anticipate where the crowd would move next, if the most influential individuals in the crowd in question were degenerate apes slinging lulz and memes.

Rarity, in particular, was something you could very much have too much of. In the early days of the NFT boom, artists and creators took their cue from the art world, and would mint unique 1/1 NFTs or create very limited editions of, say, three or five. Classical economics says that makes sense: If there are a thousand people with a desire to buy such a thing, then by limiting the edition to just five objects, you force those thousand people to compete against each other on willingness to pay, you get a bidding war started, and eventually you sell those objects for a sum of money that only the top 1 percent can afford.

The item that really kickstarted the NFT boom, a piece by a digital artist named Beeple that was auctioned at Christie's for $69 million, definitely fit that bill. Two crypto "whales" fought it out to buy the piece, and in fact it was only a weakness in Christie's online auction software that prevented the price from going even higher.

The $69 million Beeple, however, turned out to be an exception to the rule. The two men bidding on it both considered a high price to be something they actively wanted, a way of ratifying an entire asset class. The theory: Even if the piece would never again be worth as much as they paid for it, the effect that such a headline-grabbing sale would have on NFTs more broadly would be electric. That theory turned out to be true, but the main beneficiaries were not digital art collectors, or even digital artists. Rather, they were community builders—people like the fast-talking sales maestro Gary Vaynerchuk, who could create multiple brands capable of persuading hundreds of thousands of individuals to want to pay to be part of a brand-new community.

The trend had already started pre-pandemic, with the emergence of streetwear "hypebeasts" who would queue up in highly visible lines outside hipper-than-thou boutiques for the opportunity to buy a $200 T-shirt notable only for its logo. Brands like Supreme perfected the art of making *everything* a limited edition, with a high likelihood of trading hands on the secondary market for significantly more than the retail price.

Supreme would "drop" new items weekly, in carefully calibrated quantities: Enough to whet the appetite of the hypebeasts but not enough to sate it. The trick, as P. T. Barnum probably said, was to always leave them wanting more. So long as the secondary-market value of Supreme items was predictably higher than the retail value, it made sense for *anybody* to buy *anything* at the store, regardless of whether it had any value as a fashion or luxury object. Those $30 bricks, for instance, regularly change hands on resale site StockX to this day for about $250 each.

What makes the bricks so valuable? Just the fact that they are imprinted with the Supreme logo, itself a bratty art-world in-joke designed to lampoon the much more serious work of conceptualist artist Barbara Kruger. (For her part, Kruger is not amused: When asked for comment by Foster Kamer of Complex, she responded by calling Supreme "a ridiculous clusterfuck of totally uncool jokers.")

The Supreme *logo*, in other words, is where the corporate value lies—the products themselves are little more than delivery vehicles for the logo, and indeed are often made by rival brands such as Nike and North Face. As luxury goods manufacturers realized in the 1990s, it's impossible to copyright a fashion design, but it's easy to trademark a logo—so if you want to have legal recourse against counterfeiters, it's a good idea to slap your logo all over your goods.

After storied brands like Louis Vuitton and Chanel proved that consumers would covet rather than shun items sporting obnoxiously large logos, streetwear and other brands started following suit, since it's a lot more lucrative to charge through the nose for a logo than it is to invest in high-end manufacturing and try to compete on some kind of intrinsic quality.

The trick is not quality control but quantity control: So long as you don't flood the market with more branded goods than there's demand for, you effectively have a license to print money. If you play the game well, then new supply creates new demand: As people show off their new branded purchases to demonstrate their street cred, that helps to incentivize other people in their social circle to want to buy your brand as well.

If a brand like Supreme could become a billion-dollar property within years rather than decades, pandemic-era NFT brands sped up the process by yet another order of magnitude. The magic number turned out to be ten thousand: If a collection of NFTs was dropped in an edition size of ten thousand, that was large enough to be able to support a community of collectors, while still being small enough that it could have a degree of exclusivity, thereby generating a lot of desire on the part of people on the outside who wanted to be part of the club.

Early NFTs like CryptoKitties were very good at building a community but were bad at capping the edition size—just like real-life cats, they could multiply, and soon the supply of kitties exceeded the demand. The more lasting model was introduced when CryptoPunks arrived, the brainchild of a pair of Canadian software developers named Matt Hall and John Watkinson, who released ten thousand of them on day one—and that was it.

In recent history, limited-edition works have tended to be identical. Barbara Kruger, for instance, produces many editions—lithographs, photoengravings, pigment prints, flags, stools, you name it. The edition size varies—it might be in single digits or it could be thousands—but the idea is always that there are many versions of *the same thing*, and that Kruger has done her best to make them all identical.

Matt and John, as they're known in the NFT community, realized that the technology available to them allowed a much more interesting edition than that. Rather than creating ten thousand identical digital objects—easy, but boring—they created ten thousand *similar* digital objects. Each was instantly recognizable as a CryptoPunk, yet each was also unique. Certain traits were rarer than others—there were only twenty-four apes, for instance, while eighty-six punks in total sported welding goggles on their heads. (Sadly, none of the apes had welding goggles, although one had "nerd glasses.")

The idea was to create multiple layers of artificial scarcity—the punks in general were rare, but certain kinds of punk were even rarer. Most importantly, the images were pretty legible at extremely low resolution—which meant that if you used your punk as your Twitter avatar, almost everybody would understand that you were the owner of a CryptoPunk, and members of the community could even grok at a glance just how rare and special your particular punk was.

It was possible for people to use CryptoPunks they didn't own as their Twitter avatar, and it was even possible for them, if they had a modicum of cryptographic nous, to be able to mint their own NFTs and use a picture of somebody else's CryptoPunk as their officially verified hexagonal Twitter profile picture. This was annoying to some punk owners, but it was also broadly a good thing for the CryptoPunk ecosystem as a whole, since it ratified the desirability of the punks and ultimately served to entrench rather than dilute their status as resonant and valuable memes.

Creators like Matt and John certainly didn't seem to mind much: Like Domenico Dolce and Stefano Gabbana, they realized that fakes, or what was known as the "right-click problem," after the ease of downloading NFTs from the internet, were actually a fantastic marketing device. If non-owners want to be associated with your brand so much that they will show off a fake, that's a very strong signal you're doing something right. It's also free advertising for your brand, which is why Dolce & Gabbana notoriously refused to cooperate with authorities whenever the police raided a counterfeiting gang and seized a pile of fake handbags. The luxury moguls understood that the counterfeiters were doing them more good than harm.

CryptoPunks were not art, but they recapitulated much of the behavior seen in the art world for decades, especially around high-volume artists like Andy Warhol. Warhol had an instantly recognizable style, which naturally lent itself to circles within circles of prestige and value. A Warhol poster on your wall shows your affinity for the style and helps it gain that much more cultural currency—as would a copy of a Warhol painting bought for $15 from Yiwu Seqiao Painting Co., Ltd., just outside Jinhua in China. Official Warhol limited editions have real secondary-market value; original Warhol paintings even more so. Since Warhol copied his own work so frequently, earlier (and therefore more original) paintings are generally worth more than later versions, even if the later versions are bigger or more polished. Certain themes, too, are worth more than others—a "death and disaster" painting or a portrait of Marilyn Monroe is much more valuable than a commissioned portrait, and so on.

That kind of theme-and-variations approach was taken to unprecedented levels once creators started moving to NFTs. So long as the overall project could remain instantly recognizable, even in tiny thumbnail form, it could mutate into many different forms—quite literally, in the case of the Mutant Ape Yacht Club.

The ten thousand original Bored Apes were one of the hottest NFT collections of 2021; much like CryptoPunks, they had no real artistic merit, but the community that grew up around them was very loud and visible, and soon started bidding the price of apes well into the millions of dollars.

Yuga Labs, the company behind the bored apes, wasn't content to stop there—just like Supreme, it knew it could spark feverish excitement by creating new branded NFTs to collect. Yuga therefore created multiple new markets: in mutant apes, in serums that could convert into mutant apes if you owned a bored ape, and even in pet dogs known as the Bored Ape Kennel Club. Each new drop made millions of dollars for Yuga. Less than a year after being founded by four bored if overeducated Millennials in Florida, the company was being valued at $5 billion—more than double Supreme—by Silicon Valley venture capitalists.

The story of the bored apes is a bit like the story of digital assets more generally: If something scarce starts going up a lot in value, then it won't stay scarce for long. Bitcoin remains scarce, but there are now many alternatives to bitcoin—ethereum, solana, and thousands more. Apes are rare; so now you can buy dogs instead—or rocks, or penguins, or written-down items on playing cards for a game that doesn't even exist.

There's not enough demand to cover all the supply, so the speculative fervor tends to ebb from one asset to the next, with timespans often measured in weeks and the whole concept of value being eroded by caustic irony to the point of meaninglessness.

When I studied art history at the University of Glasgow in the early 1990s, my original idea for a thesis was to write about built-in obsolescence in the art world. This was the time when the "young British artists," or YBAs, were first making a big mark on the art world, with Damien Hirst exhibiting fragile, time-limited works like a cow's head being slowly devoured by flies, or a beach ball bouncing precariously above ultra-sharp knife blades. Shortly thereafter, Rachel Whiteread would make her masterwork, *House*, a concrete cast of the inside of an East End house that lived—by design—for just eleven weeks.

My interest in short-lived art was partly art historical—there's definitely an aesthetic *frisson* involved in experiencing an artwork that you know will soon cease to exist—but it was also financial. The history of short-lived art was in large part a reaction against the capitalist commodification of art objects—after all, a temporary artwork, such as a performance, can't be subject to speculative fervor, with collectors buying and selling it for ever-greater sums. And yet, even in the early nineties, there was already a feeling that built-in obsolescence was something collectors might want to pay for.

The artist Charlotta Westergren, for instance, installed a piece made of crystallized sugar above a major collector's bed; part of the art was that over the course of a couple of years, the sugar would go from being clear to being cloudy, with pieces breaking off. Eventually, the work was simply discarded—there was no point in storing it. More famously, Andy Warhol's cow wallpaper is both very expensive, if you want to buy a few rolls of it, and also designed to be pasted directly onto the wall, at which point it can never be moved or, really, sold. It will scuff and deteriorate over time, just like the silver wallpaper in Warhol's own Factory, and then that's the end of its natural life.

One more example: The Swiss artist Urs Fischer has exhibited many of his candle sculptures, which are designed to slowly burn down to the ground over the course of a few weeks. One such sculpture, an oversized portrait of art collector Peter Brant, sold at Christie's in 2012 for $1.3 million. In order to fully realize its potential, the collector will have to destroy it.

More recently, the pseudonymous English graffiti artist Banksy sold one of his works on paper in an elaborate frame designed to shred the piece should it ever appear at auction. That ended up happening in 2018—although the shredding mechanism malfunctioned, so the piece ended up half-shredded, with strips of paper dangling below the frame and the top half of the work intact.

The winning bidder cannily decided to keep the half-destroyed work she had just purchased for £1,042,000, waiting until October 2021 to return the work to the same Sotheby's salesroom, where this time it sold for £18,582,000, or just over $25 million.

It was probably inevitable that NFT purveyors would take that concept and use it to try to transform real-world objects into digital ones. A group calling itself Injective Protocol, for instance, bought a Banksy print on paper for $95,000, created an NFT of the print—which is to say, they created a digital token that refers in some way to the print—and then literally destroyed the print by burning it. They then sold the NFT for $380,000.

In the NFT era, "burning" items is a very common way of trying to maintain or create value. If you have some cryptocurrency and you sell it to a null address, that "burns" the currency and renders it irrecoverable. The effect is similar to when companies do stock buybacks: It concentrates ownership in everybody whose tokens weren't burned, and thereby makes those tokens more valuable.

The burning of the print was part stunt but was also based in a common intuition, that an object cannot exist simultaneously in two places and in two forms. In order for the NFT to be "real," there was a feeling that the original object had to cease to exist. A few months later, Damien Hirst announced his own NFT project, which, yes, involved destroying physical artworks as part of an either/or choice that collectors faced between owning something physical or owning the related NFT. Later still, a person or group known only as shl0ms detonated a Lamborghini, collected 999 burned and charred fragments thereof, and sold them off as NFTs—physical fragment not included.

What all these artworks have in common is a steadily increasing annualized return on investment. In principle, destroying an object should destroy its value. When Robert Rauschenberg created *Erased De Kooning Drawing*, he took a work on paper given to him by the great abstract expressionist Willem de Kooning, and then spent two months laboriously erasing every trace of the master's hand. (It wasn't easy: The original was in grease pencil and charcoal.) He then held on to it for the next forty-five years—he certainly didn't do it to make money.

Forty years after the Rauschenberg piece, Chinese artist and activist Ai Weiwei did something similar, spending a reported hundreds of thousands of dollars on a two-thousand-year-old ceremonial Han dynasty urn—a genuinely important historical item—and then filming himself dropping it onto hard cement, destroying it completely. "Dropping a Han Dynasty Urn" may have ultimately been monetized for more than the price of the original vase, but that wasn't the *purpose* of making it; rather, the core of the work was an oblique commentary on the Mao Zedong quote that "the only way of building a new world is by destroying the old one." And while the Banksy did end up being stupendously valuable, only a tiny fraction of that value went to Banksy himself, and the entire value-creation chain was full of randomness and contingency.

The NFTs, by contrast, were all about immediate profit. The pandemic enabled NFT artists to successfully put an immediate premium on evanescence and intangibility. The Boomer ideal of "buy a well-made pair of boots that will last you a lifetime" had evolved into a Gen Z ideal of "buy a blazingly white pair of sneakers that will lose nearly all of their value if you wear them even once." Built-in obsolescence was no longer a critique of capitalism so much as it was a desired feature of it.

Connoisseurship, in the NFT world, was worthless; art was valued not on its intrinsic qualities but rather on its status as a meme. Physical art went in much the same direction. To see a KAWS object online is to grok it immediately because it has achieved meme status. In turn, that meme status translates effortlessly into real-world value. In the digital world, the juvenile digital doodlings of an artist who posts on Instagram under the handle @beeple_crap—a man whose bio read "art shit for yer facehole"—can become worthy of being auctioned at Christie's.

We are all living, after all, in an age of artifice—a world intermediated by phones and other screens, a world that, especially during lockdown, felt vibrant and urgent and real, in stark contrast to the mundane pandemic-constrained physical existence outside the bedroom door. The compelling unreality of the virtual world has a natural counterpart in money itself, whether fiat or crypto. Assigning numbers to virtual objects is a game that feels so far removed from, say, handing over cash at a grocery store, that the connection between the two—the fungibility of money—can end up being attenuated almost to the point of erasure.

As one crypto trader put it: "I spent $7,000 tonight on a picture of a guy with a sword. I've never spent that much on an object in my life."[2] It's *easier* to spend $7,000 on a picture of a guy with a sword than it is to spend $7,000 on almost anything else.

That's partly because people have crypto wallets and real-world bank accounts, and while it's *possible* to trade back and forth between the two, most of the time people don't. Crypto investments act, in practice, as though they're highly illiquid—folks tend to trade actively within the crypto space, whether it's coins or yield farming or NFTs or something even more abstruse, while only very rarely trading crypto for dollars or vice versa.

That's one reason why some crypto enthusiasts like to make a point of "getting paid in bitcoin"—while they could easily achieve the same result just by converting some portion of their paycheck into bitcoin after being paid, in practice that's pretty rare, and they prefer such transactions to be made in a way that's automatic. The whole idea is that once the money is in bitcoin, it probably won't get swapped into dollars, and it can therefore rise in value if held over the long term.

In the short term, of course, crypto can fall—but precisely because it's such a self-contained universe, those falls cause relatively little real-world harm. If the 2022 "crypto winter" caused the $7,000 picture of a guy with a sword to become a $70 picture of a guy with a sword, that likely had very little effect on its owner's dollar expenditures, since on some level it was all play money anyway.

Even when people do sell their cryptocurrencies for dollars, they often keep those dollars in stablecoin form, in coins with names like Tether (USDT) or USD Coin (USDC). That makes trading in and out of assets like bitcoin a lot smoother and easier than dealing with bank accounts; it also reinforces the way in which crypto proceeds live in a parallel virtual world that feels far removed from reality.

The barriers to entry are also incredibly low; buying NFTs really is as easy as pressing a button. The number of ethereum (ETH) in your wallet goes down; a guy with a sword appears in your Meta-Mask wallet. It's gameplay more than it is consumption. And in any case you're really just trading one virtual asset for another; it's not like the ETH is inherently any more real, or any more valuable, than the NFT.

If anything, the opposite is the case. Holding ETH is an explicitly speculative act; there's no real reason to do so unless you hope and believe that it's going to rise in value. Holding an NFT, by contrast, confers some kind of ownership of some kind of digital object, which in turn has some kind of utility—at the very least, it has the same kind of utility that real-world collectibles have.

NFTs also have the advantage that because a lot of them are unique, or quasi-unique (your CryptoPunk is different from mine in a number of key ways), you can hold on to them during crypto bear markets without watching the market value of your holdings fall daily. In that they're a little bit like, say, venture capitalists' investments in private companies: If there was a public secondary market for such things, the price would be highly volatile and there would be periods when they would plunge in a very worrying manner. But since there isn't, investors can have more equanimity in their patience, and only worry about the market value when they really want to sell or when a particularly attractive offer comes along.

Finally, especially when the price is quoted in ETH, the numbers are just small. When it comes to NFTs in particular, the convention is that prices are quoted in crypto rather than dollars. Spending 0.5 ETH feels like less of a big deal than spending $1,500, even when ETH is trading well above $3,000. Pricing in ETH is the crypto equivalent of when a company does a stock split, reducing the nominal value of its shares to make them seem more affordable.

Finance professors roll their eyes at such stunts, but they do seem to increase demand in the real world.

For all these reasons, on top of the basic fact that fun and games are always attractive, the pandemic saw millions of people putting non-negligible amounts of money into asset classes that barely existed previously, and that didn't fit comfortably into classical models of how investments work.

One of the fundamental concepts in finance, for instance, is that of *duration*. It has a technical meaning in the bond market—it's a unit of a bond's susceptibility to changes in interest rates, which means it's a measure of risk—but the units of measurement are years, which means that it generally gets plotted along the x-axis of charts, just like time. Often bond yields are then plotted on the y-axis, which results in something known as a yield curve. When an interest rates trader looks at a yield curve, she can see at a glance the yield that the market is currently offering for any given degree of risk that she might be willing to take.

In normal times, the yield curve slopes upward, which means, roughly speaking, that the longer you tie your funds up, the more money you can make. Sometimes, however, that isn't true: Before recessions, for instance, the yield curve tends to slope downward, in a sign of pessimism about the medium- and long-term prognosis for the broader economy.

Equities, commodities, and other speculative vehicles don't have well-defined duration, but they're generally viewed as being way, way out on the far end of the duration spectrum. A long-dated bond, for instance, is just a series of cashflows—a fixed coupon payment every six months, and then a final principal repayment after, say, twenty years. Duration is a bit like the weighted average of those cashflows—a bit at the beginning, a bit at the middle, a whole lot on a certain date in twenty years' time, and then nothing.

A stock like Tesla, on the other hand, doesn't pay any dividends at all, and never has. If you're looking at the anticipated future cash-flows that a shareholder might expect to receive, there's nothing in the short term, nothing in the medium term, and *maybe* the beginnings of a small dividend payment if you go far enough out into the future. All the value of that stock, if you're trying to reverse-engineer the expected future dividends from the share price, lies in enormous hypothetical dividends way out into the future—twenty-five years, forty years, who knows. A thirty-year bond is positively safe in comparison.

At least stocks lend themselves in theory to a duration-based analysis. When it comes to SWAG assets, duration makes no sense at all, because their defining feature is that they don't generate any cashflows ever. Historically, a nice work of art has been viewed by finance theorists as a consumption good that you buy with the *proceeds* of your bond investments, more than as an investment in its own right. It's an end, it's not the means to the end. If you can sell your asset today then that's its value today, but there's no discounted cashflow analysis that will change its valuation tomorrow, because there are no cashflows to discount.

In other words, unlike high-risk securities, assets like NFTs are much more immediate in their pleasures and in their return profile. The dividends you get from owning a collectible watch or car or painting are the ones you reap when you hear the throttle open up, or glance down at your wrist, or drink your morning coffee while looking up at the eternally fresh and wondrous Charlotta Westergren painting you bought during the pandemic. (Okay, maybe that last one is just me.)

The pandemic reduced many of our quotidian pleasures to ash. The everyday experiences that syncopated our lives largely disappeared. No more concerts, no more crowded bars, no more unexpected smiles from a stranger coming in the opposite direction. I filled some of that space by buying Charlotta's painting, an act that paid substantial dividends in the form of the great pleasure I got looking at it every day. And indeed the broader art market bounced back very quickly from the immediate pandemic slump, with an unprecedented number of buyers being willing to make major purchases sight unseen, from emailed JPEGs or even just Instagram posts.

For the Extremely Online, NFTs played a similar role, but were also turbocharged with the excitement inherent whenever you buy something that has the potential to soar in value. You could own an original artwork by Grimes, the achingly cool techno-futuristic artist who seduced Elon Musk via Twitter, you could have a CryptoPunk as your Twitter avatar, you could accumulate an enviable collection of NBA moments featuring your favorite icons of basketball. Digital collectibles in many ways had *more* hedonic value than their real-world counterparts—they can't get damaged, they're effortless to share, and they confer a feeling of being ahead of the curve, of being at the vanguard of what the future is going to look like.

Collecting NFTs made investing more *fun* than it had ever been before. Community, jokes, beauty, irony—all these things came together in a way that Larry Summers's finance professors could never incorporate into their beloved Capital Asset Pricing Model. Boomers turned investing into a social hobby by trading stock tips on the golf course; Gen X didn't want investing to be a hobby at all, and just socked dollars away in index funds as part of their routine retirement planning. With Robinhood and NFTs, however, investing paid not only literal future dividends but also metaphorical present ones, in the form of the opportunity to be part of an exciting online movement.

One of the ironically perennial complaints about Wall Street is that it is too "short-termist"—it cares too much about today's earnings, or today's stock-price moves, and not nearly enough about the long term. If what you're doing is trying to save money for pension needs decades in the future, then most of what happens today is just noise, and should probably be ignored.

The ground rules of the short-termism debate are broadly agreed upon: Given that we're all trying to achieve long-term gains, what's the best way of doing that? Should we work hard every year or quarter or week or day to try to maximize our returns? Or should we put short-term noise out of our minds and try to keep as focused as possible on how well we think our portfolio is positioned for the long term? And if it's the latter, how should we judge how well we're doing?

With the pandemic came the first sign of millions of investors rejecting the terms of that debate altogether. What if we're *not* all trying to achieve long-term gains? What if we want something completely different? What if we're looking for fun and excitement and community and beauty and the feverish anticipation of enormous *short-term* gains? What would *that* kind of market look like?

In a country where most of the wealth is held by people at or near retirement age, almost none of whom have a Reddit or Robinhood account or would ever buy an NFT, such phenomena are always going to have a pretty marginal effect on capital markets as a whole. Institutional investors running hundreds of billions of dollars tend to act in line with what finance professors say is optimal strategy—or at least they aspire to do so. And while retail participation in the stock market certainly rose sharply during the pandemic, it's still unlikely to ever eclipse the sheer tonnage of money being managed by global institutions like UBS, with $3 trillion under management, or Black-Rock, with $10 trillion. Even someone you've never heard of, like Amundi, can be in charge of $2 trillion.

The spark that was lit during the pandemic, however, is unlikely to be extinguished entirely, and indeed no one should be surprised if those flames spread over time. An entire generation has been given a choice between two modes of investing—fun and immediate-gratification versus boring and delayed-gratification—and once you've tasted the former, it's hard to confine yourself entirely to the latter.

As John Maynard Keynes said, "markets can stay irrational longer than you can stay solvent"—and every time a nonsensical asset surges and creates a new cohort of millionaires, the more likely it is for other would-be millionaires to learn the lesson and try their luck with similar assets.

The great value investor Benjamin Graham liked to say that in the short run, the market is a voting machine, while in the long run, it's a weighing machine. That was his way of telling investors to ignore what other investors were doing, and to concentrate on the fundamentals. (The problem, as Keynes was fond of pointing out, is that in the long run we're all dead.)

It's easy to understand how the market as voting machine works: Prices follow demand, and when a lot of people want to spend a lot of money on a certain asset, then the price of that asset goes up. It's much less easy to understand the hidden weighing-machine algorithm, or when exactly the weighing machine is supposed to be able to arrive at its accurate long-run result.

Bond markets are definitely weighing machines: Because all bonds reach maturity, there is an end date at which you know exactly how much any given bond or group of bonds ended up paying investors in those securities. But stock markets are different. An institutionally dominated stock market has undeniable if weak tendencies toward weighing-machine status, but the Boomers won't be able to control the market after they die, and Millennials don't have the same trust in institutions. They also lack the kind of defined-benefit pensions that created many of the giant pension funds that dominate the stock market today.

As generational wealth shifts away from Boomers, then, it perforce is going to shift toward a much more online generation that has much less attachment than they do to the theories of finance professors—and that has vivid memories of the great bull market of 2020–21 and its irrational yet enjoyable murmurations. The market has always welcomed gamblers and short-attention-span day-traders with open arms—just look at penny stocks. So there will always be somewhere new for the starlings to flock to.

At various times, thanks to inflation or fiscal policy or monetary policy or old-fashioned economic growth or even just stochastic inevitability, there will be a bigger flocking than usual to such gambles.

Massive frauds, like that seen at crypto exchange FTX, can cause a similar flocking in the opposite direction. But thanks to the pandemic, millions of investors—older and richer than they were in 2020—will always remember those heady days in 2021 and think to themselves that even if they missed out the first time around, this might be their opportunity. FOMO, after all, lives eternal, as does the craving for excitement.

The Gen X predilection for passive investment might make intellectual sense, but it's not very human. In experiments, 67 percent of men administered a painful electric shock to themselves to avoid just sitting and doing nothing for fifteen minutes. The generations after mine have tasted the apple: They know what it's like to actively trade, and they've seen friends get rich doing it. That's something that can't be unlearned. Even if such behavior goes into hibernation for a while, no one should be surprised if and when short-term speculative fervor comes roaring back.

5

Workspace

THE NOUN "SPACE" has what you might call a creative-class definition—not when it's a purely physical demarcation, as in "parking space," but when it starts accumulating metaphorical undertones, as in "performing arts space," or the reinvention of your local Starbucks as a "third space" betwixt home and office. Even that parking space, for that matter, might qualify, when it's not a literal piece of square footage but is rather something more conceptual, the mere right to be able to store your vehicle in a given parking structure, even when it doesn't have a specifically reserved location.

This idea, of space as an "actualized where," a place something happens, has always been commonplace among architects and designers. During the pandemic, it started being the way in which almost everybody navigated the world. The idea that different spaces have different valences was no longer something confined to glossy magazines; it was a quotidian fact of existence. Home was where you could take your mask off.

Within the home, spaces rapidly transmogrified. Beds became offices; countertops became schoolrooms; ovens became actually used for cooking, rather than just being storage areas for various pans that couldn't fit anywhere else. Walls and bookcases became carefully curated not for their ability to make any particular sense in the context of the design of the home but rather for their ability to convey the perfect mix of personality and professionalism for colleagues and for Twitter accounts like @ratemyskyperoom. Sales of ring lights—circular LED bulbs designed to make people look good on Zoom or TikTok—surged.

The "office space" within the home was no longer a standard cuboid with a door and a desk and a window, but rather a four-sided pyramid tipped over onto its side, with the top at exactly the point of a laptop's webcam. The performative aspect of work became front of mind, complete with a heavy dose of dramatic irony, with the Zoom call participant hyperaware of all manner of chaos happening just outside the field of vision of the computer. When Adam Aron, the CEO of AMC, a meme-stock chain of movie theaters, did a live YouTube video in June 2021, he briefly lost control of his camera, which was knocked downward and revealed him to be wearing no trousers. The episode only served to solidify Aron's status as a different kind of CEO, relatable and grounded. Who among us hadn't worked in our underwear during the previous year.

Meanwhile, on TikTok, a popular trend was for people to wait until their partner was on a work Zoom call, and then take all their clothes off, walk to just outside that sideways pyramid, and film the partner's reaction. Such pranks acted as a lighthearted way of spotlighting a serious issue, which was the way in which it became effectively impossible to disentangle the personal and the professional, especially for people without entire spare rooms that could be dedicated to work.

A lot of the problem was a matter of simple arithmetic—space as measured in old-fashioned square feet, rather than space as an analytical construct. Pre-pandemic, homes were almost entirely residential—any extra space would generally go toward giving each of the kids their own bedroom, or creating a separate dining room or TV room or something like that. The "library" or "study" was much less common. Far from being a modern recognition of the ubiquity of work, it was more likely to be an atavistic pastiche of an era when gentlemen-autodidacts would have an independent income and no need of an employer. As such, it was generally found only in the top percentile of homes.

Instead, the office was always a wholly separate place, a professional zone entirely paid for by your employer, who would provide everything you needed to do your job in a place designed to be largely free of nonprofessional distractions. The commute took you away from your personal life, both mentally and spatially, while the office created a zone of employment.

When we ask what someone's position is at a company—or, for that matter, when we hire someone and then put them through an "onboarding" process—the metaphor we're using is a spatial one. Different departments exist in different physical spaces, and within those spaces the org chart is reflected in the seating plan. One of the main ways, historically, that workers have learned how to do their jobs has just been for them to physically inhabit a certain desk, a certain position. As Bloomberg columnist Matt Levine likes to say, everything is seating charts.

That was certainly true for me. My first real job was as a graduate trainee at *Euromoney* magazine, in London—probably the most intense six-month learning experience of my life. I learned how to do reporting by listening to the calls being made by the colleagues sitting next to me. I learned how to edit stories by taking marked-up printouts from editors and making the changes in the electronic copy. I learned how to design magazine pages by literally sitting next to Alison, the art director, and watching her do it.

By the time my traineeship was over, I wasn't offered a full-time job, partly because in the last week of December I had listened to all the conversations going on around me about how no one was going to come into the office on January 2, and erroneously inferred that there was no need for me to do so either. Nevertheless, I still came into the office almost every day for the following year, getting regular work on a freelance basis just because by that point I understood how everything worked.

Eventually, I was asked to design a new magazine for Euromoney Publications, not because I had any kind of portfolio or design qualifications, but just because I was *there*. Not long after that, the founding editor of that magazine—by then having moved on to a different company—offered me a job in New York.

All of this happened within eighteen months, and all of it happened by sheer force of proximity—the same force that, centuries earlier, had made the person holding the office of "groom of the stool" one of the most powerful courtiers in the land. The groom of the stool didn't have an inherently important job—his job was basically just to entertain the King while he was sitting on the toilet, and literally clean up his shit. But that degree of intimacy and access proved incredibly important, and the position was much sought-after, for very good reason.

During the pandemic, such jockeying for literal position—the corner office, or the quasi-privacy of having your back to the wall, or the desk located along a well-trafficked path that allows you to buttonhole executives as they walk past—disappeared overnight. In a largely remote working environment, with meetings and face time carefully planned out in advance, there's also much less serendipity and even *humanity*—the feeling of personal connection you can get just by holding a door open for someone.

One day in the summer of 2021 a group of my Washington-based colleagues from Axios were in New York for a meeting—one of the first times that a group of my colleagues traveled collectively for work since the onset of the pandemic. I happened to be in the office, and happened to be writing about something political. I walked over to Alayna Treene, our ace congressional reporter, had a five-minute conversation with her, and walked back to my desk energized in a way that made me realize how important those connections are. I can't for the life of me remember what we were talking about, but I can easily remember the feeling of really working *with* someone, for the first time in months.

Geoffrey West, one of the polymath scientists studying complexity at the Santa Fe Institute (SFI), tells the story of a project he worked on during the pandemic with his colleague Chris Kempes, as well as Manfred Laubichler and Deryc Painter of Arizona State University. Their weekly meetings, by necessity, were over Zoom, but at one point when the virus felt as though it was satisfactorily under control, they met in person, in a conference room at SFI. "We did more in that hour and a half," says West, "in terms of ideas and excitement and writing things down and so on, than we felt we had done in the previous year of meeting essentially every week."

Without long office-bound days and the camaraderie they engender, there's necessarily much less awareness of, and understanding of, what your colleagues are doing. Sometimes, that lack of trust can deliver an unexpected silver lining: Corporate whistleblowers reported their employers to the Securities and Exchange Commission 6,900 times in fiscal 2021, for instance—an increase of more than 30 percent on the previous year. As Matt Levine wrote after that number came out, "the mechanism here, of people feeling disconnected from their jobs and disloyal to their colleagues, is not unique to the fraud business. This story is a sort of leading indicator of a breakdown in morale and group cohesion generally as so much work is done from home."[1]

There's also more precarity. My friend Pavia Rosati has a story about her first job, working for *Mirabella*, the smart woman's fashion magazine, in 1992. She began as an intern in the fashion department and was given a full-time job as an assistant in the photo department after the previous team quit en masse.

Pavia was told to start out by logging photos, so she spent her first days doing just that: logging photos and clearing out years of un-accounted-for photos and shoots, vaguely curious about the pile of photo info sheets from various other magazine departments that was accumulating on her desk.

One day an art director came along and asked her if she had photos of the Baader-Meinhof Gang for the feature he was about to lay out. Pavia responded with a blank stare, precipitating a tirade on the subject of her incompetence from the manager in question. Barely had she started in her new job than she was staring down the end of it.

Fortunately, the editor in chief, Gay Bryant, heard what was going on and walked over to intervene. She saw the photo info sheets that Pavia had neatly pinned on her bulletin board and explained that when one of these arrived, with descriptions and details about a newly assigned article, she had to phone the various photo agencies *Mirabella* worked with, and request that they messenger over a collection of photos that could illustrate the article.

Pavia had only one question: "Is that my job?" It was—and it was Bryant's job to have situational awareness of how Pavia's job training would have fallen through the cracks, and to rescue her in real time from being branded incapable of doing her job. In an office setting, it's much easier to notice when a colleague needs help, and to act on that.

Even small changes to how we work can have huge aggregate effects on how we live. Work is where we spend ninety thousand hours of our lives, on average. It's how we're defined by others and, to a large degree, it's how we define ourselves. It's utterly central to our existence, determining where we live, how much money we have, who many of our adult friends are, and even how happy we are.

It's worth repeating the key word there: Work is *where* we spend ninety thousand hours of our lives. Work isn't just something we do, it's a place—a space that for decades has been defined in contradistinction to home. (No, she's not here, she's at work.) The workplace has its own absurdities and rituals; you can learn a lot about a company just by walking through its offices. Conversely, if you *don't* spend much time physically inhabiting a company's office, you're going to be missing something important about how that institution works, in practice, on a day-to-day basis.

As a journalist, I've experienced my fair share of executive floors—hushed, expensively carpeted spaces with multiple layers of security, a small number of enormous office suites, and an overabundance of wood paneling, even in the most austerely modern steel-and-glass skyscrapers. I've also experienced many long desks, with workers sitting shoulder to shoulder, many wearing headphones to try to achieve some modicum of respite from the sensory overload of everything going on around them. Neither feels particularly pleasant—but then again, pleasant is not the aim.

One of the many bright spots from the cinematic *annus mirabilis* of 1999 is Mike Judge's timeless comedy *Office Space*, a movie that, more than any other, identified—and created a broad antipathy toward—the drudgery of the cubicle farm, with its gray half walls and ersatz privacy. Thanks in large part to that film, subsequent iterations of office design tried hard to be cheerier, but they were just as dystopian in their own way, as immortalized in *W1A*, a BBC satire that updated *Office Space* for the jargon-filled 2010s of hot-desking and weirdly uncomfortable soft furnishings.

Pretty much all offices portrayed in Hollywood movies are bleak and deadening places. Think of the final shot of Mike Nichols's *Working Girl*, where the triumphant Melanie Griffith finally gets her own office and a secretary of her own, to the jubilation of Joan Cusack and a stirring Oscar-winning female-empowerment anthem from Carly Simon. It's written as the happiest of endings, but Nichols decides to place his camera on the *outside* of the enormous Chase Manhattan Plaza, slowly zooming back to reveal Griffith's office window as just one tiny part of a huge and soulless grid.

The antipathy derives from the fact that offices have always been the one place where density and proximity to others are understood as obviously desirable. From the point of view of the profit-maximizing corporation, it makes perfect sense to leverage the combined power of thousands of employees all living in the same city and commuting into the same building at the same time. But that's not a vision that aligns with any kind of escapist fantasy—the stock-in-trade of the film industry.

Hence all those shots of the kind of uncomfortably crowded elevators you'll never find on a Los Angeles studio lot, scenes designed to underscore the way in which the nine-to-five steals the kind of individuality and freedom that are generally represented by the wide-open spaces of the American West.

The American Dream, as encapsulated by Hollywood, is to quit your wage-slave job and follow your dream—or, failing that, at least do honest work outdoors. Peter Gibbons, the hero of *Office Space*, starts as a disgruntled software engineer with eight different bosses who's supposed to be working on Y2K bugs; the happy ending sees him in a hard hat and hi-viz vest, working on a construction site and smiling broadly as he tells his former colleagues that he has no interest in returning to office work. His white-collar job was fundamentally fraudulent and dishonest; it even drove him to crime.

His new blue-collar job, paying much less, is much more fulfilling and noble.

In both work and personal life, we're told by America's most successful storytellers, the journey to happiness involves moving away from human density. Did you grow up in a crowded inner-city apartment but then manage to find yourself a big house with a yard? Did you leave behind the rat race to live in a small cabin by a lake? Did you sell your house and retire early to live the low-budget #vanlife dream? Those are the wins. Are you still stuck in traffic or squeezing into crowded elevators or fighting with your neighbors over noise issues? Those are Ls—losses.

What the pandemic did—and this happened *very* quickly, in just a couple of weeks—was to present a vision of a realistic alternative to everything that people hate about commuting and offices. For the fictional Peter Gibbons of *Office Space*, the only way out of working at his bland tech-company office was to quit the industry entirely. The Peter Gibbons of 2020 was probably already working from home much of the time, even before the pandemic hit, but lockdown gave him the ability to dream of such an arrangement becoming full-time and permanent.

Before 2020, employees had to seek out employers who would let them work remotely—and they had to pay a price in terms of being out of sight and out of mind. If anybody thought to patch them into important meetings, they probably could barely make out what people were saying, and they certainly weren't likely to contribute anything. Once the pandemic hit, some leaders were keen to get everybody back into the office as quickly as possible—but others were happy to absent themselves indefinitely.

For most of my career, the idea of running an organization remotely was considered unserious. One of my hedge-fund sources, for instance, a swashbuckling hedge-fund manager named Marc

Hélie, was fired from Gramercy Advisors, the fund he co-founded, in large part because he liked to work on summer Fridays from his Hamptons beach house. Later on, the equally larger-than-life post-crisis CEO of AIG, Bob Benmosche, was pilloried for running the insurance giant from Villa Splendid, his five-tiered palazzo in Dubrovnik, Croatia. He defended himself to Reuters, saying he could work as well in Croatia as in New York,[2] but that to most people seemed like a stretch. And hedge-fund billionaire Eddie Lampert did himself no favors when he decided that he could run Sears from his home on an exclusive Miami island (where there's no personal income tax), traveling to the retailer's Illinois headquarters only once a year for the annual shareholder meeting.[3]

Come the pandemic, such behavior became much less objectionable. Dean Baquet, the top editor at the *New York Times*, spent most of the pandemic in Los Angeles, Zooming into meetings as required.[4] Similarly, Oracle chairman Larry Ellison decided to run his company from Lanai, the Hawaiian island he bought for $300 million in 2012.[5] Such decisions sent a signal from the top that working from home really is okay, and placed no subtle demands on lower-down workers without chauffeur-driven cars to show face at the office.

By contrast, JPMorgan CEO Jamie Dimon was commuting into his office by June 2020, despite almost having died that March after suffering a sudden aortic dissection.[6] Dimon's message was clear: He expected his senior management team in the office, alongside anybody else who had real ambition.

Not that ambition was a given any longer. Many older workers, especially, established enough in their profession that they didn't feel the need to suck up to the boss, took the opportunity to leave cities in general and two cities in particular—San Francisco and New York. Both places felt inherently dangerous and unnecessarily expensive, for people who had already climbed as far up the greasy pole as they wanted to get—and especially for those who took advantage of the pandemic to reevaluate their lives and who came to the conclusion that they were actually higher up the org chart than they wanted to be and could use a bit a simplification.

It's no coincidence that San Francisco and New York were the two cities with the highest office rents in the country, often exceeding $100 per square foot per year. High rents mean that space is always at a premium, and that corporations are always on the lookout for ways to increase density, to squeeze more employees into fewer floors. That's why WeWork grew so fast in expensive cities like New York and London: Its value proposition from the beginning was that it had the ability to fit many more workers into any given amount of space than most other offices, while providing enough in the way of sofas and free beer that the employees didn't mind—until the pandemic arrived. At that point, they started to mind very much the idea of being jam-packed into rooms that often had zero exterior exposures.

The memory of such working conditions made it easy for many employees to decide to keep their jobs while moving out of the city to somewhere with less stress and more space. The US Census Bureau measures population changes on the basis of a July-to-June year, which neatly captures the height of the Covid-induced moves that took place between July 1, 2020, and June 30, 2021. In that period, 73 percent of US counties saw more deaths than births, thanks to Covid—the largest spike in deaths in over a century. Nevertheless, 58 percent of counties saw their population go up, rather than down. New residents were moving in faster than old residents were dying.

Where were they moving from? That's easy: cities. And the bigger and more expensive the city, the faster people were moving out. The New York metropolitan area lost a net 378,000 inhabitants in a single year, while San Francisco lost 182,000, Los Angeles lost 174,000, and Chicago lost 107,000. All those numbers were unprecedented in recent history.

As a rule of thumb, the minority of counties with a population of more than half a million nearly all lost population during the pandemic, while smaller counties with less than half a million people nearly all grew. The literal Phoenix economy, the Phoenix-Mesa metropolitan area, was the biggest city to buck the nationwide trend and actually increase in population, although even there the rate of increase was significantly lower than it had been a year previously.

This was not the beginning of some great new trend of deurbanization. Around the world, people have been moving into cities for decades, and America is no exception, and that's not going to change. This was more of what market analysts might call a "bull market correction"—a brief interlude of going backward, in the context of a long-term secular increase in cities' population. It wasn't even a particularly big correction. The biggest decline, in the New York metro area, was less than 2 percent of the total population, and demand for New York property started picking up almost as soon as the Census Bureau's one-year period was over.

After all, one thing everybody learned at the height of the pandemic was the importance of location at a super-granular scale: what floor you were on (did you have any light in your apartment), what street you were on (could you hear the sirens going all night), which neighborhood you were in.

The Covid pandemic forced almost everybody on the planet to be more acutely aware of where they lived than they ever had been before. The differences between countries became enormous—but so did the differences even between neighborhoods. I always felt comfortable in my own neighborhood of Chinatown in Manhattan, for instance, where masks were ubiquitous and positivity rates were consistently among the lowest in New York. But Staten Island, just a couple of miles away, was a totally different story. Home to many front-line workers including a lot of policemen, its residents generally abjured masks and saw positivity rates that regularly broke into double digits—which is to say, more than 1 in 10 Covid tests in many neighborhoods would come in positive. At the end of 2020, Staten Island accounted for 1 in 4 of New York City's Covid deaths, while having just a twentieth of the total population.[7]

When the city's real estate rebound started happening, rents rose fastest in the neighborhoods that were popular on TikTok. And across the city—across the country—demand for New York property was increasing even where the population was decreasing, because of how the pandemic changed the arithmetic of workspace.

The very back-of-the-envelope calculation goes something like this: The average New York household fits about 2.5 people into about 1,000 square feet, for roughly 400 square feet per person. But that's not all the space available to the working adults in the household—they also have access to an office, which generally works out to about 150 square feet per person.

If the average household has one person who can work from home, and that person is accustomed to having about 150 square feet of space for working in, then the household is going to feel more cramped than usual unless it expands by about 150 square feet, or 15 percent. A 2 percent population decline will never be enough to counteract the effects of the people staying in New York demanding 15 percent more space than they had previously.

Obviously, all these numbers are very fuzzy. But the broad facts of the matter are that when you effectively add a home office to a home, either you're going to be in more of a squeeze than you were before, or else you're going to add some space. Given the amount of wealth and liquidity that was in evidence during the pandemic, it should come as no surprise that a lot of people opted for the second option—adding more space, either by moving out of the city or by moving to a larger home within the city.

Developers certainly took note. New apartments built after the pandemic hit were 90 square feet, or 9.6 percent, larger than new apartments built in the previous ten years.[8]

Those people who did upsize invariably did so by more than 150 square feet. If you're moving into a new place with a dedicated space set aside as a home office, the important thing is less the number of extra square feet you have, and more the number of windows you have. An office without a window is an unpleasant place to work, and if you're looking for a home-office space with walls and a window, well, that's what realtors call a "bedroom," and you're effectively going up an entire rung on the property ladder by adding an extra bedroom.

What that means is that for people for whom employment is a given, and who can see that working from home is going to be a greater or lesser part of their employment for the rest of their career, it follows that at some point they're going to want that extra bedroom. In a place like New York or San Francisco, that room can easily cost half a million dollars or even more, so there's a strong financial incentive to move somewhere cheaper, maybe to the suburbs or exurbs, use that new home office as your primary working space, and commute in only when you're really needed.

Suburbs and exurbs were also where most new homes were built during the pandemic. Homebuilders lost little time adapting floor plans to meet the new forms of demand—out went useless double-height cathedral ceilings; in came flexible spaces that provide aural privacy so that other people in the house don't need to hear your Zoom calls or your online exercise instructor. Ground-floor space, in particular, was reconfigured: Large double or triple garages got chopped down in size, and instead home offices got added, often with their own separate entrance. Fitting out a space like that is significantly more expensive for homebuilders than having a large uninsulated garage, but the pandemic ensured that those changes more than paid for themselves in terms of increased property values.

Such changes tend to last for decades. The downstairs powder room, for instance, came into existence as a result of the 1918 flu pandemic, as a place for visitors and tradespeople to wash their hands upon entry—a way to prevent them from unwittingly tracking germs into the house. It was a quiet grassroots public-health innovation that ended up becoming de rigueur in new builds not because of public demand for entrance hygiene (most people no longer wash their hands immediately on entering a house as a matter of course) but just because people really liked the convenience of having a bathroom on the ground floor. It's a bit like the curb cut effect: While curb cuts were introduced narrowly for the sake of wheelchair users, they very quickly became popular among the broader population who loved the way they made life easier for anybody wheeling anything from scooters to suitcases.

Something similar is likely to happen with respect to the relatively simple idea that flexibility and optionality are valuable and desirable features in any home. Almost everybody from middle schoolers onward craves the ability to carve out a quiet place where they can work, free from family distractions.

It should be noted that many of the people who tried out the suburban solution ended up regretting it. Living in a high-density city provides a large number of affordances that can easily get taken for granted and are only really missed when you start having to drive everywhere, and your choice of neighborhood restaurants becomes more depressing than exciting. Still, the sheer force of demand for new living space—which much of the time was office space under a different name, paid for by employees rather than employers—drove a terrifying boom in housing prices, which in turn placed pressure on a whole generation of Millennials, many of whom were starting families, to buy at almost any price before houses got completely out of reach as they had done in places like Vancouver or Sydney.

This wasn't a speculative bubble—almost no one was buying with the intention of rapidly flipping at a profit. It was more like a FOMO bubble: The more that prices rose, the more that people felt they had to buy now, which in turn only caused prices to rise even further. Low mortgage rates, at least until the spring of 2022, only exacerbated the situation, making it easier than ever to afford an extremely expensive house on a middle-class salary. When mortgage rates did rise, they were still negative in real terms, given soaring inflation. That helped to maintain homeownership as a very attractive proposition. House prices, after all, tend to rise in line with inflation, while mortgages are eroded by it.

In effect, a huge chunk of America's commercial real-estate budget—the amount of money that society as a whole is willing to spend on office space—got transferred into household budgets and residential neighborhoods. Companies were generally still locked into long-term leases, but broadly they found themselves with more office space than they needed to accommodate a workforce much of which was working from home a lot of the time. That gave them a desire to reduce their commercial footprint. Individuals, on the other hand, found themselves with *less* office space than they needed in homes that were never designed for such purposes, and went on a buying spree trying to acquire it.

The change will be profound and lasting, not by dint of its size but because of what it means for how white-collar professionals work, even if they had never moved anywhere. For the first time ever, inhabitants of expensive cities who hadn't really wanted to live in such places for a while—who lived there out of perceived necessity rather than out of a predilection for vibrant urban streetscapes—found themselves able *both* to move out of town *and* to keep their jobs.

The employees who moved out of town were often important enough that their employers wanted to keep them happy. Even if they weren't C-level executives like Larry Ellison, they were still the kind of people that HR definitely wouldn't want to lose, especially in the tight late-pandemic labor market. That in turn gave cover for everybody else—the people who didn't move out of the city but who still liked flexibility—to make the kind of hybrid-work demands that would have been unthinkable pre-pandemic.

Conversely, the largest percentage wage gains, and the tightest labor markets, were seen in jobs that required turning up to work. Back-of-house restaurant staff, cashiers, meatpackers, warehouse workers—all of them found themselves, for the first time, having real bargaining power over employers who were no longer capable of posting minimum-wage jobs and being able to fill them.

Most important of all were the essential workers we all lauded at the outset of the pandemic—so named because their jobs were so important, they were not subject to the lockdown rules that governed the rest of us. The work, especially at hospitals, was grueling and unsustainable, leading to significant job attrition. To make matters worse, at least in the US, the hospitals, even when their Covid wards were overflowing, were seeing a massive drop in revenues thanks to substantially all elective surgeries being canceled. Even with lots of money, staff retention would have been very difficult; without it, it was almost impossible. That was bad for hospitals and for healthcare, as workers in the industry started quitting for easier, better-paying jobs elsewhere, many of which could be done from home.

All corporations are ponderous by nature, and sometimes they need a major shock to force them to make big changes. Emergent entities, like ant colonies or slime molds or cities or even human brains, are much slower moving than the ants or neurons or other building blocks from which they emerge. The corporation is in many ways the defining emergent entity of the modern era, and can be thought of as a time-lapse sequence from Godfrey Reggio's *Koyaanisqatsi*—think of all the humans flowing into a skyscraper in the morning and ebbing out in the evening; the invisible electromagnetic tentacles connecting that skyscraper to other operations in other countries around the world; the equally invisible financial capital flowing in and out on a daily basis; the punctuated equilibria of corporate names and logos.

Think also of the stunning memorials to themselves the corporations leave behind. I can't imagine New York without the magnificent Woolworth or Chrysler Buildings, for instance, even though Woolworth barely lives on, ignominiously trading as Foot Locker, while Chrysler has become a Netherlands-headquartered frankencorporation known as Stellantis. Neither has any presence in either of those glorious pre-war skyscrapers.

When you see the corporation that way, it becomes easier to understand how hard it is for humans to change them. We're the inputs, not the outputs. Managers rise up the ranks precisely because they operate well within that organization and thrive within its particular idiosyncrasies; they're therefore unlikely to make radical changes if and when they enter the C-suite. Productivity improvements don't happen just because they're a good idea; they also need to be culturally acceptable. That's why you don't see professional basketball players shooting free throws underhand, even though doing so undeniably gets more baskets and more points.

The financial case for giving employees the option to work from home was well known by the time the pandemic hit. Back in 2013,

Stanford economist Nick Bloom authored an important paper show-ing a 13 percent performance increase when you forced workers to work from home, and a 22 percent increase when you gave them the option whether or not to work from home.[9] That paper studied call center employees—a profession much more amenable to working from home than many others. But it was highly suggestive, and also made intuitive sense. People working from home took fewer breaks and had fewer sick days; they also had a quieter and more comfort-able place to work. The big question was less *whether* there were productivity improvements to allow such a thing, and more *how* such a radical change could get adopted in large corporations, especially given the fact that, in Bloom's paper, people who opted to work from home were significantly less likely to receive promotions.

In the end, it took the exogenous shock of a global pandemic to shake up the rhythms of the corporation enough that when things settled back down, working from home was broadly, even if reluc-tantly by some executives, accepted for the first time. The change had a huge number of positive implications. Most importantly, it was what gamblers call a "freeroll" for employees. If they were happy with the *status quo ante* of commuting into the office every day, they were welcome to continue doing exactly that. On the other hand, if and when they saw value in staying at home—or working from some-where else entirely—that was now available to them, a free option.

From a corporate point of view, the total amount of office space needed went down, because at any given moment some significant percentage of workers would be opting to be elsewhere. That re-duced demand for square footage helped bring commercial rents down—or at least stop them from rising quite as fast as they had in previous years. It also allowed more companies to fit into any given central business district, and/or allowed big corporations to centralize more of their operations in their headquarters, without feeling forced to operate large satellite operations that always felt like corporate Siberia.

All transitions are awkward, of course, but it helped that almost all companies were dealing with the same issues at the same time—and it also helped that most of them were seeing record profits at the same time deep-seated institutional ways of doing things were being radically upended, meaning that shareholders at least were broadly happy in the short term.

In the longer term, it was possible to see labor once again getting an edge over capital, for the first time in decades. The job market remained super tight well into 2022, at a time when a new generation of employees was spending vastly less time with their colleagues and feeling much less connected to their employer. The way in which companies expected loyalty from their employees always left a bad taste in the mouth—back in 1999, *Office Space* made sure to skewer the way in which bosses would casually tell their direct reports, with almost no notice, that they were "going to need" them to come in to work over the weekend, for no extra pay. But even good managers, during the pandemic, found themselves increasingly exasperated at the degree of entitlement they were seeing in the workforce.

Zoomers and younger Millennials were entering the workforce very green, like all of us were at the beginning of our careers, and often had the added disadvantage of working remotely, making it much harder to learn on the job and pick things up without having to have them spelled out. At the same time, they seemed to have no humility, no expectation that they might have to spend some time learning the ropes before being in a position to make demands or even really add value to the company.

To put it another way: If workers are ants and corporations are ant colonies, those colonies were made up of two broad groups. The Zoomers and younger Millennials were behaving in unusual and even unprecedented ways, while the Boomers, Gen Xers, and older Millennials were realizing that their pre-pandemic work-life balance was suboptimal, and they were determined not to return to it. The colonies—the corporations—were large and established and could certainly accommodate a large number of individual mini-disruptions. One of the characteristics of corporations, after all, is their resilience to shocks. Nevertheless, once a whole generation of workers started behaving with an unprecedented degree of *lèse-majesté*, that posed a real risk to the time-tested model of heartless corporations exploiting hapless workers stuck at the pointy end of a highly lopsided power structure.

I'm not talking about unionization, which was the twentieth century's answer to such problems. The post-Covid workforce generally had nothing against unions, and was often happy to vote to join them, even in industries that had been union-free since inception. Such movements, however, were painfully slow and marginal—if you try to unionize Starbucks one store at a time, for instance, you soon reach the point where it's impossible to find stores with committed enough organizers.

Instead, workers managed to alight on an even more effective bargaining tool, which required no coordination at all. That was just being willing and able to quit for any or no reason, whether or not the employee in question had another job lined up.

The tool became especially powerful when it could be used *en masse*, with the majority of a team quitting simultaneously to protest working conditions. The staff of Deadspin, a popular sports blog, did that at the end of 2019, shortly before the pandemic hit; software engineers at the University of Oklahoma did something similar in June 2021, when they were required to go back to onsite work.

From an employer's point of view, such events are terrifying. Remote communication tools like Slack made it very easy for employees to coordinate with each other, and managers can often be unaware of the degree of resentment until it's too late and most of their workers have already resigned. Remote work makes it harder for managers to notice changes in morale, especially when there's a baseline level of mistrust that causes workers not to be open and honest about any grievances they might have.

Remote work also makes employment itself much more fungible, with much less cost and disruption involved in leaving one job and taking another. Employers find it harder to compete on being a "great place to work," at least when it comes to physical space: No matter how nice any given company's offices are, if you spend most of your working hours at home, then, for those hours at least, one employer's workplace is literally the same as any other's. And if you're only going into the office occasionally, then the exact location of that office becomes much less important, making it that much easier to accept employment on the other side of town or even in a different city entirely, without having to move.

Add it all up and Covid ended up precipitating a major vibe shift, one that in some cases, especially during the boom year of 2021, fully reversed the power dynamics between employers and workers. For decades, companies would post jobs, whittle down an overwhelming number of applicants using very crude filters, and eventually offer someone a job in the expectation of much gratitude and immediate acceptance. In the 2020s, many workers, especially software engineers, turned that process on its head, effectively asking companies to bid for their services. Sometimes they would accept two or even three jobs simultaneously, at full-time salaries, and their employers were fine with that so long as they got their work done. Firings became extremely rare, while quits—workers firing their employers—soared.

It didn't matter that such attitudes weren't universal. They were common enough that HR departments across the country were forced to spend a lot more time on retention and keeping employees happy, rather than being picky about whom to hire.

They were fighting a tough battle: The rat race is a suboptimal way to spend one's prime years. Among workers, a realization dawned: If work is draining you and making you unhappy, then stop doing it. Not everybody had the wealth and privilege to be able to do that, but millions of people did, and enough of them took advantage of that fact to help change, for the better, the way companies interacted with their employees generally.

The vibe shift wasn't calculated, so much as it simply manifested itself in ways large and small. I remember well the summer of 2006, for instance. I'd lost a regular gig writing about Latin American debt markets, and therefore felt the need to say yes when a fan of my blog offered me a job commuting to a suburb of St. Louis to give strategic advice to a life reinsurance company—a company that taught me quite a lot about the way American companies interact with highly valuable employees.

Life reinsurers employ a very large number of actuaries—people whose job it is to anticipate how long someone is likely to live. Actuaries have a largely deserved reputation for being boring, but their main qualification is just being good at mathematics. So this particular employer hired a large number of math nerds and paid them a very healthy salary to move to a pretty cheap part of America and work on interesting statistical problems. Mathematicians tend to be extremely good at judging how good other mathematicians are at mathematics, and so the offices soon filled up with the best mathematicians the company could find—which meant they soon filled up with a very diverse workforce, from dozens of different countries. After all, as any mathematician will tell you, innate mathematical talent is evenly distributed around the world.

The corporate offices were not all that dissimilar from what you might see in *Office Space*. They were in an office park that was within walking distance of absolutely nothing, however, so one thing they did have was lunchrooms—areas with microwaves and tables to sit at that often filled up with amazingly delicious smells from the range of cuisines being reheated.

The soccer World Cup was being held in Germany that summer, which meant that the big evening games would take place at lunchtime in Missouri. The insurance company's very international workforce naturally took great interest in the most important sporting event in the world, which also served as a universal bonding mechanism. Whether you were Spanish or Russian or Brazilian or Ghanaian, you knew the sport, you knew the teams and the players, and you were invested in what was happening. The normally whisper-quiet lunchrooms started to show real signs of life, as groups of soccer-mad employees would gather around the television to watch that day's match.

The largely American administrative staff reacted in a way that genuinely shocked me. What I expected was that they would put up large competition brackets on the lunchroom walls, maybe add some flags and other decorations, and lean into an event that was fortuitously bringing their employees together and creating lasting bonds of attachment. Instead, they *unplugged all the televisions* and announced that no one was allowed to watch any more TV for the duration of the World Cup.

What the company did was culturally insensitive and fostered a high degree of alienation within its own workforce. Tactically, it probably achieved its aims of improving worker productivity during the hours that the soccer matches were being played. And because the World Cup only happens once every four years, no one was going to quit over such a thing. At worst they would just leave the building entirely at lunchtime and watch the matches at the local bar, along with external consultants like me who had no reason to fear negative repercussions in some future performance review.

Today, almost no one would try to impose that kind of ham-handed attempt to foil employees' revealed preferences. Partially because companies are much more solicitous when it comes to trying to provide workers with what they need to be satisfied in their jobs, especially when such provision comes at zero marginal cost. And partially because it simply wouldn't work anymore: The actuaries would just declare they were working from home on match days.

The ability to work from home has severely and permanently diminished the control that corporations have over their employees' workdays (and even their non-workdays, for that matter), and the employees are the clear beneficiaries of that change. This shift is not just about demand dynamics in the labor market; it's also spatial, to a significant extent. If you put on work clothes and spend half an hour traveling to your employer's workplace, which operates entirely according to rules set by them and into which you had no input, then they are clearly in charge of everything from day one. On the other hand, if you're sitting on your sofa in sweatpants, deciding whether or not to turn your camera on during Zoom calls, and naturally being the person with full jurisdiction over your home domain, then you're inevitably going to feel more in control and less of an order-follower.

Relations between employers and employees have always been profoundly territorial, and workers have historically fought their battles literally on their employers' turf. Now that they control the physical domain of where they work to an unprecedented degree, they can taste a degree of power they haven't had in decades. Your employer might have very good reasons for wanting you back in the office. But those reasons are also self-serving, and workers—armed with newfound influence—are rejecting them.

6

The Post-Global World

THERE'S SOMETHING VERY American about the intersection of individual autonomy and physical space. Our homes are larger, our vehicles are larger, our states are emptier. Even excluding Alaska, the contiguous US has a population of about 330 million people in an area of 3.12 million square miles—about 105 people per square mile, or 260,000 square feet per person. The European Union, by contrast, contains 447 million people in 1.63 million square miles. That's 274 people per square mile, or 100,000 square feet per person.

What that means, in practice, is that we *can* expand, in ways that Europeans simply can't. If New York is too crowded, we can move to Boise, a city where job postings doubled during the pandemic and house prices rose by 50 percent. European cities responded to the pandemic by revamping shared infrastructure—banning cars from the center of Paris, for instance, given how much space they take up, and replacing them with bustling bike lanes and wider pedestrian boulevards. "Streets for people," as the slogan has it, rather than "streets for traffic." London tripled its number of bike lanes and created dozens of low-traffic neighborhoods where streets are shared by all residents rather than being reserved for cars.

Cars cause crowding, after all, both on roadways and on sidewalks. When a city has a limited amount of space per person, it makes sense to open up that space as much as possible: A lot more pedestrians than drivers fit into any given area of pavement. Parked cars are the worst: They occupy an enormous amount of otherwise usable space.

In the US, however, Covid generally pushed people in the opposite direction: *into* cars, rather than out of them. New York City replaced some on-street parking with outdoor dining, but that was about the extent of the reorganization of public space in America as a result of the pandemic.

If you make filter coffee, there's a good chance there's one action you take without even really thinking about it. You'll pour the coffee grinds into the filter, and then you'll give the filter a quick little shake, or maybe a couple of taps, to even them out and make sure they're not in a pile.

In the US, Covid's effect on personal space felt a bit like a great hand reaching down into the country and giving it a bit of a tap. Pre-pandemic, urbanists like the University of Toronto's Richard Florida liked to talk about how the world was spiky: People and money and power and creativity tended to congregate in dense cities that exhibited winner-takes-all effects. Post-pandemic, the world was very much still spiky, but noticeably less so. The locus of workspaces moved out of central business districts and into individual homes; particles—individuals, households—moved from a high-pressure area to lower-pressure areas.

Midtown Manhattan and other places that used to have the highest density felt empty, while second- and third-tier cities like Austin or Boulder became ultra-popular and more crowded than ever. The overall effect was to export the pressures normally seen only on the coasts to many other places. If you were a telecommunications company covering scenic parts of Maine or Idaho, the volume of complaints you received about inadequate broadband coverage went through the roof. Broadly speaking, what we saw was both space per person and wealth per acre becoming more evenly distributed than they were before.

That's probably good news for the US as a whole. It means that talent no longer needs to move to one of a handful of cities in order to be able to make a big difference. More to the point, it means that talent doesn't need to *afford* to be able to live in Silicon Valley or New York City anymore. It means that businesses are more flexible when it comes to accommodating and getting the best work from a wide range of talented potential employees. It means that locally based service-industry professionals can make a good living in a much wider range of towns and cities. And it means that Americans as a whole—a nation where people love being able to spread out into large amounts of personal space, especially after they've started a family—now have more opportunity than ever to do just that.

There are downsides, too. Environmentally, all that personal space comes at a significant cost in terms of carbon footprint. Spreading out means more vehicle miles traveled, as well as more embedded carbon in larger buildings. It's also possible that some of the benefits and serendipity of density might end up being lost—although, by the same token, those benefits could end up just being found in a larger number of cities.

There will definitely be an adjustment period as American capitalism recalibrates itself for the new spatial realities. During the 1998 Long-Term Capital Management crisis or the 2008 financial crisis, the president of the New York Fed could summon all the major bank chiefs to his office on Liberty Street to try to hash out a collective solution to whatever problem was facing the markets, and the biggest obstacle to getting everybody in the same room was the fact that some of them felt the need to sit in traffic instead of just taking the

4 train. There are undeniably advantages to having industries based in certain cities, just as there are advantages to being able to have impromptu in-person meetings or being able to learn how to do your job better by observing the people around you.

Still, the great shake-out has made many US regional economies much more productive than they were pre-pandemic, and that in turn makes the entire country more competitive on an international stage that was badly fractured by Covid.

The pandemic did major damage to international supply chains, throwing up barriers that had been coming down for decades. *National* supply chains, on the other hand, especially within the US, were much less badly hurt. So a continent-sized country like the US ended up with a significantly bigger advantage over its smaller competitors than it had pre-pandemic.

For globalists, after all, the pandemic was a true tragedy, one that set the internationalist dream back by decades. Before Covid struck, China and Russia were deeply embedded in a single global economy, to a degree never before seen in the history of the world. Then China implemented a zero-Covid policy that effectively stopped anybody entering or leaving the country, while Russia cut itself off from the West by invading Ukraine. By early 2022, the dream of a single global market had been entirely replaced by a new reality of onshoring and nationalisms.

Covid created or strengthened many barriers, but none more so than international borders. Banning flights from abroad was almost universally the first thing that governments did in an attempt to fight the pandemic, and restrictions often stayed in place long after they'd outlived any particular usefulness. In the summer of 2021, for instance, all vaccinated and even some unvaccinated Americans were welcomed into European countries, most of which had lower Covid rates than the US. The Biden administration promised the Europeans that it would reciprocate, but then dragged its feet: Europeans remained barred from visiting the US until November, long after peak travel season was over.

The decision to treat international travel by vaccinated Europeans as a particularly dangerous vector of disease never made any epidemiological sense. Covid doesn't care what passport you're traveling on, and even the early travel bans, in March 2020, did little to slow the spread of the disease. Instead, they underscored the severity of the pandemic, and precipitated an unprecedented global shrinkage of what might be thought of as citizens' personal radius—the parts of the world that one might come in contact with, either by going there yourself or by them coming to you.

During lockdown, that radius often shrank to literally the walls of a single apartment. But even after lockdown, it remained much more nationally bound than it had ever been before. The exquisitely fragile web of international supply chains was broken in ways that proved very difficult to fix, not least because demand for goods (as opposed to services) spiked just as the global shipping industry had managed to consolidate into a handful of hyperefficient consortiums who had finally realized that competing with each other by constantly raising capacity was a recipe for zero profits in perpetuity. Instead, by keeping capacity growth below trade growth, they could ensure premium pricing for all players.

When the pandemic hit, the shipping industry ground to a halt, putting an immediate end to the dynamic equilibrium in which the global logistics wheel was spinning. Starting that up again from a standing halt was almost impossible—nothing was in the right place—and then, to make matters even tougher, the world's trade patterns had changed radically in the face of insatiable demand from the US in particular, even as many of the world's factories were liable to be shut down by Covid on zero notice. Supply shortages rippled through entire industries like lumber or baby formula, and the clunky machinery behind the magical way in which goods could just appear at your door whenever you wanted them was revealed. Logistics companies like to be invisible: They know that the minute people start talking about them, that's a sign they've failed to do their job.

Most notably, vehicle manufacturers responded to the lockdown by idling their factories and canceling contracts across their supply chains. If the world wasn't moving, who would need cars and trucks? Turns out, just about everyone would. But by the time the auto manufacturers were faced with massive new demand for their product, their suppliers had moved on to other customers—and the hundreds of semiconductors needed to power just one modern car or truck were nowhere to be found. Those new cars that were made sold out almost immediately; customers who couldn't buy new cars found themselves paying new-car prices or even higher for used vehicles, in a classic case of supply-chain problems feeding through directly into consumer price inflation.

It didn't help that a lot of the electronics needed for cars—which are basically computers on wheels, these days—are manufactured in China and Taiwan, where Covid-related shutdowns could and did bring entire industries to a halt.

Covid didn't just create barriers to human international movement, it also spawned the terrible word "friendshoring"—the idea that companies should reconfigure their supply chains so as to locate as many of them as possible in countries that are geopolitically aligned with their home nations. Covid spawned fear and mistrust, not only of the people you come into direct physical proximity with, but of people arriving from out of state, of foreigners arriving from some other country, and so on. The pandemic lasted long enough that such attitudes had time to settle in and harden, to the point they couldn't easily bounce back even once their origin was no longer much of a cause for concern.

My wife calls it "hibernation": The way in which everybody retreated into a much smaller radius—and many of us quite liked it. People not wanting to go back to the office, people not wanting to travel for business, people not wanting to go back to interacting in crowded spaces, people not wanting to get back on the subway. For many of us, the pandemic lifestyle had real advantages over the *status quo ante*, and we were loath to give them up.

Something similar happened at the international level. Consider the tariffs that Donald Trump imposed on Chinese imports via executive order: While they were opposed by Democrats, they remained in place for years after Trump left office, as deglobalization became the bipartisan default stance. Even the promise of lower prices in the face of uncomfortably high inflation wasn't enough to break the US out of its new comfort zone of trying to be as self-sufficient as possible, or at least reliant only on its allies.

Not everybody was a happy hibernator. Bosses wanted employees back in the office; corporate executives wanted to get on planes back to China; party people wanted to go back to crowded, airless venues. Nevertheless, even those who wanted to revert to something approaching the pre-pandemic normal were acutely aware that they were making a *choice*. In an echo of the "zero-based budgeting" practiced by the Brazilian private equity firm 3G Capital Partners, middle classes around the world rebuilt the parts of their lives they had lost during the pandemic—but only if they had a real desire to go back to how things had been before. And many of them didn't.

As early as 2002, Nobel economics laureate Joseph Stiglitz found himself with an unlikely bestseller on his hands when he wrote *Globalization and Its Discontents*.[1] The book touched a nerve—a large part of the population felt left behind, or otherwise ill-served, by a trend that was perceived to mainly benefit the Davos elite. That anger was deepened by the 2008 financial crisis, with its deep recession accompanied by monster bailouts of international banks. Eventually, nativist politicians like Boris Johnson and Donald Trump gained power by tapping into that resentment. It wasn't until the pandemic hit, however, that the elites themselves—the CEOs and neoliberal politicians who had driven the globalization train for decades—finally embraced the idea of pivoting to a post-global outlook. Local supplanted global; resilience replaced efficiency.

Such changes were far from universal, but they were noticeable in the way in which different countries' economic statistics were much less correlated than they had been pre-pandemic. Nations moved in very different directions during the course of the pandemic, growing apart and attenuating shared experiences.

Across much of the western Pacific Rim, for example—China, Hong Kong, Vietnam, New Zealand, Australia, and the like—zero-Covid policies kept citizens not only in their countries but even in their homes for months or years, increasing the importance of domestic bonds (in both the household and the national sense) even as international connections slowly withered. Pre-pandemic, it might have made sense to compare Dallas to Melbourne as cities that were similarly situated in a context of global nomads and search for talent. Then one of them largely ignored the pandemic, while the other implemented extremely tough lockdowns that lasted for months. By the time they both emerged, the two cities had less in common than they ever had, and moving from one to the other—never easy at the best of times—had become vastly more difficult, both physically and psychologically.

Similarly, we've surely seen the peak of the standard European rite of passage where an eighteen-year-old goes on some cheap trip around the world for a few months, dropping in on places like Bolivia or Cambodia, having a good time, and learning not only about foreign cultures but also more broadly how to be self-sufficient for the first time after leaving the parental home. Western teens' money doesn't go as far as it used to and isn't particularly welcomed anymore; national borders are hardening, and so long as you have your phone, you're still deeply embedded in the same culture you grew up in anyway. Travel becomes something exotic to show off on TikTok, rather than a way of leaving that network behind for a while.

Much of this is for the good, especially at the corporate level. Resilient local supply chains are going to prove their worth many times over in an age of global warming and increased geopolitical unrest. A focus on local communities over ill-defined global stake-holders will ground institutions of all stripes and head off a mindset that if you're not the best in the world at something, you might as well not bother. The move away from Kyle Chayka's homog-enized "Airspace"—an interchangeable world of raw-wood tables and third-wave coffee—and toward some measure of idiosyncrasy can only be welcomed.[2]

It would be silly, however, to gloss over the serious downsides. In some cities or states deglobalization will turn out to be a profoundly negative phenomenon. Hong Kong is the ultimate cautionary tale— a place where the government, under cover of Covid, effectively obliterated all deeply treasured freedoms.

Or consider the country I grew up in, the UK. On January 31, 2020, it left the European Union; I remember walking through Piccadilly Circus in London (I was in town to shoot a TV segment on happiness, weirdly enough) in something of a daze, feeling like I was standing on an island that had just dislodged itself from solid ground and was about to drift off into some kind of irrelevant oblivion. That decision to self-inflict semi-exile from other coun-tries became a familiar feeling around the world just a few weeks later, although in the case of Covid shutdowns it made a lot more sense and felt a lot more temporary. The problem is that once ties are broken, they can take a long time to regrow—and trade ties, in particular, can be severed easily and reinstated only with enormous difficulty.

We know from the history of "import substitution" in Brazil and other Latin American countries—the 1950s version of onshoring—that attempts to do everything domestically can be disastrous and set economies back decades. On a global scale, free trade has helped to grow global GDP and reduce inequality between countries; if it's rolled back, that's going to have unavoidable negative financial consequences.

That said, there's something attractive about the idea of today's quasi-stateless international corporations being driven by commercial necessity to pick a country and stick with it, through good times and bad. The jurisdiction-shopping days when Halliburton would decide that it was moving to Dubai, or Burger King to Canada, are probably over, and are unlikely to be mourned by many.

On the personal level, for international cosmopolitan types, there's going to be a lot to get used to. I can attest at first hand that it feels *terrible* when your world shrinks, because it happened to me suddenly and unexpectedly. I did a very stupid thing in 2016 and naturalized as an American without first consulting an immigration lawyer. Four years later, after the UK finally left the EU, I decided that I really needed to renew my German passport so that I had at least one European citizenship. But when I got to the German consulate, they informed me that I'd forfeited my German citizenship when I became an American. Suddenly, my European identity—I'd been proudly doubly European all my life—was vaporized, along with any dreams of being able to easily live and work in Europe.

I'm acutely aware that simply *assuming* that I could maintain three different citizenships was the height of privilege and hubris—and that even now, with two, I'm still well ahead of the game. All the same, I don't think I'll ever forget the feeling of sitting back down in that room in the German consulate, utterly desolate, as though I was walled in now, in a way I never had been before.

The walls around us are always porous to a greater or lesser extent. It's not *impossible* that I could still end up living and working in Germany, or elsewhere in Europe. International trade and migration will continue. But the frictions are bigger now, for better and for worse. We're more rooted in place than we used to be—which is to say that we're more *invested* in place than we used to be.

I've lived in the US for more than half my life, and I'm an American citizen now. Ask anybody who's been through that process—of non-immigrant visas, and then applying for a green card, and then finally naturalization: It's not easy at the best of times, but the fact is that I really did go through it at the best of times. I arrived in the US in 1997, with Bill Clinton newly reelected as president and Tony Blair just about to get elected in the UK. My visas—first a couple of H-1Bs, then a couple of Is—were much easier to obtain than they would be today. The green card, although it felt that it took forever, in fact was positively swift by contemporary standards. And the naturalization was so easy that I *wish* it had been harder and that I'd been forced to consult a lawyer. Today, post-Trump, post-Covid, post-Brexit, there's a good chance not only that I wouldn't have been able to run that gauntlet, but that my series of employers wouldn't have even bothered to try to get me a visa in the first place.

Through most of history, individuals haven't felt particularly *stuck* if they end up living in a single country all their lives. That's just the base-case scenario, and it's one to which the world—along with its corporations—is returning. Only the Green Party really believes that it has an ideology that should be adopted by everybody on the globe; other ideologies have become much more parochial, which in general is good. (The last thing the world needs is another US president starting a war in an attempt to export democracy to the Middle East, or anywhere else for that matter.)

Globalism lies in ashes, killed by much more than just Covid, although Covid was definitely part of the fatal cocktail. The phoenixes that rise from those ashes will be many, not just one. A thousand magical creatures will attempt to take flight, and many—possibly most—will fail, or will at least look small and weak in comparison to the world-encompassing wingspan of their predecessor.

I suspect, however, that more will prove better. Globalism was a one-size solution that ended up fitting almost nobody very well. The post-global world will have more resilience, more variety, and—if it goes well—more responsiveness to local needs. Global warming is the one area where the planet needs to get on the same page, fast. But most problems are local problems—and local problems often lend themselves to local solutions, even if those solutions don't scale globally. Which is a big point in favor of smaller regional phoenixes.

Part II

Mind and Body

7

Arm's-Length Relationships

I GREW UP in London, specifically in South London, the vast expanse of suburbia south of the River Thames that North Londoners always used to pride themselves on never visiting. They had the City of London and the City of Westminster and all the sights of the bustling metropolis; we had . . . Battersea Power Station? Dulwich Picture Gallery? Crystal Palace Football Club? Not exactly Buckingham Palace or the National Gallery or Tottenham Hotspur.

One of the main things we lacked was the Tube. Sure, it does venture south of the river, but only barely: There are 250 stations in North London, leaving a mere 29 for the rest of us. To get from my house in Dulwich to the nearest Tube station involved a long walk to the Number 3 bus, an interminable wait, and then a not-short trip to Brixton. It was possible, but in practice it was always easier to just walk to the local train station, where you could take a train straight into Victoria station. For rush-hour commuters like my father, there was even a direct train into Cannon Street station in the heart of the City.

Those trains, at least while I was growing up, would often take the form of "slam-door" carriages where each car was split into a series of narrow compartments, each with its own heavy door opening directly out onto the platform. The doors only opened from the out-side, which meant that as the train pulled into the station, passengers would reach out the door's window, open the door, and hop onto the platform while the train was still moving. This was exactly as safe as it sounds, which is one of the reasons why those carriages don't exist anymore.

Why were people in such a rush to leave the compartments? The answer to that is the same as the answer to the question why every-body on an airplane stands up within a microsecond of the "fasten seat belt" light turning off when the plane has landed. When we're in an enclosed space with a bunch of other people, we naturally want to do anything we can that might put some distance between us and them.

It's a syndrome that's even more obvious in the other direction—when we have no choice but to place ourselves in spaces that will get increasingly crowded. I'd get on the Victoria-bound train at Syden-ham Hill by opening one of those heavy slam doors and entering a narrow compartment. I recall it as being two benches facing each other, each seating three people.

If I was lucky enough to enter an empty compartment I would selfishly grab the plum spot—the far corner, next to the window. That provided access to light, and a view, and, of course, maximum ventilation. It also maximized the distance between me and the next person to enter the compartment. That person would, naturally, stay by the door, following the standard protocol familiar to anybody who has ever taken an elevator.

The third entrant was the first real interloper. My compartment-mate and I, despite barely even glancing at each other, had an un-derstanding: We'd give each other space. But now, with the arrival of passenger number three, one or both of us was going to lose that space. The newcomer would have to either sit next to one of us—ugh—or, possibly worse, *opposite* one of us, causing an uncomfortable ballet of whose-legs-go-where. Logically, all three of us were equally discomfited by the inescapable geometry. Emotionally, the space belonged to the two passengers who were in it before the third arrived, and it was the third passenger who was therefore resented by the other two.

The resentment would linger in the carriage all the way to the London terminus—unless, that is, a fourth person got in at a later stop. At that point, the third passenger immediately ceased to be a newcomer, and was instantly transformed into an aggrieved native; all three of us would be duly and equally shocked at the presumption of this fourth person to impose upon our precious space. Sometimes the process would play itself out twice more, so that even the fifth occupant would feel the stirrings of native blood when faced with the arrival of passenger number six.

All of this is perfectly understandable and natural to you, even if you've never been within a thousand miles of South London: What I'm describing is a basic human trait, and it can be parsimoniously understood as an atavistic reaction to the threat of infectious diseases. The first passenger seeks out maximum ventilation; subsequent passengers maximize the radius between themselves and anybody else, being particularly uncomfortable when that proximity is face-to-face. The community that's living uncomfortably in a confined space does not want the extra risk involved with welcoming someone new—but once that person has been a member of the tribe for even a short while, any possible disease they might have brought with them will be a member of the tribe, too, and it's too late to do anything about that. The danger then becomes new individuals wanting to join.

This dynamic is so deeply ingrained in our nature that it is even found in primates. In 1976, zoologist Bill Freeland studied the literature on monkeys and found that groups tended to keep strictly to themselves, with few if any friendly interactions between troops.[1] Even unfriendly interactions tend to be characterized by a lack of physical interaction, with the smaller group generally just giving way to the larger.

Monkeys even turn out to be pretty sophisticated practitioners of Bayesian probability theory. Let's say you're a troop of monkeys, and a strange new individual makes it clear they want to join. You might be tempted to welcome them, since fresh blood in the troop helps to reduce problems associated with inbreeding, including the fact that inbred monkeys tend to have a lower ability to combat disease.

On the other hand, the very fact that this individual is alone and desirous of joining the troop is in itself suspicious. Might disease help explain why they are alone in the first place? Even if the probability of disease in any given randomly chosen monkey is low, the probability of disease in a monkey given that it's alone and trying to join a troop could be significantly higher.

More to the point, if all troops carry different background pathogens, then *any* monkey from outside the troop is highly likely to carry a different background pathogen than the members of the troop. And if that monkey had previously tried and failed to join various different troops, they might be carrying a whole range of pathogens—creating a significant risk that the entire troop might get wiped out by the admission of a single member.

The evolutionary result is that the monkeys put any potential newcomer through a series of strenuous tests before they can be admitted to the troop. The tests take a lot of time—weeks or even months. That in itself increases the probability that any disease will become apparent before the final admission decision is taken. What's more, because the tests are stressful (as is social ostracism itself), they are likely to reveal any latent infections.

Most monkeys fail the tests—and many of the failures turn out, in fact, to be diseased. This is evolution at work: better to reject a few potential incomers who might help to marginally diversify the gene pool than to accept one who could get the whole troop fatally sick.

Naturally, once a monkey has passed the tests and become a member of the troop, it, too, adopts the ultra-cautious protocol about admitting anybody else, just as men who have gone through hazing rituals at fraternities or in the military will inflict such rituals on those who come after them.

Monkey troops are, truth be told, not so different from nation-states. When countries restrict immigration, they mostly don't say that they're doing so for reasons of public health. But the stated reasons often don't stand up to logical scrutiny—in no way, for instance, is the United States already "full." Behind the rhetoric often lies xenophobia, and behind the xenophobia lies a hardwired and largely irrational fear of disease.

It's instructive to look at what happened at the beginning of the pandemic: International borders got shut down around the world, often in a chaotic manner that only served to exacerbate the total number of infections. Americans hurriedly returning from Europe in March 2020, for instance, found themselves penned into tight unmasked crowds for hours as they awaited coronavirus screening. Around the world, when border restrictions were imposed at roughly the same time as lockdowns, the restrictions remained long after the lockdowns were lifted.

One obvious example: The US barred Europeans, even if they were fully vaccinated, from entering the country well into the autumn of 2021, even as the incidence of Covid in America was far higher than in most European countries. The travel ban therefore not only outlasted the initial lockdowns, it also outlasted the Trump administration, and lived on for most of the first year of the Biden administration. It was clearly a policy with bipartisan support, even as the incoming executive branch worked hard to find other ways to repair relations with the rest of the world.

What kind of political intuition would have led Biden's White House to keep Europeans out of the US? The answer: The same intuition that causes me to resent a stranger entering my train compartment, even as I would love to be surprised by a friend unexpectedly stepping in and sitting down across from me. The same intuition that makes me uncomfortable sitting next to a table of loud unmasked diners during a pandemic, even as I'm fine sitting in much closer proximity to my own dining companions. The same intuition that saw Covid "bubbles"—the small groups of people who would hang out with each other and no one else—form almost entirely among people who were already good friends or close family.

The intuition reaches everyone: It's also found among immigrants, for instance, who often become centers of anti-immigration sentiment as soon as they have achieved a toehold in their adopted country. Whether you're in an elevator, a train carriage, a rapidly filling office, or a NIMBY—"Not in my backyard"—suburb, you've probably felt it yourself more often than you might care to admit. It has even taken its place in the standard economics literature, under a variety of different names including "status quo bias."

You're right to feel sheepish about suffering from such bias. It's irrational, for one thing, as economists have demonstrated time and time again. If you're presented with a list of health plans, for instance, wouldn't you always choose the one that's best for you? Not if you already belong to one—in that case, you're extremely likely to stick with the one you're on right now, even if it's not the one you would have chosen were you starting from scratch.[2]

More pertinently, society fails when it's based on exclusion. The way that people get excluded normally involves shameful elements of class and race discrimination. We're better than that—or, at least, we should aspire to being better than that. But at the same time, the feelings are real, and they're based not only in bigotry but also in deep-seated intuitions about public health that stretch back millennia. Indeed, the bigotry itself might well be a by-product of those intuitions—intuitions that predate even the advent of Homo sapiens and have been reinforced over centuries of bloody and painful encounters with plagues and pathogens.

In a 2008 paper long predating Covid, a group of researchers— Corey Fincher and Randy Thornhill from the University of New Mexico, and Damian Murray and Mark Schaller of the University of British Columbia—attempted to answer one of the big unknown questions in scientific literature. As they explained it, they wanted to know "why some cultures are more individualistic while others are more collectivistic."[3]

That spectrum, described as "the most important dimension for capturing cultural variation," has a lot of explanatory power, but is itself not easy to explain. Why do some cultures see in-groups and out-groups in much sharper relief than others? Why do those cultures tend to place a much greater emphasis on conformity, with much less tolerance for—or even encouragement of—rebelliousness and individuality?

The paper hypothesized that such differences between cultures can in large part be explained as differences in what they call "behavioural antipathogen defences." They write:

> To the extent that particular forms of social behaviour
> (and the specific psychological mechanisms underlying
> those behaviours) serve an antipathogen defence function,

then those behaviours (and the underlying mechanisms) are more likely to characterize the cultural populations within which there has historically been greater prevalence of disease-causing pathogens.

In English: You're going to find collectivism where there has been a lot of recent experience with infectious disease, and individualism where there hasn't. Whatever kind of innovation and progress that individualism and immigration makes possible is all well and good, but the benefits of xenophobic collectivism, in terms of keeping out disease and being able to care for the sick, can easily outweigh such theoretical returns to openness.

The researchers found historical data for the prevalence of diseases like malaria, leprosy, dengue, typhus, and tuberculosis in ninety-three different countries; they also used present-day data on the prevalence of those same diseases. What they found was a very strong correlation: The greater the degree of historical disease, the more collectivist the culture. The correlation also held, in slightly weaker form, for contemporary measures of disease. "These results help to explain the origin of a paradigmatic cross-cultural difference," they conclude, "and reveal previously undocumented consequences of pathogenic diseases on the variable nature of human societies."

Intuitively, this makes a lot of sense. Any society's culture is slow to change, so experiencing any single pandemic—or lack thereof—is not going to show up immediately in societal attitudes. Over the course of decades and centuries, however, such things become part of the collective unconscious memory. "Ring a ring o rosies, a pocket full of posies, atishoo, atishoo, we all fall down," I used to sing as a small child—as far as I knew a pleasing and melodic nursery rhyme. The meaning, however, is grimmer than any fairy tale. A ring of rosies is the rash accompanying the painful buboes that characterized the bubonic plague. A pocket full of posies refers to the scented bundles that people would go out with to try to overcome the stench of dying humans. Atishoo is a simple sneeze—a normally benign act that became fraught with dread in fourteenth-century England. And while no child would ever be encouraged to sing "we all die," somehow "we all fall down" manages to be acceptable, while meaning the same thing.

Seven hundred years later, the multigenerational trauma of the plague has finally become attenuated enough that the UK lies at the individualistic end of the international spectrum. But having a single collective identity was important enough, over many of the intervening centuries, that it precipitated a long series of bloody domestic and international conflicts.

Whether those wars would all have happened absent the long series of pandemics that befell northern Europe and the British Isles is unknowable. And it would be fatuous in the extreme to blame Europe's two twentieth-century world wars on a series of infectious diseases that happened hundreds of years previously. But taking an extremely big-picture view, pandemics clearly have the ability to shift social attitudes over multigenerational time horizons.

Those shifts are cumulative. If the Covid pandemic turns out to be a one-off thing, the long-term consequences will be smaller than if it turns out to be the first in a series of twenty-first-century diseases that all have significant public-health and macroeconomic repercussions. Even on its own, however, its ability to push countries further toward collectivism is clear.

China is the obvious example. The pandemic allowed president Xi Jinping to accelerate his program of collectivizing his country and pulling it back from any capitalist and individualist tendencies that might have been encouraged by his immediate predecessors. Similar effects were visible in countries like Vietnam and Cambodia or even in New Zealand, where the left-wing prime minister Jacinda Ardern, not yet forty years old when the pandemic hit, showed an iron will when it came to enacting ultra-strict public-health protocols, effectively telling the entire population that it wasn't allowed to leave the country for what turned out to be a period of well over two years. That was a major shift, given Kiwis' long-standing predilection for international travel—but it was broadly accepted by New Zealanders, in the name of protecting the country from disease and preventing its hospitals from becoming overloaded.

The irony here is that the move toward collectivism is being seen in precisely the countries that *didn't* experience significant excess mortality during the Covid pandemic. But perhaps that's a key way in which the causality works. Diseases incentivize monkeys to become collectivist by keeping out potential new members of their group, and the stricter they are on that front, the healthier they become.

Humans behave the same way. The word "quarantine" comes from the Italian *quaranta giorni*, the forty days that ships had to spend at anchor before they were allowed to dock in Dubrovnik. This was in the mid-fourteenth century, during the Black Death, when the port was under Venetian rule. It was a medieval zero-plague policy, calibrated to last long enough that anybody on board carrying the disease would become symptomatic—at which point the ship would be turned away.

A strong collectivist culture allows a level of cruelty that ultimately can save lives—Milan, for instance, about 150 miles west of Venice, had the lowest plague mortality rate in all of Italy, partly on account of the protocol that when one member of a family got sick, the rest of the family would be walled up in their homes with them and not allowed to leave. By trampling on individual rights and effectively sentencing the innocent to death, Milan ended up saving lives.

For centuries, then, humans have felt that proximity to others means danger; one of the first things we've always done when we come into money is increase the amount of space that we have to ourselves. Similarly, there's something contrarian about urbanist paeans to density, while the attraction of a suburban house with a front and back yard is something that doesn't need to be taught.

One way that the pandemic has changed the world is that we're more conscious of our desire for space and light and air; we understand on an intellectual and not merely visceral level where the desire comes from to spend thousands of dollars on, say, an upgrade to first class on an airliner. It's not just about exclusivity, relative positioning, and conspicuous consumption: It's also about buying the ability to board, fly, and disembark with the minimum degree of close proximity to other passengers and their exhalations.

Of course, such atavistic urges will regularly manifest themselves in ways that don't make us any safer. A large hotel room is not any more hygienic than a small one; an air freshener doesn't make the air any less toxic. And sometimes those urges prod us in downright dangerous directions—wearing a mask can feel clammy and claustrophobic, creating the desire to rip it off and breathe fresh air.

As a German, I'm acutely aware of how weird and inexplicable such feelings can be. Germans have a national love affair with *lüften*—airing out their homes by opening the doors and windows, or just getting out into the fresh air themselves. At the same time, however, they are convinced that drafts are deadly: When they're not airing their homes they generally keep them sealed up tight, just as they adamantly keep the windows closed, even in the absence of air-conditioning, in their cars and offices and (most notoriously) train carriages. The idea, as best I can understand it, is that a draft (in contradistinction to fresh air) is a way that the devil enters a space and infects you with some deadly illness.

It's not just a German thing, either. Millions of Americans are convinced that colds are caused by, well, the cold—that if you go out on a winter's day wearing insufficient clothing, you'll catch a cold. As if warm clothes prevent viral infections. Such irrational fears occur everywhere, and they don't mix well with the trauma caused by Covid.

Nevertheless, the trauma of having gone through the coronavirus pandemic has made us all armchair experts on contagion, what causes it and what doesn't. And whatever your particular theory, the one thing everybody understands is that we catch infectious diseases from *other people*.

The result is that we now live on a planet where almost everybody has traumatic firsthand experience of looking around at the people we all interact with every day, and worrying. We learned to avoid strangers, and even avoid friends. The act of hanging out in proximity to someone involved entering into a complex emotional contract with layers of trust, danger, and mutual apprehension overridden by social desire.

To a limited degree, modern technology played a role in filling the social voids caused by the virus. A slew of apps each had their moment: Discord took off like a rocket; Fortnite was huge with the teens; email listservs had their uses; private Instagram accounts would be used mainly for the comments section; various video-conferencing apps proved invaluable for distributed celebrations; and I for one spent an enormous amount of time in non-work Slack groups. Even the cursèd Facebook Messenger, I'm sure, took off somewhere. But the real killer app turned out to be good old-fashioned messaging, via WhatsApp or whichever text-messaging app you most used on your phone.

Almost everybody I know found themselves a member of more group texts, which were used much more frequently during the pandemic than we had ever experienced before. Group texts are self-fulfilling, intimate wonders: a way of keeping in touch across time zones and continents, sharing gossip, news, memes, or Wordle scores. And, of course, lots and lots of emojis, the tech innovation where emotion is right there in the name. Anything, really, to help trigger that sense of connection, of being part of a crew, of belonging, of active friendship. Because it's a group, there's less onus on any one person to participate; connections can be continually refreshed with the work distributed among those best placed to take it on.

Group texts allowed us to check in on friends when they came down with Covid or any other illness; they annoyed us, to be sure, in the way that only friendships can, but they also sustained us and gave us the human contact we needed, exactly when we needed it most. Fascinatingly, they could even sometimes be the exception to the basic human rule about mistrusting newcomers. Because additional thread members needed to be invited, usually after some kind of gut-check with the existing members, they were often welcomed. The circles of belonging widened and deepened.

Friends are generally harder to make the older you get; there's a reason why your best friends are very likely to be people you met in your teens or early twenties. But the group text changed that dynamic; during the pandemic, often your best friends were the ones you texted the most, rather than the ones you'd known the longest. Technology made friendship easier: accessible, affordable, available at your fingertips at any time.

By shunting us into the digital world, then, disease might have reinvented—or at least changed—the nature of friendship. Outside professional necessity, almost no one spent in-the-flesh time meeting new people, meaning that our digital lives *were* our real lives. The pandemic gave those digital connections the time and the opportunity they needed to strengthen and harden into something lasting, not just among gamers and early adopters and teens but among the broad population as a whole.

Real-world encounters had a millennia-long head start on their would-be usurper, of course, and weren't about to be shunted aside entirely. They will always be at the center of almost everybody's life. Yet somehow, out of the rational mistrust of others emerged a new and powerful vector of human connection—one that was easy to take for granted.

One of my favorite artworks from around the turn of the century is a suite of works entitled *Long Distance Lover* by my friend Senam Okudzeto. The piece consists of striking watercolors painted onto itemized British Telecom phone bills, each of them a record of the eye-watering amount that it cost two people to stay in touch with each other, when one was in London and the other in Accra. The piece is a reminder of the lengths that people will go to in order to have electronic connections with each other—and, today, it's a reminder of how incredibly privileged we all are to have such capabilities available to us at a marginal cost of zero.

The irony is that such technologies made it easier to keep us apart—to keep barriers up, especially between countries. Why make it easy for people to see each other in person when they can just FaceTime instead?

With the new digital connections came a loss of physical connection. To look at pre-pandemic photo albums during the pandemic months was to feel constant astonishment at the ease and regularity with which we *touched* people—an unthinking everyday occurrence that suddenly became a fraught navigation. In a reaction to the way that screens had started mediating seemingly every interaction, the years before the pandemic saw the invention of "cuddle parties"— nonsexual gatherings full of "spoon drawers" and "puppy piles" where the idea was to have lots and lots of touching for the sake of touching. Professional cuddlers would charge $80 an hour for their services and would talk about how human touch releases oxytocin and helps combat stress. Needless to say, demand for their services went to zero pretty much overnight, even if the screen-dominated stressors that had created that demand were more ubiquitous than ever.

The sexual equivalent to cuddle parties would be pre-AIDS gay bathhouses, which were similarly rendered impossible by a plague, never to return. "Anxiety buried itself into our bone marrow," wrote queer activist Leo Herrera, drawing an explicit parallel to 2020. "Covid already changed your center of gravity by six feet."[4] People who lived alone went months—more than a year, in many cases—without touching another human. We sought out distance from others, but that didn't mean we had to like it.

For the rest of us, touch became a way of showing trust: To touch someone—even to get within arm's length—was to say that I like you enough to risk getting Covid from you. When our loved ones got off airplanes, we would greet them with hugs and kisses, Covid be damned.

The massive drop in the number of people we touch on a regular basis will mean-revert over time, even if, thanks to technology, it never quite regains its pre-pandemic levels. For those of us who lived through the early 2020s, the experience of being in a crowd, of losing personal space, will always be freighted with meaning it never previously had. Some of us will seek it out, others will actively avoid it. But anybody building spaces for humans, whether they're architects or wedding planners or airlines, will have to be able to accommodate a much wider range of comfort levels than were previously normal.

In practice, what that means is that humans won't flow like they did pre-pandemic. Companies like WeWork that specialized in maximizing human density will find their work much more difficult. If you want, say, 90 percent of a given population to be comfortable in your space, it's going to have to be much bigger and more visibly ventilated than would have previously been necessary. Natural ventilation, especially, will become more prized, while contested spaces like arm rests will become more fraught.

Then there's Covid itself, which will be with us for the rest of our lives. As therapeutics improve and become more universally available, it will be less deadly—but it's still going to be something we'll want to avoid passing on to others. Self-isolation, that most extreme form of social distancing, is a practice that's not going to end. Most people will continue to practice it once they test positive, whether they legally have to or not. Navigating social spaces while infectious will similarly always be socially unacceptable, precisely because exposure to someone with Covid will remain a low-level fear of anybody out in public.

A new infectious disease is now a fact of life, after decades where infectious diseases were something we westerners barely thought about. The level of anxiety that accompanies it will vary wildly from person to person. But we'll all know people for whom it's high. Institutions who take DEI seriously—that is, "diversity, equity, and inclusion"—will need to respect such anxieties, which are statistically certain to exist in a significant percentage of their workforce. But a deadly new infectious disease, especially when it had such a seismic effect on the entire planet, will be much bigger than that.

Each of us is going to have our own attitude toward Covid and is also going to have to empathize with a vast range of other people's attitudes to the same thing. That won't be easy in the wake of a highly polarizing pandemic that caused major protests around the world, mainly from those people who downplayed its severity and were very angry about all attempts to build public policy around health concerns. My wife and I both lost friendships over Covid policy.

One big problem when it came to broad questions of civility was that while it is perfectly natural to feel sorry for someone who has a nasty disease, Covid also forced us to have opinions on vaccines and vaccine mandates, not to mention public-health measures like masks and lockdowns. That made Covid political, and in the era of Trump, everything political became loud and partisan—even in places as quiet and far-flung as Wellington, the sleepy capital of New Zealand, where an encampment protesting vaccine mandates proudly if weirdly flew Trump flags.

As Covid becomes endemic and therapeutics broadly available, the heightened emotions on both sides are sure to simmer down a little, at least so long as some scary new variant isn't raging. Still, infectious disease is back, and that's going to change the way that almost everybody alive thinks about illness.

One of the side effects of endemic disease, for instance, is taboos. The natural tendency of societies to construct norms and values that maintain public health tends to show up in other taboos, which often function as though they were infectious diseases. In some cultures, for instance, touching someone who has broken a taboo can "infect" a whole community.

Now that Covid has been top of mind for so long, don't be surprised to see attempts at tabooing other behaviors become more successful, just because we're primed to understand how such things work. Those atavistic muscles have started once again to flex, which makes it much more likely that we'll see communities start to try to build consensus on things like ostracizing people with large carbon footprints.

Take the anti-racist Black Lives Matter marches seen across the US in the summer of 2020, in the wake of the police murder of George Floyd. They're the most high-profile example of new societal norms being created on the fly, with significant success, at least in the short term.

When the first wave of Black Lives Matter marches took place in 2014, they revealed the depth of anti-racist feeling that existed in communities around the country. People of color, along with their white allies, had been witnessing systemic racism all their lives, and they were angry, and they found a unified voice that was heard across the nation. What *didn't* happen, however, was a broad change in public opinion.

The 2020 BLM protests were different. They were bigger, just for starters, and lasted longer. Protests happened not just in Black neighborhoods but in white ones, too. Most importantly, they *changed minds*, in the way the 2014 protests didn't. In 2017, US net public support for Black Lives Matter was negative—more people opposed it than supported it, by a margin of about 5 percentage points. By June 2020, support for BLM was 28 points larger than opposition to it—a massive, almost unprecedented swing of 33 points. For the first time ever, a majority of white Americans agreed that systemic racism existed.

That was partly a direct function of Covid, which was at the time killing Black Americans at twice the rate it was killing white Americans. Those kind of unignorable disparities drove home the all-pervasive deadliness of systemic racism, a force that proved tragically fatal not only in the context of police encounters but also in emergency rooms, maternity wards, and countless other institutions that are supposed to save lives rather than take them.

The uptick in racial awareness and activism was also a recognition of the effectiveness with which the whole world had just come together. It had managed to stop what it was doing, recognize a common threat to our shared humanity, and act collectively to address that threat in a set of coordinated actions the likes of which I, for one, would never have thought possible.

The world didn't react perfectly to the first pandemic in a

century—far from it—but we did react, we did bend the exponential curve of new infections, and, at least in the early summer of 2020, we were still largely united in the global fight against the pandemic. For a moment there, the virus brought humanity together—and if we could come together against Covid, there was no reason we couldn't build on that achievement and come together against racism, too.

Spoiler alert: We didn't beat Covid, and in fact Covid soon became yet another force that divided the country rather than uniting it. Much the same thing happened to BLM, whose demonstrations too frequently became associated with riots and looting, and whose demands soon started being ridiculed on the right as laughable and dangerous "critical race theory." But even if the pro-BLM polling soon fell back to pre-pandemic levels, that outcome never felt foreordained. It was *possible* that the fight for racial equality might take root across the country and manifest in a whole new set of social norms—and the proof of concept, the mechanism by which that might happen, had just taken place. It's never easy to coordinate a large group of people when there isn't a clear leader in charge telling folk what to do, but it happened twice in a matter of months—once with Covid and once with BLM—and it's bound to happen again sooner or later.

If there's one area where it needs to happen with urgency, it's climate change and carbon emissions. Already during the pandemic we saw how getting vaccinated and wearing a mask, even washing hands, became rituals of purification. Those rituals weren't universally embraced, partly because many people have a natural tendency to resist authority or anybody telling them what they have to do, and partly just because changing any kind of behavior becomes increasingly difficult the older we get.

As we age, we tend to rely less on our ability to learn things and more on what we've already learned. The pandemic ran into many strongly held priors: People who were anti-GMO foods, for example, were naturally going to have questions about mRNA vaccines. People who didn't like big government were skeptical about broad mandates. Scientists who grew up with the Hippocratic oath and years-long drug trials were skeptical about approving vaccines or therapeutics or even Covid tests for broad public-health reasons if the individual benefits weren't locked down. At the other end of the spectrum, young children were generally perfectly happy wearing masks all day—for millions of them it was just a normal part of going to school and playing with their friends, and many kept their masks on even when they became optional.

Broadly, however, almost everybody found themselves taking ritualistic steps to keep the virus at bay. Hand sanitizers became ubiquitous, and handwashing became something people *wanted* to do rather than doing dutifully. Masks were worn, distance was kept, coughs and sneezes were covered. There was a common threat, and those who didn't engage in the purity rituals, especially the voluntarily unvaxxed, were ostracized both socially and officially. No one particularly cared whether you *believed* in masks and vaccines and the like; what mattered was your actions.

As the world is forced to radically reduce its carbon emissions to save the planet from a threat much more catastrophic than Covid, similar social mores are going to be a necessary part of the way we get there. You can already see them in certain parts of society—in the future plans of vehicle manufacturers, for instance, nearly all of whom have embraced the inevitability of an all-electric future; in the pride with which architects compete with each other to design ever-greener buildings; in the high-quality low-carbon lifestyles enjoyed by the citizens of northern European cities like Amsterdam or Copenhagen or Berlin. These changes took years to happen but they did happen, which means they're possible and can be replicated in other sectors and countries.

The contribution of the pandemic is just that we've now lived through a period of severe excess mortality. We very much disliked it and we wouldn't want to go through something like that on a permanent, ongoing basis. If we all broadly adopt certain attitudes, it will be easier to achieve the necessary carbon-reduction goals. And what we learned during Covid is that behavioral attitudes *can* be learned and adopted. It's possible.

In general I'm not a huge fan of bottom-up solutions to the climate catastrophe, because they don't seem to scale very well. Even during the pandemic, it was rare to see Covid-controlling policies being driven by popular pressure, rather than from top-down scientific advice. On the other hand, the 2020 BLM movement, even if short-lived, gave me hope that societal attitudes can change quickly in a gratifyingly progressive direction. Perhaps that only happened because of the generally febrile nature of the world we were living in at the time. But if the first quarter of the twenty-first century is any guide, the world is likely to stay generally febrile for a while. Which might just provide one of the preconditions for effective progress on climate change.

8

Building Compassion

THE ECONOMIC PHOENIX started rising from the Covid ashes within a couple of months of the pandemic first shutting everything down, at a time when the mental-health ashes were only just beginning to accumulate. Covid caused an unqualified mental-health emergency, one that, for certain populations, was even deadlier than the virus itself. Almost no one on the planet was mentally unscathed by the pandemic—which is also the thing that might just cause a mental-health phoenix to rise.

The headline figures are staggering. A major meta-study in the *Lancet* found that major depressive disorders increased by 28 percent over the course of the first year of the pandemic—that's 53 million more cases, globally—while anxiety disorders rose by 26 percent, or 76 million extra cases.[1] Such increases are not unprecedented. Greece, for instance, saw something similar during the financial crisis of 2009. But they tend to be geographically localized, and often short-lived. In the case of the Covid pandemic, the mental-health depredations were global, and lasted for years.

Humans are social animals, and the lockdowns were particularly painful for the extroverted and for anybody who needs social interaction to thrive—which means pretty much all young people, just for starters. The crisis was bad enough for the American Academy of Pediatrics, the American Academy of Child and Adolescent Psychiatry, and the Children's Hospital Association to come together to declare a national state of emergency in children's mental health, citing "soaring rates of depression, anxiety, trauma, loneliness, and suicidality."[2] A lot of that came from children being taken out of shared classrooms and put into Zoom school instead.

The pandemic reminded everybody that schools are babysitting services at least as much as they are educators—and it also served to underscore the degree to which the purpose of school is to teach children how to socialize with and learn from each other. As kids get older some of that can be done through screens, but by no means all of it, and certainly not in the context of Zoom classes.

It's entirely possible that the long-term effects of artificially constrained socialization will be as big or bigger as the long-term effects of sub-par education-through-screens, insofar as it's even possible to disentangle the two. All children are different, and some are more resilient than others, but it seems uncontroversial to say that *some* of the children who found themselves stuck at home, often without even siblings, will never achieve the levels of self-assuredness and social fluency that they would have done sans lockdown. Kids who lacked a real space of their own, or easy access to screens and the internet, might easily find it particularly hard to readjust.

That said, the pandemic is in large part a shared experience across a whole generation of children and parents—they navigated it together, and they reentered life together, and even if they're three years behind in their social development, they're *all* three years behind in their social development. They felt bad when things were bad, and in general they felt better when things got better.

The effect on adults, and especially young adults, was potentially much more dire. In the twelve months ending in April 2021, the total number of fatal drug overdoses exceeded 100,000 for the first time ever.[3] The number was high but at least wasn't rising for the two years before the pandemic; as soon as the lockdowns hit, it started going up at an unprecedented rate. Those deaths were concentrated among the young.

Some professions find themselves forced to put a value on human life—philosophers, development economists, safety engineers, even lawyers, much of the time. And while there's no one universally accepted way to do that, the closest thing we have is a measure called QALY, which stands for "quality-adjusted life year." In QALY terms, the world got lucky with Covid.

Unlike the Spanish flu of 1918 or the AIDS epidemic, Covid hit the elderly the hardest—people with relatively few years left to live. If you were going to die at eighty-five but in fact as a result of Covid you died at eighty-one, then you lost four life-years; if those four years were going to be spent suffering from a nasty disease, then they wouldn't even have been particularly pleasant years. On the other hand, if you were going to die at eighty-five but in fact as a result of Covid you died of suicide or of a drug overdose at twenty-five, then you lost sixty life-years, making the scale of the tragedy fifteen times worse, for those who attempt to quantify such things. The QALY multiplier might possibly be even greater than that, given that so many of your best years were still ahead of you.

Mental illness is terrible in QALY terms even if you don't die. It substantially reduces the quality of your life-years, and it tends to last for years or even decades. The mental effects of long Covid, for instance, affect the overwhelming majority of people who get the disease.

There's no doubt that mental health declined alarmingly during the pandemic. One paper from Boston College looked at the first

nine months of a massive government survey that reached an astonishing 1.3 million American adults. It found that by November 2020,
37 percent of American adults were experiencing clinical symptoms
of anxiety, while 29 percent were showing signs of depression. Those
numbers are *four times* higher than what you'd normally expect to
find from such a survey during the pre-pandemic era.[4]

All that mental stress caused a massive increase in demand for
medical help—and the medical profession didn't have remotely
the amount of spare capacity needed to meet that demand, even
with increased efficiency due to telemedicine. Every psychologist
and psychotherapist in the country got booked out. The choice
was either to put together a rapidly growing waiting list, or else
just close up shop to new patients entirely. Some mental-health
professionals, struggling with exactly the same issues their patients
were facing, simply quit—the Great Resignation hit the medical
professions particularly hard, for obvious reasons, and therapists
were very much a part of that.

The standard of care, which wasn't particularly high to begin
with, especially for the not-rich, declined dramatically, in the face
of what one therapist described to the *New York Times* as "an overwhelming sense of malaise and fatigue."[5] Being stuck at home, with
people you never expected to be spending so much time with, amid
the stresses of a pandemic, trying to meet all your professional and
personal obligations, turned out to be simply too much for millions of people, especially when combined with the bigger-picture
societal tensions around race and politics. Something had to give;
sometimes it was a job or a marriage, other times it was sanity, or
sobriety, or even life itself. Therapists found themselves prioritizing
their suicidal patients—the right thing to do, but clearly not great
for anybody who wasn't on the brink of imminent death.

The good news, such as it was, was that the pandemic did remove much of the remaining stigma from mental illness—something that for centuries was generally criminalized or shunted away into gruesome mental institutions. In 1956, for instance, there were an astonishing 560,000 patients locked up against their will in American public mental hospitals, including JFK's sister Rosemary, who had been subjected to a disastrous lobotomy at the age of twenty-three.[6]

That changed over the subsequent decades, not entirely for the better. Partly as a result of his family situation, President Kennedy signed the Community Mental Health Act in 1963, saying as he did so that he was "proposing a new approach to mental illness."

"The cold mercy of custodial isolation," he said in a famous speech, "will be supplanted by the open warmth of community concern and capability. Emphasis on prevention, treatment and rehabilitation will be substituted for a desultory interest in confining patients in an institution to wither away."

The term of art was "deinstitutionalization"—but that's not exactly what happened. JFK's idea was for the federal government to pay for community mental-health care, but then in 1981 Ronald Reagan pushed that responsibility onto the states, which have much tighter budget constraints than the federal government. Closing down institutions became a cost-cutting measure rather than a genuine attempt to do well by patients: It was a lot cheaper to load up on tranquilizers than it was to invest in detailed nosology and personalized care.

The result was massive underinvestment in mental health, at every level of government—and the "snake pit" conditions of Bedlam and other mental institutions increasingly being reconstructed within the penal system, at prisons across the country. Even when the prisons did have adequate mental-health treatment programs, those programs were rarely continued once prisoners were released. The result was new crimes, new arrests, new convictions, and what some criminal-justice scholars began to call "life on the installment plan."[7]

When criminal-justice reform started to result in a reduction in the size of the incarcerated population, there was, once again, a massive shortfall between what was needed to care for the mental health of the former inmates and what was available. After being released first from mental hospitals and then from prisons, the mentally ill population found itself homeless, on the streets. While there was certainly sympathy for these individuals, there was also real annoyance: Visible homelessness, which is overwhelmingly a mental-health issue, is the number one problem that mayors across the country are asked to deal with—and also the number one problem that mayors across the country say they simply have no real ability to solve.

The pandemic was not a "there but for the grace of God go I" moment—very few of us, caught up in our own pandemic troubles, stopped to be grateful that we were mentally well enough to avoid outright vagrancy. It was, however, a moment where a huge proportion of the population became aware of the fickleness of our minds, and of the need to care for our mental health at least as much as we do for our physical health. Employers, including my own, started implementing compulsory mental-health days off; employees, especially from Gen Z, started new jobs on the basis that their own mental health came first and that their bosses would have to accept it or see them quit.

The goal was to reach a point where it becomes just as acceptable and just as easy to take some time off work because of mental burnout as it is to take time off work to deal with a serious physical illness. The scale of the mental-health crisis was obvious and undeniable, visible not only on the Instagram pages of celebrities like Prince Harry or Bella Hadid but also in the sheer number of professionals quitting their jobs and not reentering the workforce at all, after realizing that their job was simply not rewarding and they would be better off without it.

There was a sliver of good news, too, in the fact that even as homicide rates rose, most visibly in the form of mass shootings by troubled young men, suicide rates, at least if you exclude drug over-doses, *didn't* go up during the worst of the pandemic.[8] And suicide kills twice as many Americans than homicide does.[9] Even in Austra-lia, which probably had the longest and strictest lockdowns in the world, suicide rates remained well within their historical levels.[10]

To put it another way, while measured "psychological distress" went up sharply in areas hit by lockdowns, psychological distress is not the same thing as mental illness. Illness isn't the absence of wellness; it's not something that automatically manifests whenever your mental health declines.

One psychologist, looking at the spike in people coming to her for help, bemoaned the way in which the language of psychiatry has been coopted into the vernacular. "They're not depressed," she told me, "they're sad." You can't catch depression just from being cooped up at home for a couple of months, and the entirely understandable sadness you feel from your confinement will naturally dissipate once you start getting out and about again. Alternatively, you can self-medicate just by getting a puppy.

That's good news on two levels. It means there's no particular reason to expect a long-term increase in severe mental illness as a result of the pandemic. But it also means that the mental-health phoenix, for people on the lookout for it, might end up rising from this broad realization that mental health matters for everybody, and that a thriving company or country must, perforce, be one in a good collective headspace.

Corporate investment in mental wellness can improve productivity, reduce turnover, and ultimately pay for itself: In that sense it's quite a different proposition from standard health insurance. Some of the people who quit their jobs for the sake of their sanity are going to start new companies, or eventually allow themselves to be hired back into senior positions, and they will know better than most how self-defeating it is to wring employees out and discard them when they're spent—even if those employees would accept such treatment, which, increasingly, they won't.

Don't forget the introverts and agoraphobes, either. They got largely ignored during the pandemic, largely because many of them thrived. I might be one of them myself: When I retreated to a remote cottage on the west coast of Ireland to write this book in the winter of 2022, I got many questions asking whether I was lonely. Not in the slightest! The truth was that I found the break refreshing, and that I felt insanely privileged and fortunate that I had no dependents who needed me around, and that I could take that kind of time just for myself and my book.

I might in fact be one of the people who *developed* very mild symptoms of agoraphobia over the course of the pandemic. We didn't come down with a diagnosable mental illness, far from it. But we did discover just how happy we were at home, in contrast to others who found themselves climbing the walls.

The pandemic presented a unique opportunity to see what it's like to live and work in a very different way—to have the structure and safety of full-time employment, without most of the time and space constraints involved in commuting to a physical workplace filled with colleagues. Millions of people found out during the pandemic that they were well suited to remote work—and found an unprecedentedly broad range of employers more than willing to accommodate them. That doesn't just include people with syndromes found in the *DSM-5*; it also includes a very broad range of professionals who find themselves doing their best work, as well as being happiest, when they're far from the office. If a lot of people end up regaining a significant number of hours per week from what used to be painful commutes and annoying office politics, that could be a real mental health win right there.

Psychiatry is extremely complex and doesn't lend itself easily to generalization, but there's definitely reason to believe that a lot of the immediate problems caused by the extreme circumstances associated with the pandemic are ultimately going to be temporary. The social animal will go back to socializing; schools will go back to being full-time; fear of other people, or contaminated surfaces, will slowly abate. It strains credulity to believe the decline in mental health could remain stuck at mid-pandemic levels even when the pandemic itself is over. On the other hand, the stigma of openly discussing such issues has been diminishing for decades and shrank dramatically over the pandemic when almost everybody was affected in one way or another. That's a long-term secular trend, and it similarly seems highly unlikely that the stigma will return to where it was pre-pandemic. Once people start to be able to talk about the subject much more freely, with much less embarrassment, that makes it more likely that they're going to be able to ask for and receive the treatment they need. Just maybe, out of the mental-health ashes of the pandemic, that one phoenix might be able to rise.

It's also certain that we'll be living in a society that's getting happier. One thing we know about America is that it's broadly a happy place: If you look at the General Social Survey, a huge undertaking at the University of Chicago underwritten by the National Science Foundation, a key finding, ever since the survey began in 1972, is that roughly three times as many people say they're "very happy" than the proportion of people saying they're "not too happy." The former is about 35 percent of Americans; the latter is about 12 percent.

In the pandemic, both numbers went haywire. The "very happy" cohort plunged, to less than 20 percent, while the "not so happy"

Americans grew to outnumber their very happy compatriots for the first time ever.[11] I simply don't believe those numbers are sustainable: There's certain to be a mean-reversion, or, as the literature calls it, "hedonic adaptation." Happy humans are happy humans: Even major negative events like divorce or becoming paraplegic, while they certainly cause sadness, don't cause *permanent* sadness.

The pandemic lasted a long time and became politicized in such a way as to put almost everybody on edge literally for years. But even if Covid lasts forever, the society-wide psychological malaise associated with it cannot.

One of the things I've learned as a financial journalist is that humans tend to be much more attuned to first derivatives than they are to levels. Look at a scene and the thing that jumps out the most at you will not necessarily be the largest or most obvious part of it; it will rather be the thing that moves most visibly. When people check their stock portfolio, what they're looking for is what has changed since the last time they looked, rather than how much it's broadly worth. And when people exist in society during a pandemic, the thing they notice is how their formerly happy friends have become less happy. We expect our happy friends to be happy; we notice when they're not.

As America—and the world—returns to normal levels of happiness, we're going to see our friends getting significantly happier. We're going to notice that, and it's going to feel good—indeed, it's going to feel much better than it felt to just see them being happy day in and day out. That ride will and must come to an end, but it will be a fun ride to go on and will provide a positive hedonic tailwind to our lives, at least for a while.

We're climbing out of a deep hole—just as we've done many times before in American and global history. The mental-health horrors of the Civil War, or World War I, or Vietnam lasted for decades after the wars themselves were over. Each one broadened society's under-standing of mental injury and helped to build new and better ways of treating it.

In the case of Covid, the biggest challenge—and possibly the biggest advances—will be found in understanding the mental health of children, many of whom saw an irreplaceable part of their devel-opment simply iced out of possibility.

A substantial cohort is going to age like a tree ring from a year of forest fires—even if the years before and after are relatively nor-mal, there's still going to be a permanent mark, deep inside, from the trauma of Covid. That shared experience will manifest in many ways; I suspect educators will be the first to start identifying them.

Already in 2022, elementary school teachers were seeing an enor-mous decline in their students' ability compared to what they were used to pre-pandemic. The definitive national survey of nine-year-olds from the National Assessment of Educational Progress showed the first *ever* decline in mathematics scores, alongside the largest reading score decline in over twenty years.[12] Black children were hit particularly badly: Their 13-point decline in mathematics scores widened the Black-white gap to 33 points in 2022, from an already dreadful 25 points in 2020. (The points aren't measured on a 1-to-100 scale, but half of all students scored between 208 and 262.)

As for the rest of us, we were all affected by Covid, and collectively we have a lot of hard work to do in coming to terms with the psy-chological consequences of the pandemic. Hard work can often be rewarding; it would be wonderful if the result of all that effort were to be an increase in compassion. But that particular phoenix is barely even forming, as I write this in 2022. It will be many years, if ever, before it truly takes flight.

Part III

Business and Pleasure

9

The Two-Headed Risk Eagle

IF YOU WANT to see both ashes and a phoenix at the same place and the same time and coming from the same cause, there's no better place to look than the massive global risk recalibration caused by the Covid pandemic.

Risk, of course, is value neutral. It's the foremost driver of growth ("no risk, no reward") while also being the thing that causes untold misery every day. Risk appetite varies wildly from person to person, and can even vary wildly within a single person: Think of the person who will regularly speed down the freeway at 85 mph, for instance, but who also throws out all her wooden chopping boards for fear they might harbor germs.

That said, risk appetite rarely changes very quickly. If you happily sped down the freeway at 85 mph yesterday, you're likely to do the same tomorrow. Indeed, if people regularly do something risky, they get used to it, with the result that they stop being hyperconscious of just how risky it is. Every chef has suffered multiple burns and cuts, for instance, and a large part of becoming a professional chef involves overcoming the natural fear involved in wielding very hot and very sharp instruments with few if any safety precautions.

Something very similar happened during the pandemic. At the beginning, during the lockdown, a certain degree of altruism obtained—we were all staying home to flatten the curve, buy time, and do our part in the global fight against the virus, or at least that was a pleasant story we could tell ourselves—but that altruism was also the path of natural self-interest, given the rational fear that going out and having contact with infected yet asymptomatic individuals could prove fatal.

Within a few months, that alignment of public and private risk calculations had disappeared. People started venturing out into the world again—dating, going to work, meeting friends—and no matter how frequently or infrequently they did so, no matter whether they wore masks or not, one thing predictably happened,—which was that most of them didn't get sick. Even a full year into a virulent and badly managed pandemic, fewer than one in ten Americans had gotten the disease, which means that nine out of ten Americans had the lived experience of taking on a non-negligible quantum of risk and suffering no adverse consequences. In the earlier months, of course, that percentage was even higher.

Private risk calculations could easily swing the other way, too. Many people masked assiduously, even outdoors, and practiced impeccable hand hygiene and never ate or removed their masks indoors—and they, similarly, were extremely likely to avoid Covid. For them, the lesson was that the safety precautions worked.

Past experience, as they say, is not a guide to future results, but in reality people tend to behave as though it is. (We definitely saw that in the stock market, after the initial Covid crash, as the "stocks only go up" crowd saw their thesis confirmed over and over again.) In this particular case, a very large number of people, mostly men, found themselves taking risks and getting away with it—something that can feel very good.

A brief digression into lottery tickets: Humans are *terrible* at intuiting probabilities and risks. We don't quantify, we *feel*—which, at least in part, explains the popularity of lotteries. Over time, most jackpots tend to become harder to win—you need to get more numbers right, or the range of possibilities for each number gets bigger, or at least one of the numbers needs to be not only picked correctly but also placed in the correct position.

People are bad at grokking very big or very small numbers, but at least there's a vernacular understanding that a one-in-a-million probability means that something is basically not going to happen. By contrast, a 1-in-3,000 probability is rare but definitely within the bounds of possibility. If you have a 1-in-3,000 probability of being run over by a bus every time you step out into the street, and if you step out into the street four times a day, then you'll probably get run over by a bus within eighteen months. By contrast, if your chances of getting hit by a bus were one-in-a-million, you'd have to step out into the street four times a year for almost two hundred years before having a greater-than-even chance of coming a cropper.

This is where things get crazy: The difference between a 1-in-3,000 probability and a one-in-a-million probability—the difference between "highly unlikely" and "functionally impossible"—is the *same* as the difference between a one-in-a-million probability and a 1-in-300-million probability. In turn, that's the odds a lottery ticket has of winning the jackpot prize in either of the two big lotteries in the US, Mega Millions and Powerball.

Psychologically, taking a 1-in-3,000 risk is very different from taking a one-in-a-million risk, while taking a one-in-a-million risk is basically the same as taking a 1-in-300-million risk. That's the genius of contemporary lottery design: States can reduce the probability of winning the jackpot by a factor of 300, without having any real effect on the propensity of bettors to take a flutter. If anything, the

1-in-300-million lottery is *more* attractive to buyers of lottery tickets, because it allows for bigger jackpots and therefore bigger dreams. And really the item being bought is precisely that dream—the way in which the hours between purchase and result are filled with the hope of a life-altering event.

The lesson here is that it's ludicrous to suppose that humans will be able to effectively understand and calibrate the amount of risk they're taking with any given action. That lesson was underscored during the pandemic, when governments and news organizations around the world were faced with a constant barrage of demands from people wanting a simple answer to a simple question: Safe or Not Safe?

Is it safe to take off my mask outdoors? What about indoors? Is it safe to go to the gym if I wear a mask? Is it safe to send my kids to school if they haven't been vaccinated? Is it safe to see my elderly parent if I've tested negative? Is it safe to take off my mask for a minute to take a drink of water on an airplane? And if that's safe, why wouldn't it be safe to take off my mask for ten minutes even when I'm not drinking water?

The only honest answers to such questions were doubly unsatisfying: They would be couched in probabilistic terms that are inherently difficult to understand or act on,—and on top of that, the probabilities themselves would come with large error bars. At various points over the pandemic I toyed with the idea of giving myself a risk budget—eat indoors *or* take public transport, that kind of thing—but in practice it was almost impossible to quantify everyday activities in a way that would make that possible. Almost everybody I know found themselves, at various different speeds, getting comfortable with various different activities. Then, once an activity was included on the "Okay, I can do this now" list, it generally stayed there unless and until there was a huge surge of a new virus variant.

That mechanism didn't apply solely to pandemic-related precautions like taking off masks. As the roads emptied out in the initial weeks of the pandemic and traffic cops were nowhere to be seen, for instance, Americans found it easier than ever to ignore all speed limits. One team of men in a white Audi A8 sedan drove the 2,906 miles from the Red Ball Garage in Manhattan to the Portofino Hotel in Los Angeles—the classic "Cannonball Run"—in just twenty-six hours and thirty-eight minutes, which works out to an *average* speed of 109 mph. The men were criticized—not for driving too fast, but for possibly transmitting the virus by touching fuel pumps along the way.[1]

The result of the increase in speeding was statistically inevitable: A scary uptick in car crashes and fatalities, despite the total number of vehicle miles traveled falling substantially. What's more, the speeding wasn't simply a function of unusually empty highways. The National Highway Traffic Safety Administration (NHTSA) saw pretty much every risky behavior become markedly more common at the same time—speeding, driving without a seat belt, driving under the influence of alcohol or other drugs. The proportion of drivers testing positive for opioids, for instance, *doubled* in the six months after March 2020, compared to the six months previously. And even after traffic returned, the amount of speeding remained significantly higher than pre-pandemic levels.

The result of the increased risk-taking was, all too often, death. US pedestrian fatalities rose from 6,412 in 2019 to 6,711 in 2020 and 7,485 in 2021—an unprecedented increase of 17 percent in just two years, to the highest level in four decades.[2]

To be sure, millions of people, especially the immunocompromised, went into "risk-off" mode and stayed there. But if anything, even more people seemed to move into "risk-on" mode instead. The NHTSA has a gruesome but accurate way of measuring how many people wear seat belts: It measures something called the "ejection rate," which is the proportion of crashes where someone ended up being ejected from the car. The ejection rate spiked alarmingly from 2019 to 2020—and then stayed high thereafter.

The clear implication: Whatever your initial reason was for no longer wearing a seat belt, once you switch into risk-on mode, you generally stay there. The same is true in the opposite direction: The one demographic seeing a significant *decline* in ejection rates, for reasons the NHTSA was very interested in finding out, was women aged eighteen to thirty-four—for them, rates dropped to a significant new all-time low, and then stayed low.

If you're risking your life every time you show up for work, then other risks pale by comparison—including risks like not wearing a seat belt, or investing a substantial proportion of your net worth into meme stocks or crypto shitcoins, or taking up smoking. (The year 2020 was the first time in two decades that cigarette sales went up rather than down, with twentysomethings leading the way.[3]) Some of those risks are simply bad on both a personal and a societal level: There's no upside to increased smoking. But the underlying attitude to risk can still be positive.

While different states and countries varied widely in their re-action to the pandemic, for instance, one thing that surprised health authorities around the world was the speed with which populations wanted to go "back to normal" even as the virus was killing millions of people. The public-health authorities, by dint of their profession, naturally took it upon themselves to try to minimize the amount of death and suffering caused by Covid. Probably all of them were familiar with the trolley problem, or some other ethical thought ex-periment wherein failure to take a life-saving measure is tantamount to murder.

The revealed preferences of normal folks, however, were startlingly

different—and were much more in line with the way in which humans reacted to infectious disease before we really had tools to
mitigate it.

Within many (but not all) religious communities there was an
explicit suggestion that death and suffering are an ineradicable part
of our existence, and that the latest plague, just like all the previous
ones, was God's will. The devout didn't *want* to catch Covid, and
certainly didn't want to die of it—but they also found it easier to
embrace kismet than to try to navigate the rapidly shifting behavioral
guidelines being handed down by the government and media elites.

Disease, even fatal disease, is part of nature, something that everybody understands. Its specter turns out to be something millions
of people can get reasonably comfortable living under—after all, if
we're all going to die anyway, it can feel pointless to go to great
lengths to avoid doing so. Live the best life you can and let the chips
fall where they may: There's a simple elegance to such a formulation,
especially for people who are many generations removed from the
time when something as basic and necessary as childbirth regularly
resulted in the death of the mother, child, or both.

Behind this increased risk appetite can be found the idea that
we've built up an enviable store of risk allowance, in the form of
public-health interventions, medical advances, and simple financial
wealth—and that now's a good time to start spending some of that
down. That's something I saw during Britain's fateful Brexit vote of
2016: Almost everybody knew that leaving the EU would mean
Britain being significantly less well off than it would be within the
bloc. But the people who voted to leave also felt that they could
afford it—that it was a price worth paying.

More broadly, support for nativist and anti-globalist movements
around the world often comes from a desire for relative, rather than
absolute, prosperity. If an immigrant or a member of some other

out-group has great success and creates good jobs for the families who used to be in charge, old-timers can resent that person's success even as they do well by it themselves. Cutting the *arrivistes* down a few notches might not be in their financial best interest, but if they're reasonably secure anyway, it's something they feel they can afford to do all the same, restoring something of the old order.

It's only natural for people to rediscover their base-level priorities when loved ones die before their time, or when they see their wealth jump unexpectedly. In this case, the *memento mori*, combined with a significant liquidity injection, results in a broad recalibration of risks. The things that we used to be worried about turned out to maybe not be quite as fearsome as we had thought, given what reality was capable of throwing at us. And the opportunities to go out and refuse to be cowed by the virus—or, for that matter, by other risks, from losing income to getting lung cancer—were extremely tempting.

For those of us who live in cities, smokers and speeders and karaoke singers were a particularly visible part of the great pandemic risk shift, especially as socializing moved increasingly outdoors. Walking down a city street, especially during the "hot vaxx summer" of 2021 when everybody old enough to drink was also eligible to be vaccinated, and when new infection rates were low, was to witness a feeling of excitement and possibility—and a double-fingered rejection of fear.

That fear-off shift manifested itself in aspects of the Great Resignation, too—people quitting stable, well-paid jobs to try something riskier that potentially they might love more. But of course it was far from universal. What to one person feels like fun if risky behavior can easily look like nihilism to someone living in rational fear of the virus.

The elderly, people with weak immune systems, people with unvaccinated children at home, and just generally people who had taken to heart the injunctions to avoid the disease at all costs:—these folk numbered in the millions and felt threatened—attacked, even—by the carefree recklessness they saw around them.

The "risk-off" crowd, by their nature, were far less visible than the "fear-off, risk-on" partiers. They weren't seen snogging and smoking outside crowded bars, they didn't dress up as apes at booze-soaked crypto conventions, they didn't call attention to themselves by singing (singing!) in subway cars. In fact, they generally didn't take the subway at all.

Some of the risk-off crowd were able to move their jobs entirely online, and work from their homes, keeping human contact to a minimum. Others chose, in their millions, to drop out of the workforce entirely rather than risk going out into a world poisoned not only by a malign virus but also by a noticeable uptick in inconsiderate, antisocial, and even criminal behavior.

The state of crime, in 2019, was similar to the state of infectious disease: It was extremely low, by historical standards, and had been steadily decreasing for decades. As someone who has lived in New York for twenty-five years, I saw this happen myself. When I arrived, in 1997, crime was at all-time lows. The crack epidemic was over, no one expected to be mugged upon leaving their apartment, and the number of murders in New York City had dropped by 56 percent in just six years, from 2,245 in 1990 to 983 in 1996. I kept my wits about me, as they say, and I was fine.

In 2005, I moved into a ground-floor apartment in what used to be known as Alphabet City but that somehow had been successfully rebranded as the East Village, in an attempt to make it feel more like the genteel Greenwich Village a mile to the west. The apartment came with a small underground space that we tried with limited success to turn into a TV room; when we did the renovation, we discovered a hole behind a false wall, its contents betraying the apartment's former use as a crack den. Upstairs, the first thing we did was take all the bars off the windows. That year, the citywide murder rate, continuing its long-term secular decline, had fallen even further, to 539.

By 2017, the East Village had rather lost its charm for us, and we moved out. There were still pockets of the neighborhood of old—legendary slam-poetry venue the Nuyorican Poets Cafe, for instance, established in 1973, was still going strong in the building across the street that it had bought in 1980, while the Lower East Side People's Federal Credit Union (LESPFCU) continued to provide a vital service to longtime residents of the local city-run apartment blocks. But LESPFCU was no longer the only bank within walking distance; indeed, it seemed that every street corner boasted a branch of some multinational financial-services giant. The neighborhood had come to be dominated by bars and brunch spots catering to college students at NYU and other nearby universities, as well as a huge number of new-construction luxury apartments. The new millionaire residents had no reason to worry about crime: The number of murders in the city that year was just 292, a new all-time low, the *Economist* had declared New York to be one of the safest cities in the world, ranking ahead of places like Taipei, Milan, and Abu Dhabi, and Manhattan, in particular, was safe even by New York City standards.

As property prices soared and sushi restaurants multiplied, an understandable complacency set in: Crime would always be low and falling, and the East Village (and Brooklyn, and New York City more generally) would become one more stop along the International Hipster Trail of third-wave coffee shops and skate stores selling collectible hoodies. People living in downtown Manhattan no longer felt any need to keep their wits about them—violent crime, and even non-violent crime like robberies, became something, like infectious disease, we had basically stopped worrying about on a day-to-day basis.

Then, during the pandemic, the long-term trends reversed. For a small minority of people, increased freedom means the freedom to commit crimes. The looting associated with some of the Black Lives Matter protests in the summer of 2020 was exceptional in many ways, but it did presage a genuinely sustained and nationwide increase in antisocial behavior. Anybody whose job involved interacting directly with the public—nurses, teachers, flight attendants, retail workers, you name it—reported startlingly high levels of violence visited upon them. Hate crimes hit their highest level since 2008, with anti-Black hate crimes rising almost 50 percent between 2019 and 2020, from 1,930 to 2,871.[4]

Cities, when they work well, are an exercise in cooperation and compassion—density comes with manifold benefits, but also increases the chance that someone physically very close to you is going to do something that's good for them but bad for you. Countless written and unwritten rules and conventions have developed over the years to try to balance individuals' competing demands—stand on the right, wait your turn, face the elevator doors, don't wear a backpack onto the subway or manspread when you sit down, use headphones if you're listening to music, that kind of thing. Breaking those rules is an act of aggression, an assertion of individual agency overriding the collective good.

The pandemic expanded, quite suddenly and quite significantly, the behaviors that were considered to be antisocial and aggressive. Supermarket aisles became one-way streets; salmoning them by going the wrong way was frowned upon. Entering an already-occupied elevator became a social minefield. And then there was the whole range of ways not to wear a mask properly, with exquisite gradations of aggression depending on how ventilated the location was, how close you were to others, how many other people were masked, whether you were talking, how loud you were talking, how much of your nose might be covered, and so on. The New York City murder rate went back up quite sharply, rising to 462 in 2020 and 485 in 2021. Those numbers are still lower than, say, 2011, which certainly didn't feel particularly unsafe at the time. But as humans we're better at discerning movement than we are magnitude: A sudden rise from a low level is much more jarring (and more newsworthy) than a slow decline to a slightly higher level.

All of this was simply too much for some. The basic bargain of civility is the golden rule: Treat others as you would be treated. But the trauma of the pandemic had long-lasting consequences, especially among the Black and brown communities that were hardest hit during the early weeks when fear was at its height and therapeutics were in their infancy. For those who had been treated badly by their city and country when they needed aid the most, it was tempting to declare, or at least to believe, on a primal level, that the bargain had been broken and that society was no longer owed anything. For others, the culture wars of the Trump era turned the mask-wearing elites into an oppositional force, one to be resisted rather than respected. And for others still, the sheer exhaustion of living through the pandemic left zero mental bandwidth for caring about what the person sitting across from you on the bus might be thinking or feeling.

Meanwhile, on the other side of the encounter, people who would have brushed off pre-pandemic incivilities were receiving such things in a much more personal and aggrieved fashion. Consider the things that city dwellers got used to, in the pre-pandemic years, that weren't entirely positive. Crime rates went down, but the linked problems of homelessness and mental illness went up. While New York City as a whole was safe, certain parts of certain streets—125th Street between Park and Lex, say, or Bowery between Delancey and Houston—felt as dangerous as ever, with a very high chance of encountering someone dealing in a loud and public manner with severe mental-health issues. In the balmier cities of San Francisco and Los Angeles, entire neighborhoods started to feel that way.

Come the pandemic, of course, the risk of having an unmasked man casting spittle-flecked invective at you went from deeply unpleasant to potentially life-threatening, radically changing the calculus involved in simply walking down the street.

The great risk bifurcation, then, increased the amount of dangerous and risky behavior at exactly the same time as the appetite to encounter such behavior had never been lower. Drinking, for example, hit unprecedented heights during the pandemic, with wholesale alcohol revenues—a good proxy for the total amount of alcohol consumed—jumping more than 16 percent from $13.5 billion in February 2020 to $15.7 billion in August, and continuing to rise thereafter.

Zooming out to the very big picture, the total number of deaths in America in 2020 rose by an unprecedented 529,000 over the previous year. Covid was a very large part of that, accounting for 351,000 of those deaths. But that still leaves a stunning increase of 178,000 more people dying of non-Covid causes than had done so in 2019.[5] An American's chances of dying of "unintentional injuries," for instance, went up by 17 percent in 2020, per the Centers for Disease Control, much of which was drug overdoses. So much for life being safer when the population is venturing out less.

For Americans in the twenty-five to thirty-four age range, life became staggeringly more dangerous in 2020, and not because they were directly dying of Covid. They were already doing very badly, by historical standards, only to see the terrible become unthinkably worse. Some numbers: The mortality rate for this age group, measured per 100,000 population, was 102.9 in 2010, roughly double the equivalent number in the UK or Japan. By 2019, thanks largely to opioids, it had surged to 128.8. Then in 2020, it shot up again, by almost 25 percent, to 160.3. That's a higher number than was seen at any point during the AIDS crisis of the late 1980s and early 1990s.

If you look at the change in the total number of deaths in this cohort from 2019 to 2020, less than 18 percent of the increase was from Covid, and only 3.5 percent of all deaths in the age group were directly caused by the disease. Most of them were simply due to an increase in dangerous, self-destructive, and risk-seeking behavior—a stark signal of just how deadly Covid was on a societal level, quite aside from its lethality as a pathogen. Remember: These were, in principle, some of the most valuable lives in America—the ones where the expensive education was in the past, and decades of high-earning potential were in the future.

The essence of entrepreneurialism is a certain degree of reckless-ness. Successful founders take big and irrational risks, in a bet that has a very high probability of failure but that, repeated over and over again across the country as a whole, proves to be an unrivaled engine of economic growth. Conversely, retreating from engagement with the world is a surefire recipe for stagnation.

On the other hand, recklessness on a lifestyle level is often de-structive, while disciplined self-abnegation can generate extremely impressive results.

What happened during the pandemic was a widening of the range of risk appetites seen across the population as a whole. The 10 per-cent of the population taking the most risks were taking substantially more risk than ever, while the 10 percent of the population taking the least risk were similarly more cautious than ever before. As befits the New Not Normal, the idea of a "normal" level of acceptable risk became laughable, and more and more people started talking past each other, making a big mistake in assuming that their risk appetite was probably roughly shared by their interlocutor. Perhaps the fab-ulous avian creature rising from the ashes of Covid isn't a phoenix so much as the Russian double-headed eagle, facing in two opposite directions at once.

In the early days of the pandemic, I invoked the Covid Corollary to Weisberg's Law, which I mentioned in the Introduction: Everybody more cautious than you has gone way overboard, while everybody less cautious is not only putting themselves at risk but is acting in a deeply socially irresponsible manner.

"The virus is eroding the shared norms and beliefs that underpin both markets and societies," I wrote. "The consequences are unforeseeable, but unlikely to be good."[6]

Sadly, I was largely right. The virus created an irresolvable tension between two foundational societal norms. On one side was the ideal of freedom, liberty, and bodily autonomy. Vaccine mandates, mask mandates, and all other attempts to curtail the rights and freedoms of the individual were loudly and vehemently protested by groups who were often supported by politicians on the right of the political spectrum.

On the other side was the idea of society itself—that in times of crisis we come together to support each other, and especially the weakest among us. In normal times we pride ourselves on being polite and considerate to fellow members of our community; a pandemic is an opportunity to put such principles into practice by masking up and getting vaxxed and helping to fight the microscopic enemy through the power of collective action.

At the international level, the sovereigns easily won out over the arguments for equity and fairness. The dream of COVAX was that an international consortium of countries would develop and distribute Covid vaccines for the benefit of all, with doses going first to the neediest. But that didn't come close to happening. So-called vaccine nationalism rapidly kicked in, with Donald Trump's America being the worst offender and Boris Johnson's UK not being far behind.

The vaccines ended up going first not to the people who needed them the most, but rather to the people who were fortunate enough to live in the countries where they were developed—or, in the case of countries like Israel, who were fortunate enough to live in small, rich states that were happy to pay top dollar to jump the queue. COVAX became a charitable afterthought, a means of trying to assuage guilt through the philanthropic donation of doses and dollars, rather than a genuine global vaccine allocation mechanism.

Within countries, divisions were sometimes even worse. Loud and violent protests took place around the world in opposition to public-health measures. Self-righteousness surged on both sides, and all the venom and hostility of political castigation was brought to bear, often by politicians themselves, onto those who took the other side. Wherever you stood, it was possible to find vocal allies, and an identifiable enemy who could be blamed for whatever it was you were upset about.

I made a personal promise to myself, very early on in the pandemic, to try to dial up the sympathy and try my hardest not to judge others for making decisions that I wouldn't make. A few extremists notwithstanding, I was mostly successful: I would nod along with parents of young children who told me that they were in a particularly dire situation because they couldn't vaccinate their kids, and then nod along with parents of other young children who told me they had nothing to worry about because the virus did almost no harm to kids that age.

I realized, too, that most people didn't make risk calculations in the hyperconscious way that I and most of my friends did. As I mentioned in Chapter 1, at the end of 2021, I found myself taking the London Underground on a daily basis at the height of the Omicron surge. The rules were clear: Everybody over the age of eleven had to wear a mask over their mouth and nose—and yet a large proportion of people on the Tube, sometimes more than half, would either wear no mask at all or would do so very half-heartedly, with their nose uncovered. This in a country that's famous for its orderly queues and acquiescent "mustn't grumble" attitude to regulations.

I thought back to an article I'd read in the *Guardian* a couple of months previously, featuring a photo of four unmasked young door-to-door salespeople beaming for a newspaper photographer while on the Tube, displaying not a hint of anger or aggression (or, for that matter, a mask). Rather, they themselves felt aggrieved at what they perceived to be rudeness directed at them by mask-wearing passengers. "I don't have Covid and it's not your business," explained Charlie, one of the group.

His friend Julia then chimed in to occupy the middle ground: People on public transport should wear masks, she said. This argument wasn't particularly effective, given the fact that she was on public transport at the time, and not wearing a mask. When this was pointed out, everyone just laughed.[7]

The four work friends were in their early twenties, carving out their identity in the city, working a badly paid and thankless job in the middle of a pandemic. The messaging from the authorities was confusing—the national government had recently declared "Freedom Day," when all mandates and restrictions were supposed to have been lifted, but that didn't apply to the London Underground, which was governed by a different, more cautious authority. The youngsters didn't have any malign intent, they just had pandemic fatigue. The vaccines had arrived and, as other passengers said, that should have put an end to things.

I know what it's like to believe things just because I want them to be true. In the early weeks of the pandemic I had two friends who came down with Covid, and after they recovered I realized that I had a weirdly deep emotional investment in them suddenly having developed anti-Covid superpowers, with full presumptive immunity. I found myself feeling weirdly aggrieved that they still wore masks outdoors, and social-distanced, and were just as cautious as those of us who hadn't got the disease. Hadn't they read about the hero nurses in Liberia who recovered from Ebola and could walk through wards that were no-go areas to everybody else?

Of course, they were right and I was wrong. I wanted Covid to provide some kind of closure, if not for me then at least for the people who had it—a silver lining that, combined with the promise of future vaccines, would bring us that much closer to the much-talked-about dream of "herd immunity."

I ended up following the facts on the ground and rapidly realizing that the vaccines, while very effective, did not confer magical immunity—and that prior infection was even weaker protection against the disease. But it's *literally my job* to drink from multiple information firehoses and synthesize what I'm learning into a constantly evolving worldview. For younger people who aren't necessarily news consumers, faced with an incompetent government with a dreadful messaging strategy, in the face of rapidly shifting epidemiological epistemics, in a country that's politically polarized and riven with mistrust, in the absence of any central authority figure whose communications can be taken at face value, well, for those people it's not hard to see how a certain amount of magical thinking would end up making its way into their lifestyle decisions.

In America, it was sometimes harder to discern such magical thinking because the two tribes were quite good at keeping geographical distance from each other. There were cities where everybody was supposed to mask indoors, and overwhelmingly they did; there were states where nobody had to mask indoors, and few people did—but there were surprisingly few areas where a large part of the population was at odds with local government mandates. Partly, that was a function of elected officials doing a reasonably good job of reflecting the desires of their constituents, and partly it was just the simple fact that most of the time, most people will always be comfortable doing what most of their neighbors are doing.

Still, the blithe and the scared coexisted uncomfortably every-where—uncomfortably for the latter, at least. The risk-intolerant had a particularly fraught pandemic, and were afforded relatively little public sympathy, or even visibility. One of the reasons why the unmasked percentage was as high as it was on the London Underground and even on the New York subway was simply that a large number of risk-averse individuals stopped taking public transport entirely. Many of them never much liked it, and the pandemic was more than enough reason for them to decide they would simply not subject themselves to such things again.

If the two-headed eagle rising from the Covid ashes was often mistaken for a phoenix, that was in large part because one of the heads was bright and loud and highly visible, while the other was shrouded, sequestered, hiding indoors. Over the long term, there is reason to hope and believe that the bird will turn out to be phoenix-like after all. Constructive risk-taking can compound over time and pay unexpected dividends decades into the future; antisocial and self-destructive risk-taking, on the other hand, remains on a long-term secular decline, and it's hard to see how the pandemic could put a halt to that deeply rooted trend.

As for the risk-averse, there's reason for hope there, too. Fear is not a constant: We get used to it over time and learn to live with it and around it. That happened during all previous plagues, and it happened with Covid—the countries most afraid of the virus were those that *didn't* have it, not those that did. For those of us in the Covid-ridden west, fear generally peaked with the various waves, rising with new spikes and dying back when the case count fell.

As ever, the important thing wasn't the level of new cases, but rather the first derivative, whether they were rising or falling. A level of cases that would be cause for celebration and face-licking parties in New York would trigger doomsaying in Australia.

Eventually, people come out of their shell. Maybe they're coaxed out by their friends; maybe they just get used to the fear and decide they can live with it. The nervousness associated with being around unvaxxed or unmasked individuals is not going to be a lasting feature of the pandemic; the risk-averse head of the two-headed eagle will shrivel and die back into the ashes from which it was born. What's left might just be a phoenix after all.

Shaking the Etch-a-Sketch

THE RISE IN risk-on behavior is far from being a purely pandemic-related phenomenon. It was accelerated by the pandemic, to be sure, but it's also visible in things like the Brexit and Trump votes of 2016. Both of them were popular movements that involved a move to dangerous extremes, votes for the high-risk over the low-risk outcome.

Importantly, the Trump and Brexit votes weren't the result of a risk/reward calculation, at least not in the economic sense. Financially, the potential rewards to both outcomes were dwarfed by the downside risks. But maybe the reward came more immediately, in a non-financial way, with the humbling of the smug neoliberals and the feeling that some semblance of power and control had been put back into the hands of those who had found themselves on the losing side of the globalization game.

Some kinds of risk-taking are broadly good for any economy. Starting new businesses, or lending to them, is a prime example: It means investment in new equipment and new employees, helping not only the companies borrowing the money but also their suppliers and their workforces.

Other types of risk-taking are broadly bad for any economy. Smoking cigarettes, for example, causes misery for smokers and everybody who's close to them, as well as enormous and unnecessary medical bills.

Within the financial system, a huge proportion of risk-taking can be seen as socially useless—or, indeed, as downright harmful.[1] The housing market, which precipitated the 2008 financial crisis, is a prime example. It's fine and healthy for homebuilders to make a decent profit. But when existing homes are changing hands for many multiples of the amount it would cost to construct them, that just increases the amount of mortgage debt and housing-market speculation, while also maximizing the chances of a 2008-style crash. It even weirdly works *against* the construction of new housing, since a financialized housing system is one in which owners of houses want to keep new supply low in order to maximize the market value of their own homes. Since those owners are also voters and in control of local zoning laws, the result is a system where it often becomes almost impossible to build new housing in the areas where demand is greatest.

An uptick in risk can certainly result in a rise in inequality, and seemingly random wealth. Take options trading, for instance—something that exploded in popularity during the pandemic. Unlike stock-market investing, buying and selling options is a zero-sum game: The total amount gained is equal to the total amount lost. What's more, a lot of the winners are pre-ordained—the market-makers, who sit on the other side of every trade with an individual, make money with astonishing predictability and regularity. Some of them never have a losing day. (Gambling in a casino is risky; owning a casino isn't.)

In aggregate, then, individual option investors lose an astonishing amount of money every day, thereby demonstrating and exacerbating the natural inequality that tends to be built into markets. And yet they wouldn't do it if there weren't also a steady stream of winners—high-profile investors, many of whom post their trades to Reddit or other message boards, who really can and do make a lot of money by taking advantage of the embedded leverage in options contracts, and/or just getting very lucky and being in the right place at the right time.

Those winners in the options market join the winners in the crypto market, and the winners in the NFT market, and even, up to a point, the winners of the start-up lottery—people who wake up one morning and find themselves fabulously wealthy. The more risk appetite there is in the system, the more of those got-rich-quick millionaires will be created, and the more that the dream of getting rich quick will tempt others into the same kind of activities.

In the case of start-ups, that's arguably a good thing, for society as a whole. Venture-funded start-ups invest billions of dollars into the kind of activity that generates economic growth, high-paying jobs, and valuable new technology, including mRNA vaccines. And start-up equity is highly illiquid, which means that employees are generally forced to hold on to it, even when valuations are rising dramatically. That helps to minimize the amount of socially useless trading in the shares of start-ups.

Much of the rest of the time, however, fast riches can be surprisingly damaging. I'm not talking about damage suffered by the rich people themselves, here. While it's certainly possible to squander your millions and end up more miserable than you would have been without the money, the fact is that money really is generally good for you.

Rather, the problem with fast riches for the few is that they tend to suck in speculative capital from the many, even when that money is not being put to any kind of productive use. In most of these areas, from shitcoins to online poker, the number of winners is tiny compared to the number of losers, and even the winners don't really create much value in the world.

It's not that making money in these arenas doesn't involve real skill—it does. It's not easy to make money in options trading or crypto, or even poker. When there's a huge amount of liquidity out there, a lot of money to be made, a lot of smart, hungry young men (and even some women) decide they're going to try their hand at making their fortune. The ones who succeed get to live the dream— call in rich from their jobs, move to Puerto Rico or Singapore, and buy a Lamborghini or two. That's good for them—but it's also bad for their employers, who have just lost a super-talented employee.

It's instructive to look at the Great Resignation—the phenomenon of quit rates soaring during the pandemic—through the lens of risk appetite. The quit rate is a sign of a vibrant, healthy economy, one that embraces the risk involved in quitting one's job. Many people were quitting in order to take a higher-paying job somewhere else, which indicates that the value of their economic output was increasing.

Silicon Valley entrepreneur Dave Girouard likened the employment effects of the pandemic to shaking an Etch-a-Sketch, "removing the inertia that prevented people from changing jobs."[2] It encouraged people to find the jobs and careers they really wanted; gave them the push to leave whatever mildly unhappy situation they might have found themselves in pre-pandemic.

The hospitality industry, for instance, has always been a place with long hours, hard work, and low pay. People enter it because finding a job is quite easy, and then they stay, often for many years, because that's the default option. When the pandemic forced hotels and restaurants to close down, it gave all those employees a certain amount of perspective on what their lives had been like, and whether they had been fashioning a healthy and optimal career for themselves. The answer, often, was no—one that precipitated a move out of the industry and often out of town, too.

Sometimes, they quit in order to go into business on their own, which is even better: That's the kind of entrepreneurial animal spirits that all economies need in order to thrive. One of the big surprises of the pandemic, for me, was the number of restaurants that *opened* in the face of harsh capacity restrictions and an ultra-tight labor market. But the new-business bug was much bigger than just restaurants.

In 2021, the first full calendar year of living with Covid, 5.4 million Americans—well over 3 percent of the US labor force—applied for small-business licenses. That number represented a 53 percent jump from the 2019 baseline, and even if 80 percent of those small businesses failed, that's still more than a million new businesses created that will help to drive the economy forward.

The pandemic normalized the idea of working from home, not just for white-collar employers but also for founders. It incubated a strain of entrepreneurial YOLO that America hadn't seen before— one that infected not only childless engineers in Silicon Valley but also middle-aged middle managers in the suburbs, who often had much more experience and skill and wisdom than the recent Stanford grads dreaming of Lamborghinis.

As unemployment plunged during the Covid recovery, the risk of starting a new company fell: Not only would there almost certainly be a good job available elsewhere should the start-up fail, but employers were happy to pay a premium for people who were provably willing to take such risks. On top of that, a whole slew of companies provided pretty much all the support any start-up needed—far beyond web hosting, it was possible to pay a modest monthly fee for everything up to and including a CFO. Meanwhile office space went from being an expensive necessity to being something that many start-ups could ignore entirely.

The motivation to start a company is not always or even mainly financial. Being your own boss has obvious benefits, especially during a pandemic when obligations can pop up at home unexpectedly. Even the dynastically wealthy do it: In the tech world, founders who have made hundreds of millions or even billions of dollars from one company are regularly seen starting up another one—Facebook's Dustin Moscovitz founding Asana, for instance, or Twitter's Jack Dorsey founding Square. Those are great examples of people with a combination of human capital and financial capital using both to create real fresh value in the world, along with a lot of new jobs.

More common is the phenomenon of founders striking it rich in tech, quitting their jobs, and reinventing themselves as "angel investors"—people who provide the seed money for other start-ups. Financially, this rarely works out well, but collectively it gives a lot of small companies a lot of runway to discover whether they have product-market fit and could turn into something great. Life as an angel investor is not hard—you definitely have plenty of time to hang out at your beach house, should you be so inclined. But you're still, in some sense, contributing in a productive way to the economy.

All of these quits are what can broadly be thought of as constructive, productive quits—quits that are positive for society as a whole. The pandemic, however, also saw millions of much less productive quits—the kind of quits that might make all the sense in the world on a personal level, but are never going to show up in improved national accounts.

Many people quit just because they had Covid—a disease that can be highly debilitating and last for months if not years. If you're suffering from long Covid and barely able to get out of bed, let alone leave the house, then you're going to lose a lot of your ability to be a productive member of society. Others quit because they needed to care for the newly sick.

Much more systemically, a huge number of quits were related to childcare, given the sudden extra burdens involved in at-home schooling. Pre-pandemic, there was nothing particularly special or difficult involved in two working parents, living in a modest-sized home, having two or even three children at school. Post-pandemic, that could rapidly become an impossibility. One friend of mine told me that the only way she was able to cope was *because she got cancer* and therefore managed to take sick leave from her job.

Looking after children is not something society generally values particularly highly. Schools do it, of course, and are generally very good at it, but that core function of what they do is barely mentioned, most of the time. Instead, the focus, historically, was always on the education function—something that is undeniably important, but that also, crucially, allows teachers to be treated as trained professionals. The result is that remote schooling became something that *could* work, at least in theory: After all, the ostensible job of teachers was to teach, not to babysit. Which in turn meant that someone else had to do the job of babysitting—and that someone else was invariably a parent, often one who was already trying to hold down a full-time job of their own.

Babysitting, when separated from teaching, is the kind of job that's often given to teenagers: It requires presence, and attention, but it doesn't require a lot of skill, and it doesn't in itself contribute greatly to economic growth. Quitting a decent paid job in order to be able to do unpaid babysitting might be necessary, but it's not a positive development, and it's not going to increase the amount of productive risk being taken on in the economy.

Then there are more conventional voluntary quits—people quitting their job just because they don't want to do it. Covid accelerated these, too, insofar as it made many jobs worse, especially in the service industry. No one particularly wants to be exposed to a combination of infectious disease and caustic invective as a central part of their wage-slave job, so it's hardly surprising that those jobs proved very hard to fill once people started returning to work. There may or may not be better jobs out there, but for many people no job was a more attractive proposition than one of these bad jobs.

Involuntary unemployment is one of the most damaging things that can happen to a person, but *voluntary* unemployment is a very different matter—and started becoming more attractive than ever over the course of the pandemic, certainly as measured by the number of "idlers" on the r/antiwork subreddit. There's something extremely satisfying about telling your horrible boss that you're quitting—especially if you're someone who had the opportunity to do so during a time when the American social safety net was uncommonly generous, with expanded unemployment benefits and a nationwide eviction moratorium imposed for health reasons by the Centers for Disease Control. (After the generous unemployment benefits ran out, the "antiwork" quits were supplanted by the "quiet quit" quits, where remote workers would phone it in and do the bare minimum to not get fired.)

Quitting your job, or taking a calculated risk of getting fired from it, is, in one sense, a sign of heightened risk appetite. It shows a willingness to take the financially more uncertain and precarious road, and many Boomer employers were broadly shocked by its rise—it's not something *they* would ever have dared to do. Still, when it happens *en masse*, it reduces total earnings and therefore the amount of money sloshing around the economy. Institutions like the Federal Reserve get worried when there's a large number of healthy, working-age people who simply choose not to work: It's a sign that the economy is operating below its potential.

It's especially worrying, for economists, either when a generation's brightest talents follow that path, or when it becomes an aspirational dream. Both became true during the pandemic.

In crypto, thousands of early adopters, crypto experts, and meme surfers made enough money to quit their jobs and retire in their twenties, keeping most of their wealth in bitcoin, ethereum, and other cryptocurrencies—or, as they're better thought of, digital commodities. Those coins aren't being held in some kind of fractional-reserve bank that lends them out to needy local businesses; they're just sitting there, boasting zero economic utility unless and until they're sold. Holding a large quantity of cryptocurrency is the economic opposite of being an angel investor: It might be equally risky from a financial perspective, but it doesn't generate anything like the same positive externalities for the broader economy.

Meanwhile, the #vanlife and FIRE ("financial independence; retire early") movements converged on the idea that if your monthly expenses are low enough, then it's possible to retire in your thirties or even your twenties, with a surprisingly small amount of money.

When someone quits their job, they are no longer automatically and presumptively on the job market, looking for new employment. Instead, they ask themselves whether they have enough money (and possibly passive income) to live frugally on, either permanently or for a period of months or years. They then weigh that option against the stresses of employment. If you don't have an employer, then you have nothing tying you to an expensive urban rental. Why not just live out of a van, being sure to edit out all the miserable bits for your Instagram feed?

The #vanlife vision is much bigger than the number of people who actually decide to live on the road for a while. It's everybody who rejects the careerist norm of maximizing earnings and economic opportunity at every turn; who thinks of savings as something to be spent, rather than something to be hoarded for a hypothetical retirement decades in the future. Ultimately, it's about defining your own life by extricating yourself from the strictures of employment—not to mention the hedonic treadmill whereby every raise in salary is met by a rise in expenditures.

In that sense, the YOLO attitude accelerated by Covid aligns quite neatly with the anti-capitalist reaction to the global financial crisis of 2008. It doesn't necessarily mean less spending; in fact, it might even mean the opposite. Rolls-Royce CEO Torsten Müller-Otvös, for instance, attributed his corporate 2021 sales record to buyers seeing their friends and neighbors dying of Covid and concluding that "life can be short, and you'd better live now than postpone it to a later date." But it does tend to mean less *working*.

Work, after all, is a form of delayed consumption: a way to build up money that can be used on a future date to buy desired goods and services. For most people, some baseline level of work is necessary just to be able to have a place to live and food to eat. But one of the great surprises of the twentieth century was the way in which, as millions of people started earning vastly more money than was needed to cover necessities, they didn't work less. In fact, if anything, they worked more.

In an essay entitled "Economic Possibilities for Our Grandchildren," published in 1930, the economist John Maynard Keynes prophetically and accurately predicted a huge rise in living standards over the following century—that "the standard of life in progressive countries one hundred years hence will be between four and eight times as high as it is to-day."[3] He was right on the nose: US per capita GDP in 1930 was $8,200, as measured in 2012 dollars; by 2021 it had risen sevenfold to $59,000.

Where Keynes was wrong was in the effect all that wealth would have on the workweek. "For many ages to come the old Adam will be so strong in us that everybody will need to do some work if he is to be contented," he wrote—but then he added that "three hours a day is quite enough to satisfy the old Adam in most of us!" In other words, if you're seven times richer than you were before, you will almost certainly have ended up cutting your daily hours at least in half, if not more.

That turned out to be almost exactly wrong: Not only has the workweek stubbornly refused to shrink, but it has actually gotten *longer* for the highest earners. Senior bankers in Keynes's day, for instance, used to work on the famous "3–6–3" model: borrow at 3 percent, lend at 6 percent, leave at 3 o'clock. They made a very good income and they also had plenty of time for themselves. Today they're almost always on, worrying about markets in foreign time zones and working extremely long days, sometimes seven days a week.

One of the problems is that the way our economy has evolved, it's surprisingly difficult to make half as much money doing half as much work. If your boss offers you a raise from $150,000 per year to $175,000 per year, it's not easy to turn that into a deal where you're paid $140,000 per year but only work four days a week—partly because so many jobs barely have hours at all, and just expect the employee to be available to do whatever is needed whenever it needs to be done.

The pandemic, it turns out, was a fantastic way to reset those kind of expectations, at least in the US, and to open up a new range of possibilities. At the most obvious level, it reminded people that life is short and that they don't necessarily want to spend their prime years chained to a virtual desk. There are countries to explore, projects to dive into, dreams to chase; those things have to get prioritized somehow. It also, out of necessity, revealed a whole new universe of work that previously seemed entirely out of reach. If you can work from home, after all, you can work from anywhere.

This wasn't an obvious or necessary consequence of the pandemic, and it isn't true of other countries. The dream of working from anywhere exists more in theory than in reality, for instance: Most American companies are deeply uncomfortable with the idea of employees working from foreign countries and having the protection of, say, French employment laws. And in continental Europe, governments generally funneled money to workers via their employers, rather than opting for the direct transfers we saw in the US. The result was many fewer layoffs, most people remaining in the same job they had all along, much less turnover, and much lower quit rates. By the time most adults were vaccinated and life started going back to normal, the French workforce had actually expanded, even as the number of workers in America had declined dramatically.

Historically, when someone changed jobs, they would tend to talk a lot about how excited they were, and how passionate they were about—well, you know, you've heard it all before. The one thing no one ever said was that they took their job because it paid so well, even though that was normally the reason.

During the pandemic, the reasons people gave as to why they were taking jobs became, much more often, the actual reason why people would take jobs. Feeling good about what you do for a living started to seem a lot more important, especially when almost all jobs paid pretty well. Recruiters had to become storytellers, rather than just dollar signs—and one of the main stories they found themselves telling was the one in which the employer values diversity and difference and encourages employees to work the way they work best, rather than the way some manager would ideally like them to work.

None of these stories are 100 percent veracious, but even just telling them, over and over again, both to external recruits and in internal meetings, helps to change the way managers think. It might be naive to suppose that the corporate world became kinder and gentler overnight, but, at the margin, it might also be true.

To bring it back to risk, there has been a realization among a lot of workers, especially those who are newer to the workforce and who haven't internalized its pathologies, that the careerist path, where a person is defined by their occupation and their success within that occupation, is itself highly risky. Not only because of the risk that success will never come—although it's undeniable that winning at any job is in large part a matter of luck and being in the right place at the right time—but that your job will devour your prime years, tie you down to a resented schedule, maybe even force you to live in cramped conditions in an overpriced city you don't particularly like very much. As the English singer/songwriter Morrissey famously put it in the song "Heaven Knows I'm Miserable Now": "In my life, why do I give valuable time / To people who don't care if I live or die?"

Employers have been shunting those kind of hedonic risks onto their employees for decades, if not centuries. But the pandemic opened a glimpse of an alternative basis for the relationship between boss and worker—one involving more freedom, more flexibility, and ultimately less risk of disappointment and resentment among the workers.

Many bosses are very suspicious of such arrangements, quite possibly for good reason (and quite possibly for bad reasons, too). That said, as a new compact starts to emerge regardless, driven more by bottom-up demands than by top-down strategy, it carries with it the potential to turbocharge the economy by significantly expanding the workforce.

One of my all-time favorite economic papers came out in 2007, written by Nobel economics laureate Joe Stiglitz along with Shahe Emran of George Washington University and Mahbub Morshed of Southern Illinois University Carbondale.[4] The trio set out to ask why microloans could be so good at creating economic value even when they were issued at extremely high interest rates. After all, they noted, "How can micro activities such as backyard chicken raising yield more than 50–60 percent rate of return"—the amount they'd have to return in order for the borrowers to make a profit after paying back the interest on their loans—"when the returns to large scale vertically integrated poultry farms are in the range of 20–30 percent?"

Their answer: The loans brought women into the workforce who would otherwise not have had jobs at all. In Ghana in 1998, less than 1 percent of women were in formal employment; in 2000 in Côte d'Ivoire, only 5.6 percent of women did any work as employees. Obviously, such a society has a highly imperfect labor market, one where, for any number of reasons, an overwhelming majority of women generally find it impossible to turn their labor into money at all—until they find a microlender.

The existence of microlenders effectively brings women into the paid workforce. If you lend money to someone already earning an income, then either they need the money for some form of personal spending, or else they want to invest it in order to *increase* their income. A high interest rate can easily eclipse any increase in income that results, making such loans unattractive to workers.

For people without a paid job, however, the calculus is very different: A microloan—perhaps to buy some backyard chickens, or a sewing machine, or some other means of making money—instantly catapults the borrower into the ranks of the paid. So long as you can pay the loan back out of your income, you're ahead of the game, since beforehand your income was zero.

The economic upside of a friendlier attitude toward workers in general, and women in particular, would similarly lie in a much-expanded workforce. In America, as I write this in early 2022, unemployment is extremely low, below 4 percent, but so is the proportion of working-age people who are actually in the labor force. The labor force participation rate, as it's known, is less than 62 percent. Before the pandemic, the last time it was that low was in 1976, when women were still expected to stay at home rather than have a job.

Breaking it down by sex, the labor force participation rate for men is around 68 percent, down from levels well above 85 percent in the 1950s. And the rate for women is lower still, around 56 percent. To put that in hard numbers, there are about 160 million people in the American labor force, out of a pool of about 230 million potential workers. Some 70 million adults are not working—a number that rose by many millions during the pandemic, in an unprecedented surge of voluntary unemployment.

On one level, those millions of non-workers are a sign of precisely the rise in wealth that Keynes foresaw. They are rich enough to be able to not work, and so they don't. But these are people who don't even work Keynes's three hours a day—and many of them are both college-educated and financially insecure. It's easy to imagine that if they *could* find work, in ways that better fit into their other obligations, then they would.

The professional flexibilities that started to become mainstream during the pandemic, then, hold out one of the dreams of the phoenix economy. Poor women in Bangladesh needed little more than a $50 loan to get them into the labor force; Americans are going to need more than that. But now at least it's possible to see a mechanism whereby the labor force participation rate might stop going down and start going up again—something that would benefit everybody, whether they're working or not.

Were that to happen, it really would emerge from ashes: Covid took more people out of the workforce than even the Great Recession of 2008. Most of them left for public or private health reasons, rather than because they were fired: One way or another, the pandemic upended their lives to a degree that a job was no longer feasible. Once the health emergency is over, what will remain is a system designed—on the fly, and imperfectly, but designed all the same—to be able to accommodate the most disruptive professional event since World War II.

Broadly, that system worked vastly better than most observers anticipated at the outset of the pandemic. If it can cope with Covid, it should certainly be able to cope with idiosyncratic requests and requirements from existing and potential new employees—workers who no longer want to orchestrate almost every aspect of their lives around the needs of their employer. It's possible that will be bad for profits—but it's equally possible that the massive expansion of the potential workforce, especially during a time of subdued immigration, will create enormous, unexpected value.

The pandemic saw the US economy broken and rebuilt in record time. The 1970s TV series *The Six Million Dollar Man* was based on the conceit that thanks to bionic technology, a barely alive astronaut, Steve Austin, could be rebuilt to be "better than he was before. Better . . . stronger . . . faster." Fifty years on, our digital technology came to the rescue of an economy that had all but flatlined in March 2020. Companies running in ways that would have been familiar to the salarymen of the seventies were radically rebuilt, astonishingly quickly, to accommodate a diverse and remote workforce.

It's not easy for either companies or workers to adapt to such radical change. There will be teething pains. But there can't be much doubt that, as we saw in Chapter 2, the shock of the pandemic has put both sides on a stronger footing when it comes to their future productive potential. Over the coming decades, the US will have an advantage over countries that did a better job of keeping their pre-pandemic systems in place. There was short-term pain and disruption—not to mention an objectively unacceptable level of sheer mortality—but out of the ashes of that disruption, a digital-era phoenix will rise.

11

The Armies of the Public Fisc

ON A BALMY Chicago afternoon in November 2002, Ben Bernanke stood up to give a speech.[1] Bernanke had recently stepped down as chairman of the Princeton economics department to take a new job as a member of the board of governors of the Federal Reserve. He was not yet famous—he wouldn't become Fed chair until 2006—but among economists he was widely respected not only as an economist but specifically as an economic historian. His work on the history of the Great Depression would end up winning him the Nobel Prize in 2022.

Bernanke's job was to welcome back to Chicago its most famous economist—the man who had set the stage for half a century and more of first-rate hard-nosed economics. The occasion was Milton Friedman's ninetieth birthday, and not only did Friedman make the journey to the Windy City from his retirement home in California, but he was also joined there by his co-author Anna Schwartz, who was about to turn eighty-seven.

Friedman and Schwartz, like Bernanke, were economic historians. They started work on their 860-page magnum opus, *A Monetary History of the United States, 1867–1960*, in the late 1940s, ultimately publishing it in 1963. Its most famous and important chapter, on what they called the "Great Contraction," was a detailed historical argument that the Depression wasn't just an event that happened, the economic equivalent of an earthquake or a meteor from outer space. Instead it was *caused*—and specifically it was caused by bad monetary policy, which was largely the result of a lack of leadership at the central bank.

Bernanke's speech was mostly a recap of the arguments first made by Friedman and Schwartz some forty years earlier—what Bernanke called "the leading and most persuasive explanation of the worst economic disaster in American history." But it was also an institutional mea culpa, on behalf of the Federal Reserve. After New York Fed president Benjamin Strong died in 1928, said Bernanke, "the leadership vacuum and the generally low level of central banking expertise in the Federal Reserve System was a major problem that led to excessive passivity and many poor decisions."

Bernanke ended his speech with a promise: "Let me end my talk by abusing slightly my status as an official representative of the Federal Reserve. I would like to say to Milton and Anna: Regarding the Great Depression. You're right, we did it. We're very sorry. But thanks to you, we won't do it again."

During the global financial crisis, Bernanke's words were often thrown back scornfully in his face. Far from preventing a financial meltdown, Bernanke found himself fighting one. But this time around, the economic historian had history to learn from.

Economic firefighters, just like the people in charge of your local fire truck, have one main tool at their disposal—liquidity. ("Liquidity," in finance, doesn't refer to something wet; it refers to raw dollars, easily accessible money.) You aim it at the problem, and unleash as much of it as you can, until the crisis is over. That's what the Fed didn't do during the Great Depression, and it's what Bernanke's

Fed did do—in concert with all the world's other major central banks and finance ministries—in 2008.

The problem was that Bernanke wasn't just in charge of pointing his firehose of liquidity at the source of the problem, which in 2008–9 was primarily the banks. It was also that he had to find all that liquidity in the first place—to drill the wells, if I may stretch the metaphor probably a bit too far.

Bernanke found it easy to cut interest rates to zero, but monetary policy was still too tight at that point—there still wasn't enough cash in the system. For a host of conceptual and institutional reasons, it's very hard to cut interest rates below zero. Eventually, the Fed embarked on a program that it called "quantitative easing," or QE. Rather than just lend money to banks virtually interest-free, the Fed also started buying up huge amounts of their Treasury bond holdings for cash. The idea was to get more cash into the banking system—and thereby into the economy as a whole—rather than watch some of the country's biggest economic actors just sit on billions of dollars' worth of Treasury bonds.

It worked, to an extent—as did the forced recapitalization of all America's biggest banks with $250 billion of Treasury funds. But it was also clearly insufficient: The recovery from the crisis of 2008 was painfully slow, thanks mainly to Congress being stingy. The Fed did what it could, but Bernanke would beg Congress to spend more to stimulate the economy—as did his successor, Janet Yellen—to little if any avail.

The tightfistedness continued into the 2016 election, where Donald Trump campaigned on paying down the $19 trillion national debt. And while the debt predictably went up rather than down following Trump's $2 trillion corporate tax cut in 2017, the general reluctance to spend money remained. With Republicans controlling the White House and both houses of Congress, the ideal of small government remained, and was arguably stronger than ever.

In September 2018, for instance, I appeared as a guest on Stuart Varney's Fox Business show.[2] I was there to talk about potential government regulation of social media companies, but the segment before me featured Arkansas governor turned Fox pundit Mike Huckabee railing in an uninformed manner against the idea of a universal basic income. Something possessed me to try to correct, on air, his assertion that a guaranteed income made people less likely to find gainful employment. (The empirical evidence strongly shows that the opposite is true—that if you have the basic life stability afforded by a guaranteed income, then that makes it significantly *more* likely that you will be able find and keep a job.)

Varney, a reliable Republican mouthpiece, immediately pushed back, accusing me of being a socialist and worse. "The best way to get people out of poverty is to give them money," I said, and when Varney said that his viewers were not going to be happy about what I was saying, I replied that "It's free money. Who doesn't like free money?"

Varney's answer was clear: "The people handing it out. People like me." Nevertheless, within eighteen months, Trump supporters like Varney were enthusiastically cheering one of the largest unconditional cash transfers in the history of the planet—the first round of $1,400 stimulus checks to the vast majority of American adults.

The Trump stimulus was the result of the government finally listening to what economists and the Fed had been saying for years, which is that there are limits to what monetary policy can do in the face of a crisis. While central banks can make it easier for businesses to borrow money, that takes a long time to show up in individuals seeing greater financial security, higher wages, or more jobs. Indeed, it might never show up there at all. (When a business borrows money, it's entirely possible that it will spend all the proceeds just buying back its own stock.)

Direct government spending, on the other hand, has a more immediate effect on the economy. If you pay a contractor $1 billion to build a tunnel, that contractor will spend a large proportion of that money, directly or indirectly, on wages. Better yet, those blue-collar wages, going to individuals who tend to spend their entire paycheck, will go straight back into the economy rather than being turned into financial assets.

Even so, high-profile discretionary government spending is indirect. Government funds go to a contractor who pays a subcontractor who buys equipment from a retailer that sources from a manufacturer that pays workers to make the item in question. That's all good for business and the economy, but if the stated purpose is to help the workers, it does seem rather circuitous. Why not instead just give Americans money directly?

That's what the Red Cross started to do, to its credit, around the time I visited Rose City, Texas, in the fall of 2017. I was there to make a podcast documentary on Give Directly, a charity predicated on the proposition that the most effective use of charitable funds is nearly always to just give no-strings-attached cash to the people you're trying to help. They know what they need better than you do, after all.

Give Directly was in Rose City, a small town near the Louisiana border, after it was devastated by Hurricane Harvey. The charity was founded to help the poorest and neediest people in the world, and to this day gives away most of its money in Kenya, Uganda, and other desperately poor countries. But the principle of cash transfers works anywhere, and so, armed with $2.4 million from the Laura and John Arnold Foundation, it handed out cash to 1,594 of some of the neediest families I've ever met in America. That's $1,500 each—enough to help them get back on their feet, or at least to shore up a damaged house or buy some clothes and food.

The money turned out to be extremely helpful to the families, and a lot of my reporting trip went exactly the way you'd expect it to go. I really did see piles of useless donated clothes gathering dust in the church, for instance, and interviewed a local Texas bigwig making ill-informed (and empirically untrue) noises about how if you give poor people money they just spend it on lottery tickets and liquor.

But there was also something else going on in the background, which was that the Red Cross was giving out $400 in cash to pretty much everybody in the affected area—not just the hundreds of families helped by Give Directly, but almost half a million more.

I'm a longtime critic of the Red Cross, which covered itself in whatever the opposite of glory was after Hurricane Sandy hit the New York area in 2012. The charity was largely invisible, seemed to care more about PR than about helping the victims of the tragedy, and acted as though it had no idea how to organize thousands of volunteers and over $100 million in donations.

Five years later, however, things were very different. Rather than try to find food and clothes, the Red Cross spent most of its efforts just handing out cash. That's not trivial. People will go to great lengths to get free money, as the astonishing amount of unemployment fraud in 2020 proves. A system of unconditional cash transfers needs to be strict enough to prevent large amounts of fraud and double-dipping, while also being flexible enough to give money to the people who need it most—those who have lost everything, including proof of residence and identity.

Unsurprisingly, given the general chaos of the situation and the fact that the Red Cross was new to this game, it wasn't hard to find edge cases where things didn't go well. Some people managed to get paid twice, or more; others never got paid at all; and there were surely cases where Red Cross volunteers managed to find ways to skim off some of the cash for themselves. Nevertheless, the big picture was that the $400 checks were remarkably successful—a clear improvement over the *status quo ante*, which was for the Red Cross to raise money, spend that money on stuff it thought people would need (blankets, food, that kind of thing), and then go out into the field to distribute all that stuff. Whatever inefficiencies there might be in the cash-transfer program, they paled in comparison to the inefficiencies that had existed previously. And so the American Red Cross has continued to embrace cash transfers ever since.

When the pandemic hit, then, and the government was faced with an urgent need to get cash out the door to save the economy, two things were clear: that the Fed couldn't do it on its own, and that no-questions-asked cash transfers were by far the simplest and most effective way for Congress to mobilize resources. Out went some $300 billion in $1,400 stimulus checks—the famous "stimmies" that were subsequently credited (or blamed) for everything from fireworks sales to weird action in GameStop stock. Naturally, there was even more money for large corporations and small businesses, but the precedent being set was clear enough and popular enough that two more subsequent rounds of stimulus both repeated the exercise, to general popular acclaim.

Americans across the political spectrum loved the stimulus checks for exactly the reason that I had given Varney—everybody likes free money. What's more, Varney's complaint that he was paying for it was clearly untrue: Taxes weren't going up, and everything was being funded by borrowing, much of it from the Fed.

Cash transfers are in many ways a conservative policy—the politician who first seriously proposed a universal basic income was none other than Richard Nixon, and Milton Friedman, the conservative economist lauded by Bernanke, proposed what he called a "negative income tax" that would amount to much the same thing. Cash can be seen as deeply libertarian, compared to just about any other form of public spending. At heart, it's government getting out of the way and giving maximal freedom to the citizenry. Look at what happened when Republican politicians opposed the final round of Covid stimulus at the beginning of 2021, under President Biden: While they opposed the bill in general, they didn't focus their opposition on the universal checks.

In other words: During a period of unprecedented political polarization, a period when the two US political parties could agree on essentially nothing, they both managed to alight upon the same— correct—solution to the enormous problem facing them, which was that the pandemic had precipitated a major economic crisis. What's more, that solution was simplicity itself: Give people money.

Much of that money came in the form of stimulus checks; another huge chunk came in the form of loans to small businesses that would be fully forgiven (and therefore effectively turned into grants) if the businesses kept their employees on payroll instead of laying them off.

That solution had not been considered politically feasible back in 2009, just as it was considered politically infeasible in Europe and most of the rest of the world in 2020. Europe had a lot of welfare-state stabilizers that kicked in and kept employees on payroll even when they weren't working—that's why its economy didn't collapse. But its failure to attack the crisis with trillions of euros of fiscal stimulus also explains why the European economy started growing again in a much more faltering way than the American V-shaped recovery.

The policy of giving out money to almost everybody in the country would seem to violate the principle that there's no such thing as a free lunch: There's something *too easy* about it. But it worked. America started growing both earlier and more quickly than the more fiscally conservative European Union. And while not all countries have the luxury of being able to just spend as much as they want to get out of an economic crisis, a surprisingly large number of countries *do* have that luxury, including China, Canada,

Japan, Australia, the UK, and every member of the eurozone. The constraints aren't economic, they're political and conceptual—and, of course, historical.

What central banks did in 2009 was unprecedented, and therefore caused a lot of concern about possible unintended consequences, especially with regard to inflation. Eleven years later, when all the inflation fears of 2009 had proved unfounded in multiple different countries, it was much easier to pull out the same playbook when faced with a potentially even greater crisis. The second time around is always easier—too easy, say the people pointing to the inflation that genuinely did start taking hold toward the end of 2021, and then accelerated into 2022.

As with monetary policy, so with fiscal policy. In 2009, governments spent money to combat the crisis—but not enough. In 2020, the US broke new ground in terms of how much money it was willing to spend, and once again the fact of unprecedented action caused a large amount of worry about potential unintended consequences, principally consumer price inflation. Still, the big picture is that the government spending clearly worked; if anything it worked even better than anybody had dared to hope.

Broadly, the economic crises of both 2008 and 2020 took the form that there wasn't enough money wending its way around the economy. In 2020, unlike in 2008, the government solved that problem by adding trillions of dollars to the economy. The result was that the economy bounced back so quickly that neither supply chains nor the labor market was entirely able to absorb the resulting surge in demand, especially demand for goods rather than services. A new problem—inflation—therefore appeared, but compared to a devastating recession deeper than anything seen in living memory, it was definitely the lesser of two evils.

I should note here for anybody born after 1990 or so that recessions are not, in and of themselves, particularly terrifying things. There's a natural business cycle; the economy waxes and wanes. So long as it waxes more than it wanes, it grows over the long term— two steps forward, one step back, that kind of thing.

The job of central bankers like Ben Bernanke is to minimize the number and size of recessions—of steps back—and to keep the forward momentum going as much as possible. As Alan Greenspan famously put it in a 2011 op-ed, the free-market system overseen by modern independent central banks has done a pretty good job of creating a stable economy—"With notably rare exceptions (2008, for example)."[3] Sadly, what that has meant in practice is that small recessions are relatively rare, and massive, potentially catastrophic recessions—2008, 2020—loom in our memory.

Small recessions, however, like the one the US experienced in 2001, haven't gone away. There *will* be more of them, and while that's regrettable, it's also okay. No one has worked out how to abolish the business cycle entirely. But if and when recessions do arrive, it's imperative that they don't precipitate a crisis.

The hopeful lesson here for the future is that from now on it will be a lot easier for governments, both in the US and elsewhere, to pull the fiscal trigger and give people enough money not only to be able to weather an incipient crisis, but also to start recovering from it at maximum speed.

When Ben Bernanke gave his speech to Milton Friedman in 2002, he recognized that economists knew in theory what to do in the event of a crisis; he just didn't know how hard it would be to do that in practice. After he'd actually done it once, it became much easier to do a second time. Similarly, after Treasury secretary Steven Mnuchin gave out hundreds of billions of dollars in stimulus checks in 2020, it was relatively trivial for Treasury secretary Janet Yellen to do the same thing in 2021. We have the technology now, and we know how to use it. Which means that economically speaking, it's rational to reduce our fear of economic shocks.

Shocks can and will still happen. But I take solace from Hollywood, and specifically from action-movie sequels like the ones Mnuchin used to finance. (Between 2014 and 2017, Mnuchin racked up an impressive forty-four separate producer credits, including installments in franchises such as *Batman*, *Wonder Woman*, *Mad Max*, and *The Lego Movie*.)

In the original movie, the central banker, faced with an overwhelming financial crisis, rushes to his trusty ammo cabinet and starts firing everything he's got, cutting interest rates all the way to zero. But that's not enough, the crisis just keeps on getting bigger. So our hero is forced to invent new weaponry—unlimited international swap lines, quantitative easing, that kind of thing. He fights as hard and as nobly as he can, but it's clear he's losing both the battle and the war. The entire planet is about to be lost . . . until, at the last minute, the Armies of the Public Fisc begin to stir.

This awesome force had lain dormant for decades, lulled into an otiose torpor by well-meaning but misguided commanders. But they weren't dead. In the action-hero version of the financial-crisis movie, the Fiscal Armies turn out to be able to provide just the support the central banker needed in order to prevent catastrophe. At the end of the first movie the good guys are deeply wounded but still standing, and justifiably believe that they have successfully saved the planet. Surveying the wreckage around them, the unemployed, the evicted homeowners, the rise of populist rabble-rousing, they can hardly claim an unmitigated victory. But they did save the global financial system, and the outcome was vastly better than it might have been.

Then the sequel arrives. As in all sequels, the enemy is bigger and scarier the second time around, much less likely to be vanquished by the means we saw in part one. Of course our central banker hero does the standard stuff to try to support the economy in the face of a global pandemic—interest rates get slashed to zero almost immediately. And the new weapons like QE get brought out, too, and once again it's clear that they won't be remotely sufficient.

So the sequel turns out to be much more focused on the Fiscal Armies. This time, it's their turn to show what they're capable of. And just as in most superhero movies, it turns out that when they really want something, they end up proving themselves to be stronger and more powerful than anybody could have imagined. Fiscal policy really did save the day in the US, and the lack of it caused enormous economic problems in Europe—not to mention in all the countries that aren't able to borrow money in their own currency at zero interest rates. The man in charge of fiscal policy during all of 2020 deserves no little praise. Take a bow, Steven Mnuchin, movie producer and latter-day action hero.

Now that we've lived through the sequel, economic crises are significantly less terrifying than they were before the pandemic hit. The lingering memory of the Great Depression made us worry, on some level, that such a thing might happen again. The eggheads like Ben Bernanke promised that it wouldn't, but, well, they were economists, and only fools believe economists. Then the financial crisis arrived, and was terrifying—and *then* the pandemic hit, and was universally understood to be even worse than the financial crisis.

We've been tested, in other words, and we've found within ourselves the ability to fight off economic crises, mostly just through giving people money. There will be future economic crises, of course, and those will be bad. But we know now how to fight them: We have new and awesome skills.

In the financial crisis of 2008–9, respected economists like Mohamed El-Erian, then a senior executive at PIMCO, were telling family members to go straight to ATMs and withdraw the maximum amount of cash allowable, for fear that there would be some kind of bank holiday and only paper cash would be accepted. In 2020, economists like Nouriel Roubini started warning of a "Greater Depression"—an economic collapse even bigger than the Great Depression of the 1930s. In both cases, some level of fear was rational: After all, the experience of the Depression was that policymakers can get things disastrously wrong.

It turns out, however, that Bernanke was pretty much correct. If you understood him to mean that there would never again be another financial crisis or national economic emergency, then he was clearly wrong. But that wasn't what he meant. Instead, he was saying that central banks in general, and the Federal Reserve in particular, would never fuck things up like the Fed did in the 1930s—that they now have the knowledge necessary to make things better, rather than make things worse. And that's exactly what the Fed did in 2008 and 2020: step in and do everything in its power to minimize the pain of the crisis.

The Fed is still fallible. Its actions were partially responsible for the 2008 crisis in the first place, and while it can't be blamed for the pandemic, it can be credibly accused of being too late to its core job of taming the inflation that arrived in the back half of 2021. Economic cycles, and even economic crises, will always be with us; some of them will be the fault of central bankers. What's new is the existence of a tried-and-tested set of crisis-fighting weapons, which in 2020 proved astonishingly powerful.

Every country would rather have such weapons than not have them. Those without access to the first world's economic armory suffered unconscionably during the pandemic, unable to conjure, seemingly out of nowhere, the ability to spend their way to health—via the purchase of vaccines and therapeutics—and also to economic recovery.

On the other hand, now that we know how powerful our weapons are, we risk complacency in the face of manifest political incompetence. Next time there's an economic crisis, or what economists like to call an "exogenous shock"—and there *will* be a next time—we're less likely to see the kind of Wile E. Coyote cliff-dive that we saw global stock markets take in March 2020. To put it in superhero-movie terms, that sort of panic is based on fear that the enemy threatening the world is just too big, too powerful, too unstoppable—that there's nothing the world can do to fight it.

Now we know there *is* something the world can do to fight almost any conceivable adversary, markets will expect the superheroes to cape up and do their job. That's a reasonable assumption, in the case of central banks, but it's *not* a reasonable assumption in the case of the Fiscal Armies, which are commanded by fickle politicians. In fact, as we saw in both 2008 and 2020, politicians tend to be *extremely* reluctant to unleash broad fiscal action, and often have to be prodded into action by a plunging stock market. To put it another way: So long as the market expects the rescue to come, the rescue won't come.

This is a very weird dynamic, where boring and sober central bankers—arguably the grayest profession in the world—are willing and able to jump into immediate action. Meanwhile, politicians, who by their nature should love to bestow pork upon their grateful constituents, are strangely squeamish about handing out money to voters. It's the reverse of the situation in the 1970s and 1980s, where the job of central bankers was to counteract the free-spending tendencies of the government. It's even the reverse of the situation in the 1990s, when it was the Treasury market "bond vigilantes," rather than the central bank directly, that would punish the government for exceeding the acceptable bounds of profligacy.

Market participants know that some future shock will come—that's a known known. They also have a much better idea of what they like to call the "central bank reaction function"—which is to say, they have a high degree of certainty that in the event of such a shock, they know how central banks around the world are going to react.

That degree of knowledge is new: Central bankers have tradition-
ally cultivated a Delphic mystique, largely because they wanted to be
able to keep their options open. But jettisoning that mystique, and
making it clear what they will do in various possible futures, was part
of their crisis-fighting toolkit. (They called it "forward guidance,"
and it was designed to prevent market participants from worrying
that a rate hike could be just around the corner.)

The known unknown is lawmakers' reaction function. Markets
know that governments *can* act with speed and force to avert a crisis:
They saw it happen in 2020. But was that a unique and special case?
After all, lots of rich governments *didn't* react that way: The US was
something of an outlier in that regard and took much of the burden
of kickstarting the global recovery onto itself.

It's possible that the 2020 fiscal response was possible only because the US was in the very rare position of having a Republican
president who had broad and deep support within his own party,
who also had no compunctions about spending trillions of dollars if
he thought it would help his popularity, and who could count on the
opposition party to vote for his bill.

Democrats can normally count on steadfast Republican opposition
to any of their spending plans, and also sport an influential wing of
fiscal conservatives who are willing to oppose anything they feel might
be "too much," meaning that a Democratic president's stimulus plans
will often get scaled back to appease the party's fiscal hawks. From the
Clinton administration onward, the Democratic Party could make a
strong claim to being the party of fiscal responsibility, casting itself in
a flattering light compared to Republicans who were happy to squander trillions on wars and tax cuts. Many Democrats to this day remain
proud that Clinton was the only president since 1969 to balance the
federal budget—an achievement greatly admired in a few elite corners
of Washington and New York City, if almost nowhere else.

Opposition to large-scale stimulus from a small group of centrist Democrats wouldn't matter much if there were a chance of support from less fiscally constrained Republicans, but there really isn't. Republicans are extremely disciplined about opposing almost everything that any Democratic White House proposes. Even under most Republican presidencies, including the George W. Bush administration that found itself facing the 2008 financial crisis, the right wing of the Republican Party can be counted on to oppose large-scale expenditures, at least when they're not war related. (Hence the indelible memory of Bush's Treasury secretary, Hank Paulson, getting down on one knee to beg the leader of the House Democrats, Nancy Pelosi, to back his $700 billion economic rescue plan, after the Republicans had signally failed to do so.)

There's a case to be made that cash transfers, as practiced by the Red Cross and Donald Trump, are well aligned with small-government Republican values. After all, it doesn't take that much bureaucracy to write a check. In practice, however, "giving away free money" is anathema to nearly all Republicans, whether that money comes from taxes or from borrowing, which means that it's still going to be hard for any Republican president not named Trump to propose it at scale.

The next crisis, then, might well resemble one of those superhero movies that begins with the lead character having sworn off all heroic deeds, devoted to living a quiet life somewhere in the countryside. Bombs explode, cities fall, and the reaction is simply a shrug—the world can't count on one person to come to its rescue every time. In the movies, that person always ends up saving the planet. But next time the script won't have been greenlit by Steve Mnuchin. If the House Republicans have their way, under just about any president not named Trump, the all-conquering fiscal arsenal might well remain unused, and the movie could turn from action-adventure to tragedy very quickly.

12

Consider the Lobster Roll

ONE OF THE great shocks of the early 2020s was the return of a fearsome societal scourge that the oldest inhabitants of western countries remembered with great foreboding, even as those of us from younger generations knew it only secondhand. Infectious disease was suddenly something that everybody knew and cared about—and then, equally unexpectedly, so was inflation.

It took until 2022 for inflation to arrive, and when it did, there was no shortage of finger-pointing in terms of where the blame for it should be apportioned. Three main villains were identified: supply-chain issues precipitated by the pandemic; monetary issues stemming from fiscal policy designed to counteract the economic effects of the pandemic; and Russia's invasion of Ukraine. To those I'd add a fourth: structural changes to the economy, caused by the effect the pandemic had on how people live.

Of the two biggest direct contributors to headline inflation, one was clearly related to the spike in energy prices following the Ukraine invasion. Oil and gas markets spiked alarmingly, especially in Europe but also globally. That fed not only into obvious prices like gasoline and heating oil, and raised the jet-fuel component of airline tickets, but also contributed to food-price inflation as well. It's worth remembering: Most food we buy is grown using industrial fertilizers that are manufactured using the Haber-Bosch process for converting energy into plant-friendly fixed nitrogen.

The second major inflation component was housing, driven by the pandemic-induced need for extra space, and especially the way that homes needed to expand to encompass workspaces. When your rent is soaring at the same time that gas and food prices are going up, that feels miserable, even for people lucky enough to be able to see their paycheck growing at the same pace. Higher pay should mean you can afford more stuff, rather than just feeling as though you're running to stand still.

Then again, higher pay was a significant part of the reason that prices were rising in the first place, especially in the services sector. When the inflation numbers first started reaching alarming levels, in early 2022, food-at-home and energy costs were what I thought of as "bad inflation"—quotidian necessities whose fast-rising prices just made life more expensive for everyone, and especially for suburban and exurban Americans with large homes to cool, large families to feed, and long distances to drive to get that food. On the other hand, when restaurant prices went up, that in my mind was "good inflation"—a sign that service-industry workers at the bottom of the wage scale, especially kitchen workers, were demanding and receiving higher pay, which in turn was being reflected in higher prices.

The Great Resignation hit the lowest-paid jobs the hardest, and restaurants found themselves competing with each other for a limited supply of workers. There was no shortage of people wanting to free themselves from their kitchens and go out for a meal; instead there was just a shortage of service-industry workers willing to return to unpleasant, badly paid jobs they hadn't much enjoyed before the pandemic. Many restaurants were forced to reduce the number of days or hours they were open; with rents not coming down, that just increased the amount of money per meal that had to go to paying the landlord.

In general, rising prices are capitalism's preferred way of reducing demand for something that is in short supply. My beloved lobster roll, the food of the summer in New England and beyond, is a good example: It rises in price when lobster prices rise, but in 2022 it rose in price even when lobster prices were down. My first theory was that rising lobster-roll prices were, like restaurant meals broadly, a function of higher labor costs, but after talking to Steve Kingston, the owner of the Clam Shack in Kennebunkport, I changed my mind on that.

Kingston's seasonal workers come into the country on J1 visas— they're foreign students, from countries like Kosovo, Albania, or Mongolia, getting US work experience for the summer before returning to continue their studies. Because Kingston has been hiring J1 workers for twenty years, he's adept at navigating the system and can generally get the workers he wants at a price he's willing to pay. (In this case: $12.75 per hour, rising to $19.50 per hour for "all the overtime they can handle," which often works out to seventy to eighty hours per week in total, bringing seasonal earnings to as much as $28,000.) His workers boil and crack open more than a thousand pounds of lobster every day, extracting the meat not only for lobster rolls on-site in Maine but also for a fast-growing mail-order business.

Kingston's mail-order business was turbocharged during the pandemic by one of the fastest-growing businesses in America, a high-end delivery company called Goldbelly. When people couldn't go out to eat, restaurants turned to Goldbelly to start sending out high-quality branded meals designed to be easily prepared at home, at roughly the same price they would pay in person. (As someone who's tried the Clam Shack's eat-at-home lobster rolls, I can *highly* recommend them.)

Goldbelly's business boomed during the pandemic: Food and alcohol were the two luxuries still accessible to people stuck at home, and people were willing to pay very high prices for convenience and reliability. My favorite downtown French bistro, for instance, Raoul's, put together a burger kit at $115 and a steak au poivre kit for $205, and rapidly sold out both. The Clam Shack's lobster roll kits were priced at $125 for four rolls—a business well worth cultivating, given that the sticker price for four rolls at the restaurant itself was slightly lower, at $120.

Kingston's business was boosted even further when the Great Resignation caused other restaurants in town to close on Mondays and Tuesdays—causing the Clam Shack's revenues on those nights to be some 25 percent higher than even on the busiest Saturdays. In other words, Kingston was working flat out, selling every lobster he could boil in freshly drawn seawater.

When that happens, a business is almost forced to raise its prices. Such an action can feel a bit like price-gouging or profiteering if the costs of labor and materials haven't risen. But the Clam Shack's customers don't just want delicious seafood, they also want reliability, and the knowledge that if they make the drive down the coast, there will be a delicious lobster roll waiting for them, rather than a sign saying "sorry, sold out, try coming back tomorrow."

In a capacity-constrained world, the only way to ensure that kind of reliability is via the price mechanism. First you maximize supply, and make sure you're creating as much of your product as you possibly can. But then you have to control demand, and the only way to do that is to raise the price enough that some people would rather eat something else. Kingston, for instance, does sell cooked lobster meat, but he makes sure to charge $5 more per pound than his local competitors—to make a point about quality, but also to ensure that the most price-sensitive shoppers go elsewhere, thereby keeping demand in check.

Modern commerce often outsources price-setting to algorithms that occasionally go haywire. Nearly all of us have had the experience of looking up an obscure book on Amazon, or trying to book a flight reasonably far in advance, and seeing some insane price, possibly thousands of dollars, that seems well beyond anything that might be considered reasonable. That's just the algorithm doing its bit when supply is low, trying to avoid selling out entirely.

That experience became a lot more common during the pandemic, especially in the hospitality industry. After being cooped up in their homes, people around the world wanted to travel again—but the global tourist infrastructure wasn't ready for them. Many hotels were still shuttered or couldn't find staff; the ones that did manage to reopen had often lost years or decades of institutional knowledge and continuity, while also trying to navigate Covid protocols that inevitably eroded many of the grace notes that epitomize any luxury experience. Such service is called "high touch" for a reason, and it's much more difficult to execute when all touch is suspicious.

And yet, in the face of declines in quality that were most obvious to the hotel operators themselves, prices just went up, and up, and up. Hotels that would normally charge $250 or $300 per night were seeing their revenue-management algorithms generating prices of $1,000, $1,500, or more.[1]

Some hotels capped the amount they charged, deciding that they simply weren't capable of living up to the expectations that accompany a four-figure nightly price tag. After all, a hotel room that feels nice at $300 can be deeply disappointing at $1,500—and hotels don't like to disappoint their customers.

With or without price caps, hotels were booking out at astonishing prices—and their customers, broadly speaking, weren't disappointed. Going *anywhere* was worth it, whatever it cost—and households were sitting on record levels of cash. Restaurants discovered the same thing: They feared that their customers would balk at massive price rises, but those fears never materialized. The prices went up, the customers paid more, the staff earned more, and a new equilibrium was found. Some customers were priced out, of course—but that was a feature, not a bug, in the context of businesses that were stretching to provide good service to those who remained.

Economists talk of "price elasticity of demand"—the amount that something can go up in price before you're no longer willing to buy it. For decades, prices were kept low not because people weren't willing to pay more, but because of competition. I might be *willing* to pay $1,000 to fly to California on JetBlue, but if Delta will fly me there for $500 I'll happily do that instead. After the pandemic hit, businesses were much less keen on competing with each other for market share simply because they didn't have the staffing to grow. Filling up airplanes wasn't the problem; finding pilots to fly them was. As a result, the mechanism keeping prices low evaporated, just as frugality more broadly was dissipating in favor of a general desire to grasp the nettle and live life as much as possible. Home Depot is selling a $299 Halloween skeleton with animatronic LED eyes? That'll sell out in hours, thank you very much—in July.

A quote from John Maynard Keynes started cropping up in many places during the pandemic: "Anything we can actually do we can afford." It's a line from a BBC radio address he gave during the Second World War, when he was talking about his plans to rebuild the country.[2] As Keynes told the story, he was talking to "an eminent architect" about his pretty grand ideas, which included giving "every substantial city of the realm the dignity of an ancient university or a European capital." Theaters, concert halls, dance halls, galleries, restaurants—all would be built from the ruins of the war.

The architect was presumably excited by all this new work—but also had one big worry. "Where's the money to come from?," he asked the great economist. Keynes simply brushed the question aside. Britain had architects; it also had bricks and steel and cement, and skilled tradesmen. So long as Britain was *able* to rebuild, it could *afford* to rebuild.

Keynes was at pains to draw a distinction "between the problem of finance for an individual and the problem for the community as a whole." It was entirely possible for a person to be able not to afford something, even if collectively the country could still afford to do it. This is one of the central insights of Keynesianism. But after 2020, the question of what counted as affordable at the household level was recalibrated in the minds of millions. A lot of middle-class Americans had more than enough savings to splurge on experiences. The question then became: Should they spend that money now, or should they continue to save it so they could spend it at some point many years in the future? The experience of living through Covid acted as a heavy thumb pressing on the "spend now" side of the scales.

It seemed as though a large chunk of America suddenly started reading Ecclesiastes, a book written long before the invention of the 401(k) plan: "So I commend the enjoyment of life, because there is nothing better for a person under the sun than to eat and drink and be glad. Then joy will accompany them in their toil all the days of the life God has given them under the sun."[3]

Sara Suvada, a Starbucks shift supervisor and barista from Michigan, told the *Wall Street Journal* that spending $5,000 on taking her husband and daughter to Disney World was money well spent, saying that "The memories are worth more than gold." Her comments were echoed by another park-goer, a twenty-nine-year-old mom from Kentucky, who had the attitude that "I can always make more money."[4]

The *WSJ* article was about the way in which Disney was making more money from its parks than ever, even with attendance down from pre-pandemic levels. The company's "yield management" algorithms were clear: Willingness to pay a lot of money was higher than ever, and it was much more profitable to have slightly fewer visitors paying a lot more per visit than it was to cultivate volume with annual passes. (Disney stopped issuing new annual passes in 2022 and would agree to renew old ones only at ever-higher prices and with ever-greater numbers of blackout dates.)

Americans have always been the world's greatest consumers, armed with a "we can afford to do this" attitude that was turbocharged in the pandemic, when money seemingly arrived effortlessly from everywhere and millions of people discovered they could afford to not work at all. Many took the opportunity of the lockdown to look back upon their lives and question the mindset that the highest priority was always to navigate a seemingly endless list of tasks that needed to be continually aced in order to avoid destitution and despair—pay for shelter, put food on the table, stay healthy, save for retirement, find a well-paying job, etc.

For these people, the pandemic was the shock to the system that allowed them to break out of the disaster-avoidance mindset, take a look at their lives, and realize that they actually had a decent amount of wealth and stability,—which meant, therefore, they had the ability, for once, to follow their passions.

That mindset is inherently inflationary. On the demand side, it reveals itself in ever-greater willingness to pay for goods and services; on the supply side, we see fewer people wanting to do the kind of jobs, especially in the service industry, that are necessary for such experiences and products to exist. More demand and less supply means higher prices—and then the expectation of higher prices in the future drives extra demand in the present, as people buy things now before they get more expensive.

Is that kind of inflation something to worry about? My general feeling is that no, it isn't. When it comes to discretionary purchases, or even people removing themselves from the workforce because they feel like it, price inflation is sometimes just a way of revealing a country's changed preferences. There was an old price equilibrium, and now there is a new one; if the new one is higher than the old one, then there will be an interim period of inflation, and that's fine.

More broadly, insofar as price inflation is a function of hourly workers getting better wages, it's the good kind of inflation, redistributing wealth from people with excess disposable income to people at the lower end of the income scale. Bad inflation, by contrast, is driven by rises in commodities: there's negative utility in driving extra revenue to murderous petrostates.

In 2022, we saw both types of inflation. But commodities cycles come and go. And if you strip out commodities and temporary supply-chain effects, the rise in consumer prices was in very large part a sign of revealed preferences and healthy optimism. You could even see, in the shadows of the consumer price index, the outlines of a phoenix rising from the ashes.

In her autobiography, Agatha Christie talks of her life as half of a middle-class couple in 1919, earning £900 per year between salary and passive income. That was nothing special—it was roughly equivalent to about $65,000 today. But they stretched to a live-in maid, at £36 per year, and even a nurse, on top, for their first child.

"Looking back, it seems to me extraordinary that we should have contemplated having both a nurse and a servant," writes Christie. "But they were considered essentials of life in those days, and were the last things we would have thought of dispensing with. To have committed the extravagance of a car, for instance, would never have entered our minds. Only the rich had cars."[5]

Of course, servants were only an essential part of life for people who weren't themselves servants. Christie's maid made about $2,600 per year, in today's money—a level of poverty, even after accounting for room and board, that has since rightly been outlawed.

Over the intervening century or so, the price of labor has gone steadily up—which is to say, average earnings have risen, along with most people's quality of life. When an American goes to Geneva or Stockholm and is shocked at restaurant prices, they're seeing what happens in a more egalitarian society that pays its bottom-tier workers a living wage.

In general, economies improve when labor-intensive services become more expensive. There are exceptions to this rule—the US healthcare system springs to mind—but in general we want to move away from a world where certain things are cheap because labor is cheap, and toward a world where labor is valued and valuable.

The US, during the pandemic, advanced more in terms of hourly wages than it had in many years beforehand. Some of those advances were eaten up by inflation—but the structural changes were profound, with the country flipping for the first time in decades from one where workers chased jobs, to one where employers chased workers. What's more, corporate profits stayed strong: There was no indication that paying higher wages was bad for stock-market earnings.

Inflation, then, while definitely unpleasant, can be seen as another one of those liminal states—something we need to get through in order to arrive at a better place. It's not always that way—there's no shortage of economic histories that feature purely destructive, rather than constructive, inflation. But consumer prices in the US rose at an annual rate of more than 9 percent in both the late 1940s and the early 1950s, and in both cases that was a sign not of economic malaise, but rather of economic vibrancy. The 2020s feel more like that than they do the 1970s, and there's no reason why the inflation of 2022 shouldn't presage a great and broad economic expansion like that seen in the 1950s and 1960s. If that happens, Covid will be able to take a chunk of the credit.

There's even a precedent: The Black Death caused working men's wages to soar in the Middle Ages. The same phenomenon, on a smaller scale, could yet transform labor economics for decades.

13

New Money

MONEY, AS A concept, is a slippery, protean beast. It's a real, physical thing, for starters: It can be folded up, inserted into envelopes, dropped into a jukebox. It's a store of value, a medium of exchange, a unit of account. It's also the flip side of debt, or credit. My favorite economics paper, by former Minnesota Federal Reserve president Narayana Kocherlakota, makes the case that money is memory—it's society's way of keeping track of who owes what to whom.[1] If you've read anything about the history of money, you might vaguely remember stories about large stones on the island of Yap being money, and those stones retaining their value and utility as money even when the boat they were on sank and the stone disappeared under the waves forever. Differences as to the nature of money lie at the heart of some of the deepest and most intractable arguments in economics—the Austrians versus the Keynesians versus the Modern Monetary Theorists, for instance.

One thing we can say for sure: The more you think about it, the harder money is to understand. That's why it lends itself so easily to late-night undergraduate bull sessions, and also why we will never see a time when utopians aren't trying to reinvent it in one way or another, whether that be through the issuance of local scrip designed to be used to buy your neighbor's turnips or whether it's by inventing complex games for computers to play, creating markets of eternal fascination to people like the Winklevoss twins.

For 99.9 percent of the population, however, money has always been simple. It's what you need to earn to pay for stuff. The more you have, the more you can buy, either now or in the future. You guys worry about the ontology of wealth; I'll worry about making rent this month.

Even during crises, that conception of money tends to hold firm. I got my start as a finance blogger thanks to my years writing about sovereign debt crises—think Mexico in 1994, Korea in 1997, Russia in 1998, Ecuador in 1999, Argentina in 2001, and so on and so forth. One of the defining features of such crises is that a country has borrowed money from private-sector creditors (think Citibank) and also directly from other countries (think France)—and then finds itself in a situation where it can't pay everybody back in full and on time. What's it supposed to do?

Creditor countries, the largest of which is often the US, are collectively referred to as the Paris Club. They have a distinctive way of thinking about this question, which they reframe like this: Bail-outs or bail-ins?

In a bail-out, the creditor countries allow the debtor countries to roll over their bilateral debts—that is, the sums they owe to other governments—and will even occasionally grant outright debt forgiveness on some portion of the monies owed. Because the amounts due to other countries thereby fall, the crisis-hit country has more ability to continue to service its private-sector debts: its bonds and loans held by the likes of BlackRock or JPMorgan Chase. The "bail-out" is therefore not only a bail-out of the debtor country; it's also a bail-out of the creditor countries' private-sector lenders. That way the crisis doesn't spread from the banking sector of the country in trouble to the banking sector of richer nations.

In a bail-in, by contrast, the creditor countries insist that whatever kind of debt forgiveness they offer has to be met by "comparable treatment" from global banks and the rest of the private sector. Everybody takes a loss, which in turn helps to ensure that banks and bond investors do their homework on countries before lending to them, instead of simply assuming that if something goes wrong, they'll get bailed out anyway.

There are countless complexities within this system, which I shan't bore you with, and the fights about the right and fair thing to do in any given situation can get blazingly hot. But the overarching model is simple. There's a finite stock of precious money, some of which is controlled by governments and some of which is controlled by the private sector. Those institutions are willing to lend out that money, but they want it back, with interest. Depending on how systemically important the borrowing country is and how much money it borrowed, failure to pay back the money risks precipitating multiple crises in countries around the world—so everybody fights aggressively to get what they consider to be their fair share of whatever might conceivably be on offer. Money is the field of battle, a constant, a given; all sides play by its rules.

In 2008, however, that conception of money started to fall apart. Classically, if the US government wanted to support American banks, it would do so by propping up troubled borrowers—by moving money in the direction of the debtors. In the late 1980s, for instance, the US Treasury masterminded the creation of billions of dollars in so-called Brady bonds, named after the Treasury secretary at the time, Nick Brady. The bonds were the sovereign debt of Latin American countries, but they were partially guaranteed by Treasury bonds issued by the US, and they refinanced a pile of dubious loans that, if allowed to go into default, would have rendered much of the American banking system insolvent.

That then became the standard playbook: In 1994, for instance, Treasury secretary Robert Rubin cracked open an obscure slush fund called the Exchange Stabilization Fund to bail out Mexico—which, of course, was a back-door bail-out of Mexico's lenders, who were in large part American banks. The point was that the US needed a certain amount of money to enact the bail-out, so it went looking for the money, and found it, and used it.

In the financial crisis, that playbook was jettisoned. Once again there was a huge pile of bad loans—in this case, subprime mortgages. And once again, if those mortgages were to turn bad, that would more than wipe out the capital of most large American banks—and many small ones, too. So the obvious move was to prop up subprime borrowers, restructuring their debts in such a way that the borrowers would both keep their houses *and* keep the banks afloat.

In fact that was the original plan: The so-called Troubled Asset Relief Program, or TARP, was designed to buy troubled assets like subprime loans from the banks, shoring up their capital while giving the government the ability to sell those loans to investors committed to avoiding foreclosure if at all possible. That didn't happen, however. TARP was deemed to be too small to save the banks by buying their bad debt, and so instead it was used to bail out the banks directly. They kept their bad loans, but the government credited their accounts at the New York Fed with so much new cash that solvency worries largely disappeared. One day, Treasury secretary Hank Paulson decided that the banks needed to have more money; the next day they had it. Not all the banks were happy about this, but they had no choice in the matter. TARP money was an instrument that the government created and used to fight the crisis, and the banks were forced to accept it whether they wanted it or not.

Armed with that precedent, the US government turned to money creation early in the 2020 crisis. In mid-April 2020, millions of Americans woke up to find out that $1,400 had magically appeared in their bank accounts, placed there by the Trump administration as part of the first Covid stimulus plan. No longer was the US obeying the same money rules as everybody else; now, money was obeying orders being handed down by the government, the only entity capable of pulling such a move.

The US dollar is a fiat currency: It is issued and governed by the authority of the nation, but most people, most of the time, don't think about it that way. That started to change with the 2008 financial crisis. It's no coincidence, for instance, that Satoshi Nakamoto, the inventor of bitcoin, wrote this in February 2009, when the crisis was at its peak: "The root problem with conventional currency is all the trust that's required to make it work. The central bank must be trusted not to debase the currency, but the history of fiat currencies is full of breaches of that trust."[2] Without the crisis, it would have been much more difficult for Satoshi's invention to capture the imagination of so many technologists in the way that it did—and even Satoshi himself might not have been nearly as invested in the project as he was.

The US government wasn't finished with its project of transforming the dollar from a bedrock fact of life to a powerful instrument of policy. The dollar represents the apex of what Credit Suisse money expert Zoltan Pozsar calls "inside money"—that is, the credit model of money, where wealth is the amount you're owed. If you have $100 in a checking account at a bank, then your asset is the bank's liability: The bank owes you $100, payable on demand at any time. On the other hand, if you place a $100 note in a safety-deposit box at the same bank, then that's "outside money." That money is no one else's liability, beyond the circular tautology that the US government promises to give you $100 if you present them with the note.

The overwhelming majority of dollars in the world are "inside money"—normally money that is owed by some kind of financial institution. That includes all the dollars owned by the world's central banks as foreign reserves. The Brazilian central bank, say, doesn't keep piles of greenbacks in a vault somewhere in Sao Paulo; if it did, it couldn't easily use them to support its currency, or for any other standard central bank operations. Instead, like all other central banks, it keeps its dollars in an account at the Federal Reserve Bank of New York.

The fact is that *all* dollar-denominated accounts are ultimately based in the US. While it's certainly possible to open a dollar account at a bank in Zurich, your bank's dollars—the ones they owe you—aren't in Switzerland, they're in America. Indeed many of them are on deposit at the New York Fed, too.

Because substantially all financial institutions need to transact in dollars, and because all dollars need to be held in the US, virtually all the world's financial institutions are overseen by American regulators. That's why it's always been so difficult to send money in and out of Cuba, for instance, wherever you live and whatever currency you want to transact in. The Americans have a law against it, and they will have no compunction in prosecuting any financial institution that breaks that law, whether it's American or not.

The US has always been at the forefront of using its financial hegemony as an instrument of foreign policy. There are just as many banks with branches in London as there are banks with branches in New York, but you don't see the UK fining foreign banks hundreds of millions or even billions of dollars for the crime of dealing with countries that the British Foreign Office doesn't like. Even so, the

Americans were always respectful of the principle of sovereign immunity. They might go after French bank BNP Paribas for dealing with counterparties in Sudan, but they wouldn't go after France itself.

In early 2022, however, the Biden administration, emboldened by the monetary successes of the pandemic, embarked upon what hedge-fund manager Dylan Grice accurately described as "the weaponization of money"—and trained its new financial weapon directly on fellow sovereigns.

First came Afghanistan, which had some $7 billion in sorely needed reserves when the Taliban took control of the country in 2021. The Biden White House effectively confiscated all that money, earmarking half of it for humanitarian aid to Afghanistan, and reserving the other half for the potential benefit of the families of American victims of 9/11.

The commandeering of Afghanistan's sovereign wealth was followed just a couple of weeks later by a similar operation aimed at Russia, after the invasion of Ukraine. Russia's sovereign "inside money" was effectively frozen as part of an unprecedented global effort to cut the country and its major oligarchs off from the international financial system. Wherever there was Russian wealth—whether it was in the form of foreign exchange reserves or bank accounts or "outside money" like yachts or Picassos in the Geneva free port— western governments moved to seize it, to literally impoverish the entire country. The immediate effect was an implosion of Russia's domestic economy, the victim of a monetary weapon with truly awesome power.

Within a week of Russia invading Ukraine, there was no longer any doubt that the dollar, and its central role in international trade, was a tool that would be used by American authorities in ultra-aggressive furtherance of foreign-policy objectives—especially when those objectives were shared by monetary authorities in the EU, the UK, Switzerland, and elsewhere.

On some level, Russia was just being treated in the way individual criminals are treated in all jurisdictions, their assets prone to being seized or frozen. But the scale and scope of the Russia sanctions were orders of magnitude greater than anything ever seen in a criminal prosecution, and were much more comparable with the kind of sums that governments spend on wars or stimulus packages. (To put things in perspective: Russia's 2020 pandemic stimulus totaled about $70 billion, while its central bank reserves, rendered useless by sanctions in 2022, were roughly ten times larger than that.)

Western governments had even more control over money and trade flows than a narrow reading of the official sanctions would suggest. Financial institutions and large public companies are by their nature conservative; with new Russian individuals and companies getting added to the sanctions list on a daily basis, none of them were likely to want to do business with even perfectly legal and legitimate Russian clients or customers. Even when Russia was allowed to sell oil, for instance, finding someone willing to buy it was extremely difficult.

The changing perception of money, from bedrock unit of economic existence to volatile munition, took place against a backdrop of inflation higher than anything that had been seen for forty years—inflation that had been caused by the pandemic. Inflation, more than any other economic phenomenon, erodes trust in money, and as Russia invaded Ukraine, it was running very hot indeed, thanks to the way in which Covid had disrupted supply chains as well as the overwhelming fiscal and monetary responses from the government. The war in Ukraine only made things worse, causing commodity price spikes and even more supply-chain disruptions as corporations found themselves having to avoid the largest country in the world, and not even fly over it.

Money became a central part of the New Not Normal—something that almost everybody had simply taken for granted, but that suddenly felt like it had a tomato-seed-like tendency to skitter away from any attempt to grasp it. What does money *mean*, when $1,400 can just show up in your bank account one day and then your salary gets shrunk by 7 percent the following year just because of inflation? In an era of the unexpected, millions came to the realization that money was contingent, a social construct rather than an objective reality. In a society that for decades had been centered on the almighty dollar, that was disconcerting to say the least. The pandemic changed the world's (or at least America's) conception of money itself.

The dollar still retained its hegemony as the world's reserve currency, and it also retained its utility as a measure of relative wealth. When I first moved to the US from the UK in the mid-1980s, I learned quickly that social class was a lot simpler here: To all intents and purposes, the more money you had, the more social status you had. Individuals judged *themselves* by how much money they earned or owned, and centered their lives on maximizing it.

By the time the pandemic hit, things were already much more complex, with resentment displacing aspiration on the right, while on the left slogans like "every billionaire is a policy failure" captured the imagination of a generation that was happy to describe itself as being socialist. The concept of shared peace and prosperity seemed naive in a post-Trump world of walls and border controls, and pretty soon the dollar itself was being used to drive countries further apart rather than bringing them together.

The technocrats changed, too. The two individuals charged with protecting the primacy and stability of the dollar are the secretary of the Treasury and the Federal Reserve chair, and those two individuals quite explicitly made it clear that they had bigger things to worry about than the conceptual status of the dollar. There was the pandemic, of course; there was an unprovoked war in Europe that was started by a nuclear power; and then there was the broad thrust of both fiscal and monetary policy in the United States, which for the first time focused on the poor as much as the rich, and people of color as much as the white majority.

At the Federal Reserve, for instance, the classic role of the central bank—"To take away the punch bowl just as the party gets going," in the words of former Fed chair William McChesney Martin— was recognized as, effectively, taking away the punch bowl just as Black Americans were about to be offered good jobs. In order to begin to counteract decades of systemic racism built into the deep structures of the economy, the Fed had to say—and did say—that it would be willing to see above-target inflation for a matter of years, if necessary.

In that sense, the conventional wisdom of America's most powerful technocrats—led by a Republican, Jay Powell, at the Fed—constituted a sharp move away from the hard-money Clinton-Rubin-Greenspan era, instead creating a degree of uncertainty about the status of the dollar that was quickened by rhetoric about bitcoin and other monetary alternatives. Even people who didn't buy into the bitcoin dream could still think the crypto evangelists had a point about fiat currencies. Such people started wondering just how stable the dollar really is, especially when "audit the Fed" conspiracy theorists were doing their best to fan the flames of mistrust.

The dollar is still, by a long shot, the mightiest currency around. It might be wobbling a tiny bit at the edges, but it's not even smoldering, let alone in ashes. That said, *mistrust* in the dollar is rising sharply, along with mistrust in almost all institutions, and that mistrust grew rapidly during the pandemic for understandable reasons. In turn, that's going to make it harder for the Fed to do its job.

The core task of any independent central bank is to keep inflation under control. That's easier said than done, however. The Fed and other central banks really only have two things they can use to bring inflation down, once it appears. One is interest rates; the other is the institution's own credibility. And there's a case to be made that the latter is more essential than the former.

The one thing that no central bank wants is for out-of-control inflation to become a self-fulfilling prophecy—a phenomenon sometimes referred to as the "wage-price spiral." In a non-inflationary economy, prices are largely static. But once businesses and individuals start to expect inflation in the coming months, they will expect all prices—including salaries—to generally be steadily rising.

Let's say I run a factory that turns sprockets into widgets. If I expect to have to pay more for next year's sprockets, that means I'm going to have to raise the price of my widgets this year in order to have the money necessary to pay the increased price. So the price of widgets goes up today, just as a result of my inflation expectations about what's going to happen tomorrow.

Something similar happens with wages. For most of my career, my salary was presumptively static. In an inflationary environment, on the other hand, companies find it hard to tell employees that their wages will not keep up with inflation, and semi-automatic pay rises start to happen on an annual basis, quite aside from performance-based raises and promotions. Naturally, companies need to raise their prices not only to be able to pay higher prices from their suppliers of parts, but also to be able to pay higher prices to their suppliers of labor—their employees. Thus does a wage-price spiral become entrenched.

One of the most important things that a central bank can do, then, is to manage expectations. If the central bank governor is a sober and trusted individual who can credibly promise that inflation is going to be low next year, then businesses are much less likely to raise prices today. What's important is less the central bank's ability to keep a lid on inflation, and more the existence of a broad *belief* in that ability. Interest rate hikes work well when they persuade businesses that inflation is not going to be a medium-term problem; they're much less effective when they don't.

The pandemic therefore made the Fed's job much more difficult, by reducing the effectiveness of the expectations channel in constraining inflation. Simply asserting that inflation will be kept in check is no longer a self-fulfilling prophecy, and in fact risks eroding the central bank's credibility even further should the prediction not come true.

Covid wasn't the sole cause of this problem. The financial crisis, the Ukraine war, the reappearance of inflation, even Donald Trump's incessant attacks on Fed chair Jay Powell, all contributed to the growing suspicion that the dollar and the Fed were not things that could always be trusted. But Covid in particular created an atmosphere where people started to expect the unexpected, where recent history was a terrible guide to the immediate future, and where formerly comforting technocratic reassurances were met with an unprecedented degree of suspicion and even foreboding.

Wartime is enervating—just like the worst days of the pandemic, it is characterized by a need for hypervigilance and the constant real risk that untimely death will find you despite all the precautions you're trying to take. That kind of fear tends to make it hard to concentrate on long-term visions or projects. The business world is similar: The world's largest and strongest and most innovative companies tend to be based in stable, predictable economies. Navigating a fickle monetary system is a full-time job in itself, and leaves less room for longsighted corporate strategy.

Insofar as the stability and hegemony of the dollar is something that stops being a baseline assumption and starts to become a low-grade or even high-grade source of worry for the business world, that will serve to erode one of the key comparative advantages that American companies have historically had over their foreign competitors.

It's not just American companies that will be affected, either. Global multinationals are deeply embedded in the dollar-based system and will be hurt just as much. But at least they will have the resources to be able to hire new employees to address this new source of risk. Smaller companies, both inside and outside the US, could find themselves tossed about much more on monetary swells, with much less ability to navigate them.

On the other hand, what's bad for big business might end up being good for actual people. The pandemic-era causes of monetary instability were also just plain good causes, on a humanitarian level—whether it was putting money into Americans' bank accounts when they needed it most or using the international financial system as a nonviolent means of punishing the unprovoked aggression of Vladimir Putin.

It's broadly a good thing if governments in general, and the US government in particular, have the option to be able to make full use of their monetary powers. The monetary show of force we saw after Russia's invasion of Ukraine was the kind of response that no superpower would ever want to take off the table—strong, effective, but also stopping well short of a shooting war between NATO and Russia that could end, literally, in global annihilation. The cost of such an act is orders of magnitude lower than the cost of an actual war, both financially and in terms of human life. If the solidity of the dollar has taken a blow, then think of it as acting a bit like a crumple zone in a car. If it protected the lives of countless potential victims of World War III, then that's a trade-off well worth making.

The world's central bankers, and the ones at the Federal Reserve in particular, are committed to restabilizing its currencies and eradicating inflation. The attempt to become more attuned to the needs of marginalized communities is still in place, but it's always going to be less important than the central mandate of price stability. Prepandemic, that price stability was largely taken for granted, and the Fed could talk about being okay with inflation running above target for a year or two if that would help the victims of structural racism. Now it's not clear whether they still have that luxury.

The pandemic and inflation didn't burn the American monetary system to ashes, far from it. The dollar remains strong—problematically so, for multinational companies seeing their foreign revenues steadily shrinking in dollar terms thanks to currency effects. Nevertheless, there's an undeniable sense that the monetary sands have shifted beneath us, and that we're nowhere near the solid ground that, with hindsight, we were complacently occupying for the past few decades.

The good news is that we've found an important new tool of foreign policy, and even of domestic fiscal policy. The bad news is that it makes capitalism that much more difficult. Capitalists have overcome much bigger obstacles than this, but looking forward, the winners of the New Not Normal economy—the phoenixes of the coming decades—are surely going to have to have some kind of newfound ability to navigate protean currencies.

14

Inequality

EVERY YEAR SINCE 2007, the World Economic Forum has put out a Global Risks report to coincide with its annual meeting at Davos. That's a big week for worthy reports, many of which are accompanied by press conferences at a luxury hotel in the sleepy Alpine town that annually transforms itself into a feverish zone of plutocratic hobnobbing. There's the International Labour Organization's World Employment Outlook, the Edelman Trust Barometer, the Oxfam inequality report, and so on.

All of these publications seem to get fatter every year, so they always try very hard to put the most important news in bright colors at the front, where it might get noticed by VVIP devoting thirty seconds to flipping through a document that took dozens of people an entire year to compile.

The format of the Global Risks report, at least for its first fourteen years, was largely fixed. It would list the top five risks facing the world along two axes: the most likely, and the most dangerous. A pandemic was never in the top five most likely risks, but it was the fourth most dangerous risk in 2007, and the fifth most dangerous risk in 2008.

Both the most likely and the most dangerous risks change significantly every year. That doesn't mean what you might think it means—that the risks themselves are incredibly volatile. Most of the risks—not only pandemic risk but also things like natural disasters or global aging or greenhouse gas emissions—don't actually change significantly year to year.

What's really changing is not the risks themselves so much as the degree to which the Davos elite care about them. Look under the hood of the report and you'll discover that even though it's collated by big insurance companies whose livelihoods depend on being able to quantify the likelihood and severity of big risks, the actual results come from something called the Global Risks Perception Survey, in which 841 "business, government, civil society and thought leaders" from "the World Economic Forum's multistakeholder communities" are asked to fill out a questionnaire asking what they're most worried about.

It therefore probably comes as little surprise that after pandemics dropped off the chart in 2009, they did reappear for one year, in the slightly changed guise of "infectious diseases." That year was 2015, immediately following the Ebola outbreak in Sierra Leone and Liberia.

The report methodology largely explains why "income disparity" came from nowhere to top the list for three straight years, from 2012 to 2014. Those were the years in which the sluggish economic recovery from the global financial crisis, combined with healthy market returns for the Davos ultra-rich, made rising inequality impossible to ignore, at least for thirty-six months or so. Then again, after being impossible to ignore, it was promptly ignored: Inequality never again made an appearance on the chart.

Maybe that's because, after 2016, the worst consequences of income inequality had already come to pass, and at that point there was little that anybody could do to fix the problem. Popular resentment of elites broke up the European Union, with Brexit, and then propelled Donald Trump to the presidency of the United States.

There's even a case to be made that the 2008 financial crisis caused the Covid pandemic, in a way that the World Economic Forum's global risks chart only glancingly hints at. By their nature, financial crises tend to result in slow and painful recoveries, which is exactly what we saw with the years following 2009—combined with a quite startling rise in the stock, bond, and property markets, thanks to zero interest rates.

That highly visible widening of inequality set the stage for Brexit and Trump, and one of Trump's first actions was to dismantle the National Security Council's Global Health Security and Biodefense unit. Tom Bossert, the security adviser who had pushed hardest for a biodefense strategy against pandemics, left government service entirely, as did Timothy Ziemer, who was in charge of the US response to a pandemic. At the same time, Trump's aggressive stance toward China meant that the two superpowers largely stopped cooperating on health issues, and no Americans from the Centers for Disease Control, or anywhere else for that matter, were part of China's initial response to the Covid outbreak in Wuhan.

Counterfactuals are always dangerous, but it's *possible* that a full-strength US pandemic response unit, under a relatively China-friendly President Hillary Clinton, could have helped the Chinese authorities to nip the Wuhan outbreak in the bud, and/or could have massively slowed its international spread. At the very least the virus would have spread less quickly in the United States under a president who didn't believe that magical thinking would make it go away.

Covid hit international radar screens too late to make it into the WEF's 2020 risks report, which only mentioned "outbreaks of emerging infectious diseases, such as SARS, Zika and MERS" on page 76. By the following year, Covid wasn't a risk, it was what the report classed instead as a "clear and present danger," alongside such things as "digital inequality," "terrorist attacks," and "human environmental damage."

On some level it's silly to try to make apples-to-apples comparisons between such wildly different risks as income inequality and global thermonuclear war, to watch them rise and fall on the WEF rankings as though they were competitors in some great risk fight. On the other hand, as an anthropological exercise, monitoring the rankings is highly informative. Even after the pandemic hit, the Davos elite were not particularly exercised about inequality—they had more urgent things to worry about, like, well, the pandemic.

The fact is, however, that the pandemic massively exacerbated global inequality on almost every conceivable scale and axis—within countries, between countries, between the powerful and the powerless, between rich and poor, north and south, Black and white, men and women, the sick and the healthy. Because there was a global public-health emergency going on, the deterioration was not noted as perhaps it should have been—although as we saw from 2012 to 2014, even when it's top of mind, that hardly means that the powerful are likely to do anything about it.

That's partly because the powerful are a large part of the problem. One profound form of inequality is deviation from equality in the sense of "all men are created equal"—the idea that every citizen has the same birthrights, privileges, and inherent dignity as every other citizen. The idea, most famously and pithily expressed by Thomas Jefferson in the Declaration of Independence, can be traced back at least as far as John Locke's *Two Treatises of Government*, published in 1688.

Locke's achievement was to dismantle the position of his intellectual opponent, Sir Robert Filmer, who had proclaimed that men are born into servitude, within a pre-existing hierarchy with God at the top and the earthly sovereign one layer down. (Locke was aided in his fight by the fact that Filmer had been dead for twenty-seven years when his pro-authoritarian treatise was finally published, under the title *Patriarcha*, in 1680.) Locke's side of the argument might have become "self-evident," at least to Thomas Jefferson, by the time the Declaration was written in 1776, but it certainly wasn't self-evident before 1688. Truth be told, it wasn't exactly self-evident to Jefferson either, a man who owned—and claimed dominion over—more than six hundred enslaved humans during the course of his life.

Even today, the power of Jefferson's preamble lies in its rhetorical force rather than its empirical provability. Inequality is all around us, from birth to death; it's built into every system of government in the world. (The United States certainly doesn't consider *all* men to be created equal; in fact it goes to great lengths to deny the perquisites of US citizenship to the overwhelming majority of people in the world.) However, both Jefferson and most modern Americans can discern a Lockean ideal behind the inequality—the "state of nature" where, truly, everyone is equal and no one is superior or inferior to anybody else. Members of such a society might, collectively, in their own self-interest, form some kind of government from the bottom up—much as Jefferson did in 1776. Such government gains its legitimacy from the consent of those governed and not from any God or sovereign inheritance.

The pandemic coincided with, and perhaps gave cover for, one of the biggest rollbacks of such consent in modern memory. If all countries exist somewhere on a Lockean spectrum, then many of the largest—most notably China, the largest of all—moved noticeably toward its authoritarian end, away from freedom and democracy.

China was never exactly democratic, of course, and the Uyghur genocide in Xinjiang predates the outbreak that started in Wuhan in late 2019. Still, President Xi Jinping took full advantage of the pandemic to increase the surveillance state, crack down even further on freedom of expression, and even ban video games for anybody under the age of eighteen, except for one hour per day on weekends and holidays.

China's zero-Covid strategy was extremely harsh. Authorities would regularly isolate people overnight, wherever they happened to be—in a Uniqlo store, in a strange office building—just on suspicion that they might have been exposed to someone who was exposed to the virus. A woman on a second date found herself stuck with her date and his parents for thirty days when their city abruptly went into lockdown.[1] The authorities in Xi'an moved more than 45,000 people into government-run quarantine during a single lockdown.[2]

One hospital refused to admit a patient with chest pains, since he was in a medium-risk district; he died of a heart attack. The hospital's caution is easily explained—just look at the fifteen-month prison sentences handed down to two doctors who treated patients without following the correct Covid protocols.[3]

Ultra-strict lockdown policies, often enforced by groups of patriotic volunteers, were strengthened by a blanket ban on any criticism of those policies on social media, let alone any dispassionate journalistic coverage. Such censorship helped to entrench the Chinese Communist Party's control not only over how its citizens live but even over how they think.

Most notable and most shocking to western observers, China used the pandemic years to extend that control not only on the mainland but also in Hong Kong. Under the Sino-British "one country, two systems" treaty of 1994, China promised that it would continue to allow democracy and freedom of expression in the city through 2047—but then, in 2020, the Chinese government effectively tore up that treaty by passing a broad national security law that gave Beijing full command of a city of 7.5 million freedom-loving people.

The opposition to the law was loud and extended, but also futile: By the end of 2021, the democratic opposition and the pro-democracy press had been effectively eradicated, the Tiananmen Square memorial statue at the University of Hong Kong had been unceremoniously taken down, and the city had utterly lost its status as the cosmopolitan jet-setter's base of choice on the western rim of the Pacific Ocean.

Using its zero-Covid policy as the stated reason, China forced all visitors, as well as any Hongkongers arriving from overseas, to quarantine in a hotel room for twenty-one days, at their own expense, before being allowed to enter the city. Accommodations in designated quarantine hotels ranged from a 100-square-foot space in the Bridal Tea House Hotel for HK$490 (US$63) per night, up to a 1,785-square-foot suite at the Mandarin Oriental for HK$55,000 per night—about US$150,000 for the full twenty-one-night stay. Wherever you chose, your key card worked only once, and leaving your room was grounds for immediate arrest.

Given Hong Kong's centuries-long status as an entrepôt whose comparative advantage had always been its unrivaled web of connections to other cities and countries, the travel restrictions cut straight at the heart of its identity and made the city significantly less attractive as a place to live and do business, especially for English-speaking international financiers who could live anywhere they liked. That was a feature, not a bug, as far as Beijing was concerned. If you're running a country that rigorously polices individual expression, you don't particularly want a large number of rich westerners, and especially rich westerners' kids, inculcating your youth in the ways of freedom and democracy. You also don't want to make it *too* easy for the existing population to flit back and forth between Hong Kong and Vancouver or London or Sydney or New York or Taipei, thereby being constantly reminded of what Hong Kong so painfully lost when Beijing took control.

Hong Kong retained its fully convertible currency, as well as a legal system that foreign investors could rely on for impartiality in commercial disputes, so it kept much of its status as a financial center. That was part of Xi's calculations: As the rise of China helped Beijing and Shanghai to solidify their position among the world's most important financial centers, it became clear that freedom and democracy were far from being necessary prerequisites for financial success. In any case, China had become rich enough that it could afford to crack down on certain forms of wealth creation, if doing so would bolster the position of the Communist Party. That's why Xi started putting the screws on domestic technology billionaires and ended the practice of Chinese companies listing their shares on the New York Stock Exchange, at roughly the same time he was cracking down on Hong Kong.

Looking at the way in which authoritarians around the world consolidated power during the pandemic reminded me of the way in which individuals quit their high-paying jobs after realizing that money wasn't making them happy: In both cases, the rich and powerful gave up money for something they desired even more. Wherever there was a lurch to authoritarianism, the economy invariably suffered as a result, but this seemed to be taken as a price that the government, at least, was willing to pay in order to consolidate power. It's only money, after all.

Hungary and Poland, for instance, both EU member states, saw their economies deteriorate after they started looking very much like they had one-party rule under right-wing strongmen. Both also built an apparatus of corruption, which helped to mitigate any economic losses for the architects of autocracy themselves.[4] Turkey went even further under President Recep Tayyip Erdoğan, who proved himself entirely capable of destroying the nation's currency and economy in the service of consolidating his power over all civic institutions.

In poorer countries, outright coups became common for the first time in decades. In the span of less than a year, from mid-2021 to early 2022, there were successful coups in Mali, Burkina Faso, Guinea, and Sudan—on top of attempted coups in Niger and Myanmar. In Chad, an attempted insurgency failed to install a new regime, but succeeded in killing the president, Idriss Déby.

Most historically, Russia invaded Ukraine in February 2022, a shockingly unthinkable act pre-pandemic, and one that was so surprising that the morning it happened, the Moscow stock market index plunged by 50 percent from an already-depressed level. (The violence of intraday market moves doesn't give a good indication of how momentous a certain precipitating event is, so much as it gives an indication of how unexpected it was.)

The virus acted as an accelerant in all these cases. As Joseph Stalin famously said, "a single death is a tragedy; a million deaths is a statistic." The pandemic caused a million deaths by September 2020, then another million by January 2021, and another million the following April, and another million by July, and yet another million by October. The millions just kept on coming, an ongoing tragedy of such enormity that it was almost impossible to conceptualize.

The effect was numbing and couldn't help but undercut the post–World War II liberal dream of an international order based on a universal respect for individual human rights. When countries like New Zealand locked down and shut themselves off from the rest of the world in order to protect the lives of their citizens, it looked like—it was—a noble gesture, based very much in the Lockean ideal of individual equality. If some significant percentage of your population dies unnecessarily, when you as a head of state could have taken steps that would have prevented those deaths, that puts you in a desperate moral position.

Large-country leaders, however—Trump, Putin, Bolsonaro,

Johnson—had no patience for trolley-problem ethical conundrums. They knew that so long as *some* deaths were inevitable, there was no way of tying any individual death to the decisions they made. Sure, that person might have been saved by a more aggressive government policy, but then again, they might not have been. Who's to say.

There's definitely a consistent logic at play here. Decisions to kill a certain identifiable person are terrible. There's much less moral opprobrium, on the other hand, attached to decisions that are statistically certain to result in many deaths, especially where the identities of those who will die is unknowable. A decision to raise the speed limit would be one example: Only a tiny minority of voters consider such an act to be tantamount to murder.

The result is a weirdly skewed moral calculus with respect to the pandemic. When people die from a disease, that's a death from "natural causes," but when people are asked to wear masks indoors, that's an active government-imposed constraint on the way that people live their lives.

That explains why, politically, lifting restrictions was far more popular than imposing them—something the medical profession never really came to terms with. While epidemiologists were happy to opine on optimal public-health policy, they largely failed to keep up with political reality, which was that voters *did* blame politicians for mandates, but they *didn't* blame politicians for deaths.

In turn, that gave politicians an effective carte blanche to act in ways that were clearly detrimental to the most vulnerable members of society. No longer were all men created equal: If you were unfortunate enough to enter the pandemic while living in crowded conditions, or suffering any of a huge list of comorbidities, or being immunosuppressed, or working in a hospital, or simply just being old, then in country after country you very rapidly learned that you were a second-class citizen with meaningfully less fundamental dignity than a "karen" in a supermarket who was annoyed at being asked to wear a mask.

Mandates are broadly egalitarian: They apply to everybody, treat all lives as equally valuable, and attempt to protect everybody. When states either refuse to implement mandates or make a big show of dismantling them, they're effectively throwing their weakest citizens under the bus for the benefit of those who would prefer to just take their chances in a survival-of-the-fittest contest.

Base-level human equality is predicated on the idea that everybody is born with inalienable rights, including the right to life and the right to liberty. Chinese authoritarianism respects neither; the country's mandates come not from respect for the individual but rather from the conviction that the individual must subjugate herself and her desires for the greater good of the collective. Elsewhere, in places like the US, UK, Sweden, and Brazil, the right to life found itself being subjugated to a conception of liberty that almost entirely ignored the role individuals play as vectors and spreaders of infection.

The virus itself then made matters much worse, as the Delta and Omicron variants pushed their way past vaccine defenses, making vaccination something that was very good at keeping vaccinated individuals out of the hospital but much less good at preventing those individuals from infecting others. As Covid then spread, it didn't target the young and healthy, like the Spanish flu of 1918. Instead it proved most lethal among the segments of the population who were already being left behind in terms of their wealth and power within society.

Being poor, in and of itself, was top of the list of comorbidities associated with dying of Covid. In many countries it's impossible to get large-scale data on the income of individual Covid patients, but the largest healthcare system in Mexico, the Instituto Mexicano del Seguro Social (IMSS), is the exception: It has data on the daily earnings of all its affiliated workers, who comprise all the private-sector employees in the country, as well as their families.

A *Lancet* study looked at more than one million IMSS participants who went to a clinic with Covid-like symptoms and who were tested for Covid.[5] None of these were among the very poorest Mexicans: They all had some kind of private employment and had access to healthcare. Still, the variation in outcomes was stunning.

If you tested positive and were in the bottom 10 percent of earners, you had a roughly 40 percent chance of ending up in the hospital and a 17 percent chance of dying. If you were in the top 40 percent of earners, by contrast, your chances of being hospitalized fell to less than 15 percent, and your chances of dying were only about 4 percent.

The final conclusion: After controlling for all variables, including medical comorbidities, being in the lowest 10 percent of incomes made Mexicans *five times* more likely to die of Covid than their compatriots in the top 10 percent.

The Mexican findings align with what was seen elsewhere. In Belgium, for instance, a different study found that there was a twofold difference in death rates between Covid-positive patients from the lowest and highest income deciles. The smaller ratio makes sense: What counts as poor in Belgium would be middle of the pack in Mexico. A separate meta-analysis of infection fatality rates across entire countries—including all the poor and all the rich—found that at any given age, someone with Covid was twice as likely to die of the disease in a developing country than they were in a high-income country.[6]

Those statistics hide variations within countries. If it had been possible to conduct the Mexican study with all Mexicans, rather than just formally employed private-sector workers, the ratio would probably have been higher than five to one. And if it were possible to look at fatality rates for people with Covid globally, across countries, you'd see a higher ratio still. Health outcomes are very highly correlated with earnings, and income inequality remains at staggeringly high levels. The average adult in the top 10 percent of earners in the world makes about $100,000 per year, according to the World Inequality Lab's definitive annual report, put together by star economists Lucas Chancel, Thomas Piketty, Emmanuel Saez, and Gabriel Zucman.[7] If that adult is in the bottom 50 percent of earners in the world, she only makes about $3,000 per year—and will, on average, have a significantly larger family to support.

The pandemic didn't hurt the incomes of the bottom 50 percent broadly—in rich countries, especially, the poorest citizens generally saw their wealth go up rather than down, thanks to generous government fiscal policies. For the bottom 10 percent, however, things were dire.

The World Bank has one priority above all others: poverty reduction. For that reason, it keeps close tabs on the number of people in extreme poverty—people living on less than $1.90 per day. (That's less than $700 per *year*.) In any given year, the extreme-poverty number tends to go down by about 25 million people. In 2019, it was estimated at 655 million people; by simple extrapolation of the medium-term trend, it was expected to fall to 635 million in 2020. Instead, it rose. It didn't just rise a little, either; it jumped more rapidly than in any other year that the World Bank has estimates for.

The Bank's best estimate for the number of people who were living in extreme poverty in 2020 is 732 million, well over double the population of the United States. The single-year increase in poverty more than wiped out all the gains since 2016, and the cohort in extreme poverty in 2020 is roughly 100 million people larger than it was going to be, absent the pandemic.

To put that number in perspective, the total number of people who died of Covid, globally, in 2020 is probably less than 2 million. The human misery caused by the pandemic, in other words, is much greater than what the broad economic statistics or the death and hospitalization count shows. Year in and year out, even as the annual death rate from Covid starts to decline, the extreme poverty rate is likely to remain about 100 million people above its pre-pandemic trend.

The same is true for poverty more broadly, defined as people living on less than $5.50 per day. That population rose to 3.3 billion people in 2020, 169 million of whom wouldn't have been there were it not for the pandemic.

Mass immiseration didn't only afflict the poor. Women and girls, including transwomen, experienced a huge increase in gender-based violence during the pandemic. They often found themselves living with abusers from whom they had no escape—just as the social support systems put in place to protect them had broken down in a world of lockdowns and medical triage. Helplines saw a huge increase in calls, but often were hamstrung in their ability to provide help; India's National Human Rights Commission cited domestic violence counts 2.5 times higher than their pre-pandemic level.[8]

Government support for employers and employees was also gendered, by its very nature: You can't support what you don't know exists, but in some parts of the developing world, more than 90 percent of women workers are in the informal sector. Those women found themselves falling through the cracks, left without any means of earning any kind of livelihood, and without any means of turning to the government for help.

Not that workers in the formal sector did great. A comprehensive World Bank study of global incomes in 2020 and 2021 showed that *every single centile* of the income distribution earned less money in both years than pre-pandemic.[9] That is to say, if you're one of those salaried professionals who can work from home and who earned just as much money in 2020 and 2021 as you did in 2019, then you're *well* ahead of most other people around the world who were making the same amount. In fact, Americans in general were one of the very few countries where incomes broadly went up rather than down over the course of the pandemic, at least in nominal terms.

Involuntary unemployment skyrocketed, rising 20 percent to 224 million in 2020, per the International Labor Organization, from 186 million in 2019. It then stayed elevated in 2021 and showed no sign of reverting to its pre-pandemic lows.

Inequality was extreme on the vaccine side of things, too. As muted, downbeat celebrants rang in the 2022 new year, in the shadow of the Omicron wave that swept the world that winter, less than half of the global population was fully vaccinated, and less than 7 percent of people had received a booster shot that would give them decent protection against the new variant.

The rapid development of effective vaccines against Covid was arguably the greatest scientific achievement of the early twenty-first century—but developing a vaccine, on its own, is woefully insufficient.

In order for a vaccine to have broad uptake across any population, four different things need to go right. The government needs to be able to get its hands on enough vaccine for everybody; it then needs to be able to distribute it to every corner of the country, keeping it at the necessary temperature all the while; the distribution and logistics network then has to be able to muster the resources necessary to get the vaccine into every local arm (or at least one of every pair). Finally, and most importantly, the owners of those arms have to *want* to get vaccinated—or, at least, not want to not get vaxxed.

Getting around all these obstacles and still ending up with a healthy overall vaccination rate is incredibly difficult in poor countries. Just the first one alone was a major problem for most of Africa, for instance—in the initial months that vaccines were available, substantially all vaccine doses were hoarded by rich and middle-income countries, plus India, whose Serum Institute had a license to manufacture the Oxford University vaccine distributed in the rest of the world by AstraZeneca. Placing orders was easy, filling them was hard: By mid-2021, for instance, COVAX, the organization dedicated to the equitable distribution of vaccine, had purchased 2.4 billion doses—and shipped just 95 million.[10]

Worse, many of those 0.095 billion shipped doses found themselves unable to get shepherded past the next two obstacles before their expiry date. COVAX was so shambolic and unpredictable that large quantities of vaccine would arrive in countries like Chad and Benin that lacked the organization and infrastructure to get the vaccine into arms. In the latter, for instance, 110,000 doses ended up expiring because the country was only able to vaccinate 267 people per day.[11]

Exacerbating the situation further, once countries started being offered substantial amounts of vaccine, it had become abundantly clear that the mRNA vaccines were significantly more effective than the others, and most government leaders—not to mention citizens—were understandably reluctant to be fobbed off with a second-best option. Because of supply constraints in the manufacture of the Pfizer and Moderna vaccines, there simply wasn't enough of them for all the billions of unvaxxed people in the world.

Given all the logistical obstacles facing the world's poorest countries, it was vital that the final hurdle—vaccine hesitancy and vaccine resistance—be much lower in the developing world than it was in rich countries like Germany or the US. Sadly, that wasn't the case. While some countries—Ethiopia, for instance—were very eager to get vaccinated, others, like Liberia, were very hesitant. For entirely understandable reasons, their level of trust in foreign institutions and pharmaceutical companies was low. Much the same reasoning explains why the people of Hong Kong in general, and the elderly in particular, were extremely reluctant to get vaxxed: They just didn't trust the Chinese government.

All these obstacles don't perfectly compound; sometimes they cancel each other out. If there are a hundred people in a village and only fifty want to get vaxxed, for instance, then when the traveling nurse arrives with only fifty doses, she can get all of them into arms. In general, however, there's a chicken-and-egg relationship between vaccine hesitancy and unvaccinated populations. People tend to behave in much the same way as their neighbors, and if their neighbors are happy being unvaxxed then they probably will be, too. Wait long enough, and eventually unvaxxed status starts becoming a part of people's personal identity, and at that point, changing their mind becomes almost impossible. Simply being unable to vaccinate populations early can make it significantly harder to vaccinate them later.

Vaccine inequality is terrible for health outcomes in unvaxxed countries and regions; it's also terrible for health outcomes in vaccinated countries and regions because vaccine-resistant strains find it much easier to develop in unvaxxed populations. It has the potential to be simultaneously the outcome and the cause of a new pandemic strain. That's a central reason why, after a century of very good fortune when it comes to infectious diseases, the expectation for the next few decades is much less hopeful.

You can't have inequality without having winners to contrast against the losers, and the biggest winners of the pandemic were, to no one's great surprise, the greatest winners of the pre-pandemic years. Which is to say, the billionaires.

It's not particularly helpful to look at the income of billionaires in the pandemic, although it did go up. In the US, for instance, the top 0.01 percent of the population saw its disposable income go up by about $1 million per year between January 2019 and December 2021. But the ultra-rich—who had, to all intents and purposes, a 100 percent vaccination rate—don't really care about income. In fact, they tend to want to minimize their income, since the lower their income the less tax they need to pay. If they need spending money, they can just borrow against their wealth. And it's what happened to billionaire wealth over the course of the pandemic that was nothing short of staggering.

A bit of perspective: Back when the World Economic Forum was most worried about increasing inequality, in the wake of the global financial crisis, billionaires for the first time were increasing their wealth at a rate of $1 trillion per year. That was shocking even after taking into account that they lost about $2 trillion in the 2008–2009 stock market crash: It only took them a couple of years to make that money back, and their wealth just kept soaring thereafter. In total, over the fourteen years from 2007 to 2020, including the financial crisis, billionaire wealth rose by $4.9 trillion, in real 2021 dollars. Call it an average of about $350 billion per year.[12]

By contrast, over the nineteen months from March 2020 to October 2021, including the stock-market crash of the early pandemic, the same billionaires saw their wealth rise by $5.5 trillion. That's about $3.5 trillion per year, a rate of wealth appreciation an entire order of magnitude greater than the already-obscene historical norm.

Total billionaire wealth surpassed $14 trillion during the pandemic—and that's just the high-profile, mostly western billionaires we know about, as enumerated by *Forbes* magazine. The true number is certainly much larger. It includes brand-new crypto billionaires, like CZ, the founder of Binance; secretive Americans like Jeff Yass, the founder of Susquehanna International Group, whose wealth is estimated by the investigative reporters at Project Brazen at more than $100 billion; and a whole passel of shadowy oligarchs. On top of that are individuals like Vladimir Putin and Khalid Sheikh Mohammed, who effectively control the wealth of entire countries and should probably be added to the list somehow.[13]

The rise of the billionaires created indelible "let them eat cake" moments, none more so than the time Jeff Bezos took a multibillion-dollar joyride into space, in a rocket that couldn't look more like a giant penis if it tried.

By the time the pandemic began, Bezos had already appeared on stage with Mathias Döpfner, the CEO of German publishing house Axel Springer, to receive a corporate award and answer some softball questions. One of those was the standard "how do you give back" gift to any interviewee—Döpfner asked Bezos how he, as the first person in history to be worth more than $100 billion, could "spend that money reasonably" and "do good."

If you're a billionaire in the public eye, you and your comms people *love* this question. It's a great opportunity to paint yourself not as a rapacious capitalist disrupting entire industries and upending the way of life of millions of people, but rather as someone who has thought deeply about the potential of great wealth to make the world a better place, and who is excited to put those plans into action. And yet, somehow, Bezos managed to make news with his answer for all the wrong reasons.

Döpfner didn't know it at the time, but his question came less than a year before Bezos would take to Twitter to announce that he and his wife MacKenzie were divorcing, in a move that had seismic force in the world of philanthropy. MacKenzie, with the billions she received in the divorce, immediately became arguably the most aggressive and imaginative philanthropist in the world, approaching her wealth and good fortune with a level of humility that historically has been notably lacking from the plutocratic classes.

Most charitable foundations are set up to live in perpetuity and keep grantees on the back foot: Charities spend untold hours retroactively justifying previous grants so as to maximize the chances of getting future ones. MacKenzie Bezos, reverting back to her maiden name of

MacKenzie Scott, did the exact opposite. She didn't set up a foundation at all; instead, she found a handful of trusted advisers to help identify needy causes, and started writing enormous checks, which arrived entirely unexpected. Rather than worry about "her" money being "wasted," she realized that the people running charities were no less qualified to spend money than she was, and probably were much more qualified. So she just outsourced the decisions to them, no strings attached, to the tune of roughly $9 billion in just the first two years.

Scott's generosity was a double implicit rebuke to her ex-husband. First of all was the simple fact that she was able to give away so much money only by divorcing him: Her inability to support charitable causes in a large-scale way while being half of the richest couple in the world was lost on no one. More pointedly, her post-divorce generosity could be seen as a direct response to the way in which Bezos answered Döpfner's question.

"The only way that I can see to deploy this much financial resource is by converting my Amazon winnings into space travel," said the billionaire who prides himself on his drive and imagination. "That is basically it."

The message: It wasn't that he didn't *want* to give his money to those less fortunate than himself, so much as that he couldn't even conceptualize doing so, given the sheer magnitude of his resources. The only path visible to him, when it came to spending down his fortune, was to burn it up going into low-earth orbit—something he finally did, during the pandemic. (The eleven-minute flight, during which about eighty humans died of hunger and about a hundred more died for lack of access to basic healthcare, was responsible for roughly three hundred tonnes of carbon emissions, more than the average Mexican emits in a lifetime.)

When he came back down to planet Earth, the e-commerce billionaire's message was even clearer. "I want to thank every Amazon employee and every Amazon customer because you guys paid for all of this," Bezos said in a press conference that was streamed live across the planet he had just risen above. "Seriously, for every Amazon customer out there and every Amazon employee, thank you from the bottom of my heart very much. It's very appreciated." It was a clear-eyed if tactless acknowledgment of the inequality that had propelled the world's richest man into space—himself being the lucky beneficiary, while Amazon's hundreds of thousands of warehouse workers provided the necessary labor.

When I worked for Reuters, my colleague Ryan McCarthy and I created a website called Counterparties that was a bit like the Drudge Report for finance—just links to interesting stories, with commentary usually confined to little more than a hashtag. Ryan was a master at creating those little tags, and the most useful one of all was #billionairewhimsy. Sometimes it would describe pure consumption decisions—a Qatari sheikha's decision to drop millions of dollars on a massive Richard Serra installation in the middle of the desert, say, or Larry Ellison's purchase of a decommissioned Soviet fighter jet, because, if you can, why wouldn't you. Or, for that matter, Jeff Bezos's desire to spend well over $40 million building a five-hundred-foot-tall clock inside a West Texas mountain that ticks only once a year and is designed to last for at least ten thousand years.

More often, the hashtag would describe investment decisions, if they were made mostly for, well, *whimsical* reasons. Hong Kong billionaire Li Ka-shing investing $120 million into Facebook in 2007 because it made him feel young would count,[14] or Rupert Murdoch setting up an iPad publication because he saw it in a dream,[15] or Warren Buffett buying his hometown newspaper despite being on the record that such assets didn't make sense at any price. (He was right: He ended up selling it at a loss nine years later.[16])

Financial-information billionaire Mike Bloomberg put it pithily during his stint as mayor of New York, when his eponymous company bought *BusinessWeek* magazine. Told by advisers that the magazine could end up costing him $25 million per year in losses, he retorted: "Do I look like a guy worried about losing $25 million?"[17]

Bezos's investment in Blue Origin, a for-profit space-tourism company, falls very much into that category. It's the kind of thing that you can do, when you're a billionaire, especially since such investments can sometimes turn out spectacularly well.

In 2004, for instance, Elon Musk, already dynastically wealthy after his exit from PayPal, invested $6.5 million into a small electric-vehicle start-up called Tesla Motors. Over the subsequent years he put in more—about $70 million all told, roughly the price of a decent LA mansion or a pretty good Picasso. Eventually that investment would make Musk the richest person in the world, and—much more importantly—would transform the entire global auto industry forever.

Not all transformative plutocratic investments are for-profit. The Rockefeller Foundation, for instance, alongside a few others, invested about $600 million over the course of half a century into the project broadly known as the Green Revolution. The development of disease-resistant wheat, and later rice and corn, first in Mexico and then globally, has been credited with preventing a billion deaths from hunger. The individual hero of the story is the scientist Norman Borlaug, who won the Nobel Peace Prize in 1970, but the money that funded his research ultimately came from Standard Oil's monopoly profits.

Other billionaires' charitable foundations can be thanked for the American system of public libraries and even the creation of the national 911 emergency response system—as well as marriage equality in the US and the passage of a law mandating bike helmets in Vietnam.

For all the good that billionaire wealth can sometimes do, however, the ashes of increased inequality are clear. Nearly all the WEF's global risks are exacerbated by inequality—even natural disasters like earthquakes and tsunamis carry much greater loss of life when they hit areas plagued by avoidable poverty. Inequality causes hunger, disease, and stunting—the irreversible condition where children don't grow fast enough for their age when young. That doesn't just make them shorter as adults, it also makes them sicker, poorer, less proficient at learning, and more prone to chronic disease. In countries like Burundi and Eritrea, more than half of children under five are stunted. In Guatemala it's 47 percent, in Yemen it's 46 percent, in Libya it's 38 percent. In the US, it's much lower, at 3.4 percent, but still almost three times the 1.2 percent rate in Estonia.

Inequality worsens biodiversity loss and water crises; it also sparks coups and wars, which in turn cause mass migration, refugee crises, and a xenophobic tilt in politics in destination countries. Inequality even increases fiscal imbalances, when only the bottom 99 percent actually pay taxes.

For thousands of years, inequality has also driven some of humanity's most magnificent achievements, from the pyramids of Egypt to the Great Wall of China; from the treasures of the Medicis to the Panama Canal. Inequality allows the few to marshal the resources of the many; allows big bets and bigger wins.

Inequality is an unrivaled driver of long-term thinking. That can be selfish—the first job of dynastic wealth, for instance, is to preserve itself across generations. The Habsburg family were extremely good at that—they ran a huge chunk of Europe for 645 years (!) from 1273 to 1918—but today's dynasties tend to keep a much lower profile and do a better job of spreading their wealth around the world so that it can't be confiscated by an incoming government.

Beyond self-perpetuation lies a desire to make a mark on history, to be remembered for posterity. The Habsburgs, many of whom were immortalized by the greatest portraitist of all time, Diego Velázquez, definitely managed that. Nowadays, paintings seem a bit small. Instead the first move of the ultra-rich is to slap their name onto something grand that's designed to last forever—a major cultural institution, say, or a high-profile philanthropic foundation that only ever gives away 5 percent of its funds per year, and therefore will never die.

Whether they set up a foundation or not (the likes of Mark Zuckerberg and Laurene Powell Jobs prefer LLCs, which are more flexible), one constant theme is *ambition*. Zuckerberg says that he wants to cure all disease by 2100. His Facebook co-founder Dustin Moskovitz, along with the likes of Elon Musk and Jaan Tallinn of Skype, has been pouring millions of dollars into "x-risk" research, with the aim of identifying and preventing the risks that could literally wipe out humanity entirely. One such risk, that computers will attain consciousness and destroy humans, is purportedly being addressed by a group called OpenAI, backed with billions of dollars from Musk and other tech luminaries, as well as Microsoft.

They're encouraged in such endeavors by my favorite thinker about philanthropy, Stanford University's Rob Reich. Reich makes the point that foundations—and, by extension, the very rich more generally—can and should play a vital role in any democracy: "to engage in high-risk, long-run policy innovation and experimentation."[18] Public companies can't do that—they have a fiduciary duty to their shareholders, and they're generally focused on keeping up their quarterly earnings. Politicians find it hard, too: Experiments fail, which is a bad look at the next election, especially when they're expensive. Philanthropies, by contrast, can try out ideas; if they work then they can be scaled up with much less risk by government, and if they fail then there's no one they're accountable to, so (ideally) there are no negative professional consequences.

Take social impact bonds, for instance. The idea behind them is simple and smart: A significant number of the men released from prison will end up committing crimes again and going back. That's really expensive for the state, which not only pays tens of thousands of dollars per year to house inmates in prisons, but has massive criminal-justice costs on top of that. Plus, of course, crime hurts the community in which it's committed. It therefore makes sense to spend thousands of dollars on anti-recidivism programs—*if* they work as well as they say they do.

Goldman Sachs came up with a market solution to this problem. It found an organization it believed would be cost-effective in terms of reducing recidivism—which is to say, the organization's costs were low enough that even if it only prevented a fraction of its clients going back to prison, that would represent a savings much greater than the amount it spent. So Goldman issued social impact bonds to investors who believed in the program, and used the proceeds to cover its costs. If it saved as much money as it promised, then the investors would get their money back. If it didn't, they would take a loss.

The scheme was underwritten by Bloomberg Philanthropies, which is to say, Mike Bloomberg. The investors who bought the bonds in the pilot schemes didn't actually have any money at risk: If the recidivism didn't drop as much as expected, Bloomberg would pay them back.

Politically, this kind of program is an extremely hard sell, especially since it would be a profit center for Goldman Sachs, a bank famously described by journalist Matt Taibbi as "a great vampire squid wrapped around the face of humanity, relentlessly jamming its blood funnel into anything that smells like money."[19] As a philanthropic bet, however, it makes all the sense in the world for Bloomberg Philanthropies. If it works out consistently, at that point government could be persuaded to fund such plans at a much larger scale—and if it doesn't, then there's no egg on the foundation's face. It's good to take bold risks, and not all risks pay off.

In the end, the social impact bonds didn't work nearly as well as Bloomberg and Goldman had hoped; both the structure of the bonds and the anti-recidivism program they were funding turned out to have unexpected weaknesses. I don't like to think of the experiment as a failure, though; I think of it as a fantastic example of matching risk with risk appetite, which is the fundamental equation that drives nearly all growth and progress. Bloomberg's wealth gave him the risk appetite to be able to take risks; indeed, he almost certainly thinks that if his philanthropies *don't* regularly take risks that end up failing, that's a very good sign that they're being far too risk averse.

Inequality is like MSG for risk: It dials up the magnitude of whatever flavor of risk there is. Downside risks become bigger and worse; upside risks become bigger and better. The pandemic's effects on inequality are therefore the perfect example of how Covid isn't just the foremost illustration of what a New Not Normal world can look like; it's also a force accelerating those changes. The post–WWII world—the world following the worst and largest downside tail event of them all—was one of surprisingly low volatility overall. That wasn't sustainable, and now it's over.

That said, in the US particularly, there's reason to believe that the MSG inequality sprinkles might create fewer ashes and more phoenixes, at least when compared to the rest of the world. The US isn't an island, and global risks are global, but domestically it was one of the few countries to see inequality go down rather than up over the course of the pandemic.

UC Berkeley superstar inequality researchers Emmanuel Saez and Gabriel Zucman, along with their colleague Thomas Blanchet, put a huge amount of effort into calculating the effects of the pandemic on US inequality in particular. Their main finding will come as no surprise to anybody: While the 2020 recession was very sharp and painful, it only lasted a couple of months and then the recovery came at a blistering, unprecedented pace. To no one's great surprise, the rich recovered first, the poor last.[20]

But then comes the more surprising bit, which is that the poor actually did *better* than the rich overall. In January 2020, the average disposable income for an American in the top 10 percent was $268,900 per year, while the bottom 50 percent had just $24,200 of spending money on average. A common way to measure inequality is to just look at the ratio between the two—in this case 11.1.

By December 2021, the top 10 percent had seen their income rise to $280,600, while for the bottom 50 percent it had gone up to $26,300. The ratio of the former to the latter had decreased to 10.7.

At the height of the pandemic, the contrast was more striking still. In March 2021, the ratio was $288,400 to $40,900: The former was just seven times larger than the latter. Alternatively, look at 2021 as a whole and then compare it to 2019 as a whole: The *entire bottom half* of the US income distribution—more than 60 million households— saw its income rise, on average, by an astonishing 20.3 percent.

A lot of that increase came in the form of Covid relief checks— stimmies—that were always designed to be temporary. But even looking past government aid, the bottom 50 percent saw its average pretax income rise by 11.7 percent in 2021—and that's in real terms, after accounting for inflation. The following year, inflation did erode some of those gains, but not most of them.

Growth, invention, and other upside surprises are often connected to a surplus of risk capital sloshing around the system—which is exactly what we saw during the pandemic. Thousands of outré projects were funded in 2020 and 2021, most of which were destined to fail, but some of which, statistically speaking, are certain to succeed spectacularly. That part of the inequality equation is global, although the US does attract much more than its fair share of such funding.

More interesting is what's happening at the bottom end of the US income distribution. The influx of capital into the working classes, and the level of social stability that came with it, was a liberating force for millions. The eviction moratorium, imposed by the Centers for Disease Control for health reasons, probably had an even bigger effect. Suddenly, the famous precariat—the people living paycheck to paycheck, often being exploited in the gig economy while paying off huge student loans—found themselves with a level of stability many of them had never experienced before.

Safe in their rental accommodations, flush with stimulus money, making no payments on their student loans thanks to a moratorium that was in place for more than two and a half years, and placed on almost an equal footing with everybody else who was stuck at home, the members of America's childless precariat in particular found themselves blessed with the luxury of time.

Much time is wasted, but a surprisingly large amount of wasted time turns out to be the raw material that can end up changing the world. Think Keith Richards, inventing guitar tunings in his bedroom that the world had never previously imagined. Unstructured time is the godmother of creativity and invention, and more people had more of it during the pandemic than at any time in living history. They also had at their fingertips an entire internet's worth of knowledge and precedent—the glorious long tail of YouTube, the bottomless Discords of Web 3.

The greatest play of all time, *Macbeth*, was probably written during the pandemic lockdown of 1606, giving new weight to the lines about how Scotland is full of "sighs and groans and shrieks that rend the air," a "violent sorrow" so common as to become a daily fact of life. When Shakespeare talks of how "good men's lives expire before the flowers in their caps, dying or ere they sicken," he's describing the effects of Macbeth in the terms his contemporaries would use to recount the bubonic plague they were living through.

It's certainly not *expected* that a plague will produce a masterpiece like *Macbeth* (or *King Lear*, which was written at the same time). But the law of large numbers does come into play: A pandemic—especially an Extremely Online pandemic—is a little bit like the famous thought experiment of giving a million monkeys a million typewriters. It would in a sense be surprising if strokes of genius did not take place somewhere, if not artistically then commercially or academically or scientifically. The New Not Normal means an increase in black-swan outliers, which are one of the main drivers of human progress.

I have no crystal ball; I don't know what form that inspiration will turn out to have taken. But I fully expect the post-pandemic years to surprise the world with ideas formed when time was in surplus and money worries were at an all-time low. The late social entrepreneur Leila Janah liked to say that "talent is evenly distributed but opportunity is not"; looked at through that lens, the pandemic acted as a way of increasing equality of opportunity, at least in the US. Maybe it even helped to create the next Leila Janah—someone who can build on her legacy of providing opportunity to people who lack it, working on the dream of ultimately extending those opportunities to all people at all times.

We don't have equality of opportunity yet, in the US or anywhere else. But during the pandemic we probably got closer than we've been in a long time, and I'm very much looking forward to seeing the dividends that result.

Epilogue: You Only Live Once

PERIODS OF GREAT stress and mortality often precede periods of growth and innovation. World War I gave way to the Roaring Twenties; the end of World War II kicked off what the French call *Les Trente Glorieuses*, Thirty Glorious Years of global growth and prosperity. Covid, devastating and unwelcome as it was, arrived as the world was stuck in something of a rut—economists liked to talk of the "Great Moderation," or of "secular stagnation," or even of a "new normal" where expectations would be permanently lowered and humanity would have to resign itself to the fact that its eras of great progress were all in the past.

The pre-pandemic world was extremely efficient. Global logistics networks delivered goods just in time; employers paid their workers just the amount necessary; one workplace-optimization tool (Agile) was supplanting another one (Six Sigma). In fact, it was *so* efficient that any advances were marginal: Productivity growth in both Europe and the United States was at levels so low they hadn't been seen in peacetime since the advent of the industrial revolution.[1] We were very close to what topologists call a "local maximum"—a point from which you can't go any higher without first going lower.

Then the pandemic arrived and broke almost everything. Countries around the world *literally stopped*. Covid broke bodies and minds and time itself—and then it revealed just what we were collectively capable of. We rebuilt, faster than anybody expected, in brand-new ways. Millions of us took the opportunities afforded by forced lock-down to reexamine what we were doing with our lives and reorient them in ways that maybe we should have done years earlier. After all, we're path-dependent creatures of habit, and sometimes it takes a major shock to jolt us into action.

You saw the effects in yourself, in your friends, and in your employer, too. Almost overnight, set ways of working were torn up, replaced by something thrown together on the fly that turned out to work much better than anybody would have anticipated. The whole experience was chaotic and *definitely* suboptimal—that's always the experience when you're coming down from a local maximum. I remember in-terviewing the chairman of a major global consultancy about remote work and spending the first few minutes trying to get him up to speed on how to use Zoom. To this day I shudder whenever someone sends me a calendar invite with a Teams link. But, as we saw in Chapter 2, the sheer velocity of problem solving and reinvention surprised nearly everyone. (No one ever sent me a calendar invite with a Teams link pre-pandemic.)

I've avoided the term "post-Covid" to describe the new world we find ourselves in because Covid isn't going anywhere, so maybe I'll just call it the phoenix economy instead. The phoenix economy, compared to the pre-pandemic world, will be unpredictable—Not Normal. It's unlikely that Covid will be the last major pandemic to ravage the world. Geopolitical tensions will rise, and will flare into wars, many of which will be caused in one way or another by global climate change, which has moved from being a future threat to a pre-sent danger. Inequality, uncertainty, and precarity will become more common.

In the face of all these troubles, the biblical imperative to eat, drink, and be merry—perhaps you prefer the more secular version about the pursuit of happiness—will take on extra urgency.

My name, Felix, comes from the Latin. It's hard to translate, because in our modern world we make distinctions that the ancient Romans didn't see—between happiness and luck, between luck and success. In the ancient world, those were all the same thing: Fortune smiled on you, one way or another, or she didn't. In the modern world, successful people are often affronted if they're accused of being lucky, and just because someone's lucky doesn't mean that she's happy. In the phoenix economy, the terms will start to become more similar again. Bets will be placed, often very large ones, and some of them will turn out to be successful, conferring wealth and happiness on the lucky winner; many others won't be so fortunate. The similarities to WallStreetBets or crypto—the feeling that you're in a place where randomness and skill and blind luck all intertwine in a way that can't be disentangled—are clear; maybe the people who flocked to such activity during the pandemic were just getting a head start on the rest of us.

In a world where even money itself can't necessarily be trusted, wealth becomes less attractive. Savings are just deferred consumption, and there's always a risk that either you or the savings won't be around tomorrow to do the consuming. As that risk rises, the natural tendency is to spend more today. Either Fortune will look after you tomorrow, or she won't. We've already seen an increased demand for space and for experiences. If that demand stays strong in the light of increased uncertainty about the future, that will help provide a powerful economic wind in the phoenix's tail, driving it upward, further into the unknown.

Economists have a concept called the "marginal rate of time preference"(MRTP), which is expressed as an interest rate but which basically shows how willing you are to delay gratification today in order to get more tomorrow.[2] For most of my life, my MRTP has been very low. In fact it was clearly *too* low, in the case of some wine I bought over a decade ago and laid down for a special occasion at some point in the future. It was a good idea in principle—but what I didn't anticipate was that my taste in wine would change, and my future self wouldn't actually *want* to drink that kind of red wine. When the pandemic hit, I started opening a bunch of "good" bottles with great vigor. It was a way to brighten up the lonely days of lockdown, but it was very consciously also driven by a "life's too short" feeling. I certainly didn't buy those bottles to outlive me!

As our MRTP rises, our desire to consume today rises with it. The pandemic marked the end of a period of ultra-low financial interest rates, and it similarly marked the end of a period of ultra-low personal discount rates.

At the top end of the spectrum, billionaires who previously kept their heads down and lived in low-key luxury started buying out the world's stock of superyachts, stocking up on trophy properties and artworks, and broadly started spending much more than they had previously. Sure, there might have been more of them, and they might have been richer in aggregate, but they all had enough money all along to spend this way—they just didn't feel the need to do so. Among the middle classes, as we saw in Chapter 12, there was a noticeable jump in propensity to spend. If anything, that jump was even more visible at the bottom end of the income spectrum—although it might have been there all along, and the relatively poor just didn't have enough money, before the stimulus checks and wage hikes came along, to be able to spend as freely as they could during the pandemic.

To be clear: I'm not talking about the kind of optimistic boomtime spending that individuals engage in when they have a rational expectation of being richer tomorrow than they are today. You can get the same kind of increase in spending from the kind of lol-nothing-matters fatalism that we saw in Chapter 4, or just from the feeling that, given the number of unknown unknowns out there, it's best to enjoy your money now, when you have the opportunity to do so.

Spending money is just the beginning of how people start to behave in an unpredictable, Not Normal world. They're more likely to quit their job; they're also more likely to get married or get divorced. If inequality is the MSG of risk, heightening both the upside and the downside, then the phoenix economy effectively sprinkles MSG across our quotidian lives, amplifying the flavors of the present and heightening our experience of the world.

The reason I'm ultimately an optimist, when it comes to this new economy, is not just the nominative determinism of a man named Felix. Nor is it really based on any kind of economic analysis. Rather, it's because I see a rise in compassion and generosity, and because I believe that where those two things are strong, very good things tend to follow.

In the phoenix economy, you're no longer able to count on the kind of things you used to be able to take for granted. Tragedy and triumph will both become more common. But underlying it all is a renewed appreciation for life itself—our own, and everybody else's, too.

Acknowledgments

This book owes its existence to many people, but first on the list has to be Bridget Matzie, my agent, who had the very first idea for it. Bridget teamed up with the astonishingly patient David Kuhn, who signed me up in 2008 and never once hurried me to write anything—until April 2020, when the stars aligned. The proposal we finally put together would never have happened without them urging me along—but it also would never have happened without key words of encouragement and advice from Genevieve Bell, whose ideas about viewing the pandemic through the lens of big themes created the whole structure of this book.

Just as patient as David Kuhn is the amazing Hollis Heimbouch, at Harper Business, who first pitched me on writing a book for her in February 2010. Few people seem to enjoy writing books, but I guess I'm in the minority, thanks largely to Hollis, whose enthusiasm for this project has made it a true pleasure.

I was overoptimistic on one front, however. My day job is writing Smart Brevity with the amazing team of writers and editors at Axios, and it turns out that switching back and forth between bullet points and discursive long-form paragraphs is . . . hard. My eternal thanks and gratitude to Nick Johnston and Aja Whitaker-Moore, at Axios, for letting me take three months off to get most of this thing written, and just generally for being the best bosses that any journalist could ever hope to have. Special thanks, too, to my friend and colleague twice over, Emily Peck, for her constant enthusiasm for the project and also for sparking the idea, over cocktails at Grand Central Terminal, that became my beloved Chapter 3.

Quite possibly the reason that most people don't enjoy writing books is that most people don't have the luxury of writing their book in Roundstone, Ireland, one of the friendliest and most gorgeous places on the planet. Many thanks to Anne and Simon for their amazing place on the pier—seriously, stay there, it's called Roundstone Quay House, you'll love it. It's just lucky I was there in the winter, because the view from the window made it all but impossible to write anything during daylight hours.

Really, I just wanted to hole up to write a book, but this being the Connemara, I was greeted at every turn with a truly humbling degree of kindness and hospitality, most of which took place at O'Dowd's, home to a pint of Guinness that even Guinness skeptics will love. If you're ever in Roundstone, do pop in to Coffee Cottage and get a bowl of soup and a coffee from James and Aoife, the best baristas in town—although I must admit that my own writing was fueled mainly by the truly spectacular Anam coffee roasted by Brian O'Briain in the Burren. Brian, you are a genius and I know you roast the best coffee in Ireland because I was informed of this fact by the most impeccable source, the unique and amazing Cliodhna Prendergast, who, along with her brilliant husband, Patrick, plied me with food and drink and friendship and who introduced me to the astonishing Ballynahinch Castle. (Yes, you have to stay there, too.) I cannot wait to repay some tiny fraction of your hospitality the next time you guys are in New York.

Outside Ireland, I have to thank Simon Clark and Andrea Yaryura, Matthew Rose and Louisa Bokkenheuser, Jon Fine and Laurel Touby,

John Greally and Geraldine McGinty, Guan Yang and Marian Lizzi, Jolie Hunt, Larry Coben, John Avlon, Nassim Nicholas Taleb, Delphine Guenin, the WITI crew, the Wordlechainers, and, especially, the entire Bickford-Lansbury clan, you guys are amazing. Plus Zach Gage, whose perfect games certainly wasted my time but also kept me sane.

Most of all, however, none of this would have even been conceivable, let alone possible, without the constant support and encouragement of my wife, Michelle Vaughan. It was Michelle who responded to me telling her about David's email by telling me that I had to write the book; it was Michelle who took on way more than her fair share of household work; it was Michelle who pushed me to go to Ireland on my own for three months. Thanks for everything, Michelle. I love you, and I promise to do a lot more cooking from now on.

Notes

Prologue

1. For the details in the Prologue, I am indebted to the Pueblo Grande Museum and Archaeological Park, operated by the City of Phoenix.

Introduction

1. See Mary Williams Walsh, "A Tidal Wave of Bankruptcies Is Coming," *New York Times*, June 18, 2020, at https://www.nytimes.com/2020/06/18 /business/corporate-bankruptcy-coronavirus.html.
2. Nouriel Roubini, "The Coming Greater Depression of the 2020s," Project Syndicate, at https://www.project-syndicate.org/commentary /greater-depression-covid19-headwinds-by-nouriel-roubini-2020-04.
3. James Altucher, "NYC is dead forever," at https://jamesaltucher.com /blog/nyc-is-dead-forever-heres-why/.
4. Global Health Security Index 2019, at https://www.ghsindex.org/wp -content/uploads/2020/04/2019-Global-Health-Security-Index.pdf.
5. John Kay and Mervyn King, *Radical Uncertainty: Decision-Making Beyond the Numbers* (W. W. Norton, 2020).
6. Douglas Adams, *The Restaurant at the End of the Universe* (Pan Books, 1980). The fact that Adams's list of professions was still fresh forty years later is a sign of just how slowly the world normally changes.

Chapter 1: The New Not Normal

1. El-Erian started calling an end to "the new normal" in 2016. See Mohamed El-Erian, "The End of the New Normal?," Project Syndicate, February 2016, at https://www.project-syndicate.org/commentary/the-end-of-the -new-normal-by-mohamed-a--el-erian-2016-02.
2. Lewis Carroll, *Through the Looking-Glass*, Chapter 5.

3. Dodai Stewart, "The Year in Limbo," *New York Times*, December 18, 2021, at https://www.nytimes.com/2021/12/18/style/year-in-review-2021.html.

4. Ben Dolnick, "(Let Us Out of This Clause)," *New York Times*, July 6, 2020, at https://www.nytimes.com/2020/07/06/opinion/parentheses-coronavirus-writing.html.

5. Kate Fox, *Watching the English* (Hodder & Stoughton, 2004).

6. "'Stay at home!': Italian mayors send emotional plea to residents," *Guardian News*, at https://www.youtube.com/watch?v=KxtGJsnLgSc.

7. See the polls showing that, by a 62 percent to 24 percent margin, Australians wanted to scrap the zero-Covid policy and end restrictions when vaccination rates hit a certain target, at https://www.smh.com.au/politics/federal/voters-back-national-vaccination-targets-to-ease-restrictions-20210824-p58lk5.html.

8. Mary Douglas, *Purity and Danger: An Analysis of Concepts of Pollution and Taboo* (Routledge, 2002).

9. Leslie Jamison, "Since I Became Symptomatic," *New York Review of Books*, March 26, 2020, at https://www.nybooks.com/daily/2020/03/26/since-i-became-symptomatic/.

10. The Emanuel clip in question can be found at https://www.youtube.com/watch?v=Pb-YuhFWCr4.

11. As quoted in Tom Philpott, "The Biblical Flood That Will Drown California," *Mother Jones*, August 26, 2020, at https://www.motherjones.com/environment/2020/08/california-flood-arkstorm-farmland-climate-change/.

12. See Romer's May 2020 conversation with Tyler Cowen at https://conversationswithtyler.com/episodes/paul-romer-2/, where he outlines a plan to use "the sovereign immunity of the states" to allow companies to sell tests that aren't approved by the FDA.

13. Steve Coll, *Private Empire: ExxonMobil and American Power* (Penguin Press, 2012).

14. See Felix Salmon, "The fall of an empire," Axios, November 1, 2020, at https://www.axios.com/2020/11/01/the-fall-of-an-empire.

Chapter 2: The Great Acceleration

1. See Felix Salmon, "Inflation, recession, pandemic makes for messy reality," Axios, July 30, 222, at https://www.axios.com/2022/07/30/inflation-recession-pandemic-putin-biden.

Chapter 3: From Ladders to Trampolines

1. Fred Schwed, *Where Are the Customers' Yachts? Or, a Good Hard Look at Wall Street* (Simon & Schuster, 1955). It's still in print to this day.

2. Robin Wigglesworth, *Trillions: How a Band of Wall Street Renegades Invented the Index Fund and Changed Finance Forever* (Portfolio, 2021).
3. Howard Marks, "Thinking about macro," at https://www.oaktreecapital.com/insights/memo-podcast/thinking-about-macro.
4. Kevin Roose, "He's a Dogecoin Millionaire. And He's Not Selling," *New York Times*, May 14, 2021, at https://www.nytimes.com/2021/05/14/technology/hes-a-dogecoin-millionaire-and-hes-not-selling.html.
5. See https://twitter.com/WHO/status/1237777021742338049.
6. Yes, that's an actual Bullard paper. James Bullard and John Duffy, "Learning and Structural Change in Macroeconomic Data," FRB of St. Louis Working Paper No. 2004–016A, at https://papers.ssrn.com/sol3/papers.cfm?abstract_id=763926
7. Kyle Chayka, "The meme economy," January 29, 2021, at https://kylechayka.substack.com/p/essay-the-meme-economy.
8. Charles Duhigg, "The Pied Piper of SPACs," *The New Yorker*, June 7, 2021, at https://www.newyorker.com/magazine/2021/06/07/the-pied-piper-of-spacs.
9. Michael Lewis, *Liar's Poker: Rising through the Wreckage on Wall Street* (W. W. Norton, 1989).

Chapter 4: lol nothing matters

1. Bruce Robinson, author and director, *Withnail & I* (1987).
2. See https://twitter.com/nathanielpopper/status/1494772157448011777.

Chapter 5: Workspace

1. Matt Levine, "Fraud Is No Fun Without Friends," Bloomberg, January 13, 2021, at https://www.bloomberg.com/opinion/articles/2021-01-13/fraud-is-no-fun-without-friends.
2. See Adam Tanner, "AIG chief defends holiday," Reuters, August 27, 2009, at https://www.reuters.com/article/insurance-aig/aig-chief-defends-holiday-idUKLNE57Q03K20090827.
3. See Hayley Peterson, "Sears' reclusive CEO explains why he rarely visits the office—and instead lives at his sprawling $38 million estate that's 1,400 miles away," *Business Insider*, March 27, 2018, at https://www.businessinsider.com/sears-ceo-eddie-lampert-responds-to-critics-of-his-management-style-2018-3?r=US&IR=T.
4. See Kali Hays, "New York Times Editor Dean Baquet Has Been Running the Gray Lady from L.A.," *Los Angeles Magazine*, July 26, 2021, at https://www.lamag.com/citythinkblog/dean-baquet-los-angeles/.
5. See Avery Hartmans, "Billionaire Oracle founder Larry Ellison has reportedly moved to the Hawaiian island he mostly owns, the latest high-profile

departure from Silicon Valley," *Business Insider*, December 14, 2020, at https://www.businessinsider.com/larry-ellison-oracle-lanai-island-hawaii -move-2020–12.

6.   See David Benoit, "JPMorgan's Jamie Dimon and His Brush with Death," *Wall Street Journal*, December 24, 2020, at https://www.wsj.com/articles /jpmorgans-jamie-dimon-and-his-brush-with-death-you-dont-have -time-for-an-ambulance-11608821876.

7.   See Zack Fink, "Staten Island Accounts for 25 percent of City's Recent COVID-19 Deaths," NY1, December 9, 2020, at https://www.ny1.com /nyc/all-boroughs/news/2020/12/09/cuomo--staten-island-accounts -for-25--of-city-s-covid-19-deaths.

8.   See Gregory Schmidt, "Luxury Rental Buildings Take 'Working from Home' to the Next Level," *New York Times*, July 23, 2022, at https:// www.nytimes.com/2022/07/23/realestate/co-working-luxury-rental -buildings.html.

9.   Nicholas Bloom et al., "Does Working from Home Work? Evidence from a Chinese Experiment," *Quarterly Journal of Economics* 130, no. 1 (February 2015): 165–218, at http://dx.doi.org/10.1093/qje/qju032.

Chapter 6: The Post-Global World

1.   Joseph Stiglitz, *Globalization and Its Discontents* (W. W. Norton, 2002).

2.   Kyle Chayka, "Welcome to Airspace," The Verge, August 2016, at https://www.theverge.com/2016/8/3/12325104/airbnb-aesthetic-global -minimalism-startup-gentrification.

Chapter 7: Arm's-Length Relationships

1.   W. J. Freeland, "Pathogens and the Evolution of Primate Sociality," *Biotropica* 8, no. 1 (March 1976): 12–24, at https://doi.org/10.2307 /2387816.

2.   See Miriam Krieger and Stefan Felder, "Can decision biases improve insurance outcomes? An experiment on status quo bias in health in-surance choice," *International Journal of Environmental Research and Public Health* 16, no. 6 (June 19, 2013): 2560–77, at https://www.mdpi .com/1660-4601/10/6/2560.

3.   Corey L. Fincher, Randy Thornhill, Damian R. Murray, and Mark Schaller, "Pathogen prevalence predicts human cross-cultural variability in indi-vidualism/collectivism," *Proceedings of the Royal Society B* B.2751279–1285, at http://doi.org/10.1098/rspb.2008.0094.

4.   Leo Herrera, "Weird," September 26, 2020, at https://www.instagram .com/p/CLPddziBFe0/?hl=en.

Chapter 8: Building Compassion

1.   "Global prevalence and burden of depressive and anxiety disorders in 204 countries and territories in 2020 due to the COVID-19 pandemic, *The Lancet*, October 8, 2021, at https://doi.org/10.1016/S0140 -6736(21)02143-7.

AAP-AACAP-CHA Declaration of a National Emergency in Child and Adolescent Mental Health, at https://www.aap.org/en/advocacy/child-and -adolescent-healthy-mental-development/aap-aacap-cha-declaration-of-a -national-emergency-in-child-and-adolescent-mental-health/.

2.   National Center for Health Statistics, Provisional Drug Overdose Death Counts, at https://www.cdc.gov/nchs/nvss/vsrr/drug-overdose-data.htm.

3.   Rebekah Levine Coley and Christopher F Baum, "Trends in mental health symptoms, service use, and unmet need for services among US adults through the first 8 months of the COVID-19 pandemic," *Translational Behavioral Medicine* 12, no. 2 (February 2022): 273–83, https://doi .org/10.1093/tbm/ibab133

4.   Tara Parker-Pope, Christina Caron, and Mónica Cordero Sancho, "Why 1,320 Therapists Are Worried about Mental Health in America Right Now," *New York Times*, December 17, 2021, at https://www.nytimes.com /interactive/2021/12/16/well/mental-health-crisis-america-covid.html.

5.   See KQED, "Did the Emptying of Mental Hospitals Contribute to Homelessness?" and "Rosemary Kennedy: The Tragic Story of Why JFK's Sister Disappeared from Public View," at https://www.kqed.org/news/11209729 /did-the-emptying-of-mental-hospitals-contribute-to-homelessness-here and https://www.kqed.org/pop/22432/rosemary-kennedy-the-tragic-story -of-why-jfks-sister-disappeared-from-public-view.

6.   See Vern Pierson, "Hard truths about deinstitutionalization, then and now," Calmatters, March 10, 2019, at https://calmatters.org/commentary /2019/03/hard-truths-about-deinstitutionalization-then-and-now/.

7.   Tom Bartlett, "The Suicide Wave That Never Was," *The Atlantic*, April 21, 2021, at https://www.theatlantic.com/health/archive/2021/04/pandemic -suicide-crisis-unsupported-data/618660/.

8.   See Our World in Data, "Suicide Rate vs. Homicide Rate," at https:// ourworldindata.org/grapher/suicide-vs-homicide-rate.

9.   Australian Institute of Health and Welfare, "Mental health impact of Covid-19," at https://www.aihw.gov.au/reports/mental-health-services /mental-health-services-in-australia/report-contents/mental-health -impact-of-covid-19.

10. See Christopher Ingraham, "New data shows Americans more miserable than we've been in half a century," January 28, 2022, at https://thewhyaxis .substack.com/p/new-data-shows-americans-more-miserable.

11. "Reading and mathematics scores decline during COVID-19 pandemic,"
     National Center for Education Statistics, at https://www.nationsreportcard
     .gov/highlights/ltt/2022/.

Chapter 9: The Two-Headed Risk Eagle

1. See Dennis Romero, "'Cannonball' coast-to-coast drive record set amid
    virus shutdown," NBC News, April 11, 2020, at https://www.nbcnews
    .com/news/us-news/cannonball-coast-coast-drive-record-set-amid
    -virus-shutdown-n1182011.
2. Pedestrian Traffic Fatalities by State, GHSA, at https://www.ghsa.org
    /sites/default/files/2022-05/Pedestrian%20Traffic%20Fatalities%20
    by%20State%20-%202021%20Preliminary%20Data%20%28January
    -December%29.pdf.
3. "FTC Report Finds Annual Cigarette Sales Increased for the First
    Time in 20 Years," at https://www.ftc.gov/news-events/news/press
    -releases/2021/10/ftc-report-finds-annual-cigarette-sales-increased
    -first-time-20-years.
4. See the 2020 FBI Hate Crimes Statistics, at https://www.justice.gov/crs
    /highlights/2020-hate-crimes-statistics.
5. See National Center for Health Statistics, Mortality in the United
    States, 2020, at https://www.cdc.gov/nchs/products/databriefs/db427
    .htm.
6. Felix Salmon, "Coronavirus ushers in era of uncertainty," Axios, April 2,
    2020, at https://www.axios.com/2020/04/02/coronavirus-economy-market
    -uncertainty.
7. Andrew Anthony, "To mask or not to mask? Opinion split on London
    underground," The Guardian, September 19, 2021, at https://www
    .theguardian.com/world/2021/sep/19/to-mask-or-not-to-mask-opinion
    -split-on-london-underground.

Chapter 10: Shaking the Etch-a-Sketch

1. Adair Turner, "How to tame global finance," Prospect, August 27, 2009,
    at https://www.prospectmagazine.co.uk/magazine/how-to-tame-global
    -finance.
2. See Dave Girouard's tweet thread at https://twitter.com/davegirouard
    /status/1452333296415911936.
3. John Maynard Keynes, Essays in Persuasion (W.W. Norton, 1963), pp.
    358–73.
4. M. Shahe Emran, A.K.M. Mahbub Morshed, and Joseph E. Stiglitz,
    "Microfinance and Missing Markets (March 2007). Available at https://
    ssrn.com/abstract=1001309.

Chapter 11: The Armies of the Public Fisc

1. Remarks by Governor Ben S. Bernanke at the Conference to Honor Milton Friedman, University of Chicago, Chicago, Illinois, November 8, 2002, at https://www.federalreserve.gov/boarddocs/speeches/2002/20021108/.
2. There's video, if you want to watch the whole exchange, at https://www.mediamatters.org/stuart-varney/watch-fox-panel-become-speechless-after-guest-defends-universal-basic-income.
3. Alan Greenspan, "Dodd-Frank fails to meet test of our times," *Financial Times*, March 29, 2011, at https://www.ft.com/content/14662fd8-5a28-11e0-86d3-00144feab49a#axzz1I5YYNcgb.

Chapter 12: Consider the Lobster Roll

1. See Colin Nagy, "The Revenge Travel Edition," Why Is This Interesting, July 1, 2021, at https://whyisthisinteresting.substack.com/p/the-revenge-travel-edition.
2. John Maynard Keynes, "How Much Does Finance Matter?," The Listener, April 2, 1942.
3. Ecclesiastes 8:15, New International Version
4. Robbie Whelan and Jacob Passy, "Disney's New Pricing Magic: More Profit from Fewer Park Visitors," *Wall Street Journal*, August 27, 2022, at https://www.wsj.com/articles/disneys-new-pricing-magic-more-profit-from-fewer-park-visitors-11661572819.
5. Agatha Christie, *An Autobiography* (Collins, 1977). I am indebted to Timothy Lee for finding the exact form of the mildly garbled quotation that often does the rounds; his excellent post on this subject can be found at https://fullstackeconomics.com/why-agatha-christie-could-afford-a-maid-and-a-nanny-but-not-a-car/.

Chapter 13: New Money

1. Narayana Kocherlakota, "Money Is Memory," Federal Reserve Bank of Minneapolis, October 1, 1996, at https://www.minneapolisfed.org/research/staff-reports/money-is-memory.
2. Satoshi Nakamoto, "Bitcoin open source implementation of P2P currency," February 11, 2009, at https://satoshi.nakamotoinstitute.org/posts/p2pfoundation/1/#selection-9.0-9.50.

Chapter 14: Inequality

1. "China Holds the Line on 'Zero Covid,' but Some Wonder for How Long," *New York Times*, January 21, 2022, at https://www.nytimes.com/2022/01/21/world/asia/china-zero-covid-policy.html.

2.   Li Yuan, "The Army of Millions Who Enforce China's Zero-Covid Policy, at All Costs," *New York Times*, January 12, 2022, at https://www.nytimes.com/2022/01/12/business/china-zero-covid-policy-xian.html.

3.   "Two doctors in Lu'an, Anhui, were sentenced to 1 year and 3 months in prison for treating fever patients without authorization," CCTV, October 26, 2021, at https://news-cctv-com.translate.goog/2021/10/26/ARTI9ywBW9HSgTkNpPoeuI8z211026.shtml?_x_tr_sl=auto&_x_tr_tl=en&_x_tr_hl=en-GB&_x_tr_pto=wapp.

4.   Anne Applebaum, "The Disturbing New Hybrid of Democracy and Autocracy," *The Atlantic*, June 9, 2021, at https://www.theatlantic.com/ideas/archive/2021/06/oligarchs-democracy-autocracy-daniel-obajtek-poland/619135/.

5.   "The income gradient in COVID-19 mortality and hospitalisation: An observational study with social security administrative records in Mexico," *The Lancet*, November 10, 2021, at https://doi.org/10.1016/j.lana.2021.100115.

6.   "Assessing the Burden of COVID-19 in Developing Countries: Systematic Review, Meta-Analysis, and Public Policy Implications," BMJ Global Health, at https://gh.bmj.com/content/7/5/e008477.

7.   Credit Suisse Global Wealth Report 2021, at https://www.credit-suisse.com/media/assets/corporate/docs/about-us/research/publications/global-wealth-report-2021-en.pdf.

8.   National Human Rights Commission, "Human Rights Advisory on Rights of Women in the Context of COVID-19," October 7, 2020, at https://nhrc.nic.in/sites/default/files/Advisory%20on%20Rights%20of%20Women_0.pdf.

9.   Nishant Yonzan, Christoph Lakner, and Daniel Gerszon Mahler, "Is COVID-19 increasing global inequality?," World Bank Data Blog, at https://blogs.worldbank.org/opendata/covid-19-increasing-global-inequality.

10.   T. V. Padma, "COVID vaccines to reach poorest countries in 2023—despite recent pledges," *Nature*, July 5, 2021, at https://www.nature.com/articles/d41586-021-01762-w.

11.   Benjamin Mueller and Rebecca Robbins, "Where a Vast Global Vaccination Program Went Wrong," *New York Times*, August 2, 2021, at https://www.nytimes.com/2021/08/02/world/europe/covax-covid-vaccine-problems-africa.html.

12.   The best single place to find all of this data is the methodology note to the annual Oxfam inequality report. The 2022 version is at https://oxfamilibrary.openrepository.com/bitstream/handle/10546/621341/tb-inequality-kills-methodology-note-170122-en.pdf.

13.   Project Brazen, the multimedia journalism outfit started by Bradley Hope and Tom Wright, has a great newsletter called Whale Hunting

that does a great job of sniffing out these folks. See https://whalehunting
.projectbrazen.com.

14. Russell Flannery, "Li Ka-shing's Midas Touch," *Forbes*, March 7, 2012,
at https://www.forbes.com/sites/russellflannery/2012/03/07/li-ka-shing
-midas-touch/?sh=8c0fb88429e4.

15. Amy Chozick, "After a Year, Tablet Daily Is a Struggle," *New York Times*, February 5, 2012, at https://www.nytimes.com/2012/02/06/business/media
/after-a-year-the-daily-tablet-paper-struggles.html?_r=2&ref=media
&pagewanted=all.

16. "Billionaire Buffett Dumps Newspaper Holdings at a Loss," Agence
France-Presse, January 29, 2020, at https://www.courthousenews.com
/billionaire-buffett-dumps-newspaper-holdings-at-a-loss/.

17. Michael Barbaro, "Bloomberg Testing the World of Opinion," *New York
Times*, February 28, 2011, at https://www.nytimes.com/2011/03/01/
nyregion/01bloomberg.html?_r=2&adxnnl=1&ref=nyregion&adxnnlx
=1299006634-j0Vk/Fg5BQJwk1Wyc6kV3Q.

18. Rob Reich, "What Are Foundations For?," *Boston Review*, May 28, 2013, at
https://bostonreview.net/forum/foundations-philanthropy-democracy/.

19. Matt Taibbi, "The Great American Bubble Machine," *Rolling Stone*,
April 5, 2010, at https://www.rollingstone.com/politics/politics-news
/the-great-american-bubble-machine-195229/.

20. Thomas Blanchet, Emmanuel Saez, and Gabriel Zucman, "Real-Time
Inequality," NBER Working Paper No. 30229, July 2022, at https://eml
.berkeley.edu/~saez/BSZ2022.pdf.

Epilogue: You Only Live Once

See "Solving the Productivity Puzzle," McKinsey Global Institute, February 2018, at https://www.mckinsey.com/~/media/mckinsey/featured
%20insights/meeting%20societys%20expectations/solving%20the
%20productivity%20puzzle/mg-solving-the-productivity-puzzle
-report-february-2018.pdf.

1. Mark A. Moore and Aidan R. Vining, "The Social Rate of Time Preference and the Social Discount Rate," Mercatus Center, November 2018,
at https://www.mercatus.org/system/files/moore_and_vining_-_mercatus
research-_a_social_rate_of_time_preference_approach_to_social
_discount_rate_-_v1.pdf.

Index

About the Author

FELIX SALMON is a writer and podcaster. Currently chief financial correspondent at Axios and host of the weekly Slate Money podcast, he was previously the finance blogger at Roubini Global Economics, *Condé Nast Portfolio*, and Reuters. He earned an MA in Philosophy and Art History from the University of Glasgow and has won journalism prizes including a Loeb Award and the American Statistical Association's Excellence in Statistical Reporting Award. He lives with his wife, the artist Michelle Vaughan, in Manhattan.